Revolutionary Spirit
A View of the Scotch-Irish
Influence in America

William L. Brown, Jr.

ISBN 1-891708-48-1   19.95

Copyright © 2005 by William L. Brown, Jr.

Pebble Publishing, Inc. • P.O. Box 2 • Rocheport, MO 65279
Phone: (573) 698-3903 • Fax: (573) 698-3108
E-mail: info@pebblepublishing.com
Online: www.pebblepublishing.com

Visit our bookstore in historic Rocheport, Missouri.

Dedication

This book is dedicated to

My wife, Claudia

My daughters, Anne & Elizabeth

My mother, Virginia

And in memory of

My sister, Julie

My father, William L. Brown, Sr., D.D.S.

My aunts, Betty Jane Brown McCauley & Kathryn Smalley

& my cousin, David Vaughn McCauley

Acknowledgments

I would like to thank Paul E. Stroble, Ph.D., for his unselfish help in creating a proper outline for this book and Julie Tenenbaum for her excellent typing and editing skills. Special thanks to Brett Dufur for his willingness to take on this project and for his expertise in editing and publishing.

Author's Note

This book covers some of the historical conflicts that occurred between the Catholic and Protestant faiths in an earlier time. This author in no way intends to criticize either of these contemporary religions, wishing only peace, understanding, and good will between them.

Thomas Jefferson predicted that all Americans would abandon these two religions of the Gospel of Jesus Christ within one generation of his death. Jefferson, of course, was wrong. During his lifetime, though he lived a public life, he rightly expressed the wish that his religious beliefs remain a personal and private matter. Throughout his life Jefferson carefully preserved copies of his correspondence, insuring that after his death, his opinions (including those on religion) would be on public display.

Thomas Jefferson's thoughts on religion deserve our attention. They would be a counterpoint to the Scotch-Irish Presbyterian influence in America.

Table of Contents

Foreword

Revolutionary Spirit is primarily a family history, but hopefully it offers historical and spiritual insight that is of general interest.

The members of this family migrated to the New World because of religious persecution in the Old World. Their experience would instill in them a desire for religious reform in the New World. Nonetheless, they continued to believe in a living God that was ever present in their lives, providing guidance and support.

As a counterpoint, Thomas Jefferson personally rejected God as a living influence in his life. He believed that the disciples had "disfigured and perverted" the "sublime and moral philosophy" of Jesus of Nazareth by trying to make him more than a philosopher. Jefferson would reformulate the Bible—by cutting out those portions containing what he called the corruptions of the disciples, reducing the rich texture of the sacred and holy scripture to a text of philosophy—and this is now referred to as *The Jefferson Bible.*

Although no cause and effect can be presumed between Jefferson's lack of faith and his actions, the carefully preserved record of his life is open for examination. To America's benefit, Thomas Jefferson would clearly understand and promote the enlightenment ideals of individual freedom, but the historical record shows Jefferson's judgments and actions have been flawed and misguided in dealing with many other issues.

The Davidson, Ewing, and Brevard families of *Revolutionary Spirit* had experienced an earlier struggle for independence in the countries of their origin. They would also participate in the successful fight for independence in America. Their reliance on God would support them from generation to generation. The first public statement proposing American independence would be published under the signature of Ephraim Brevard. Brevard's uncle, Rev. Alexander MacWhorter, was one of the "fighting parsons" of New Jersey, who crossed the Delaware with George Washington and was present at the battles of Trenton and Princeton. William L. Davidson would command the Hornet's Nest and would help drive Lord Cornwallis from North Carolina during the Revolutionary War. William L. D. Ewing would fight under the command of Andrew Jackson during the War of 1812. He would later help prevent Abraham Lincoln's participation in a duel that could have ended Lincoln's life at age 33. Rev. Finis Ewing's associate, Rev. James Smith, would play a role in the religious life of both Andrew Jackson and Abraham Lincoln.

Even though this family would look to God for assistance, they did have their share of adversity. Rev. Finis Ewing's eldest son, William L. D. Ewing, would be a troublemaker in his early adult life in Vandalia, Illinois, before becoming a successful Illinois politician. Finis Ewing was a political ally of Senator Thomas Hart Benton of Missouri and would be slandered by Benton's political adversary David Barton. In the twentieth century, Adlai Ewing Stevenson would draw criticism for the contradictions of his political life and the conduct of his private life.

During the American Revolution, Thomas Jefferson would write with determination for American freedom, but he was not physically a man of action. The Brevard, Davidson, and Ewing families were a part of the Scotch-Irish migration to America in the first half of the eighteenth century. The Scotch-Irish, with God's help, would take strong action in the struggle for American freedom—a struggle that began with the Revolution and continued into the twentieth century.

Introduction

The true spirit of the American Revolution in North Carolina was not a sudden revelation of human kind's self-doing. It was born out of one thousand years of struggle and suffering. This spirit took root in the Old World—in the Highlands and Lowlands of Scotland and in the countryside of France. Through succeeding generations (several of which were in Ireland), its germination progressed and was swept across the great ocean, to be carried into the foothills of the Blue Ridge Mountains. Then with one final shove, this spirit came to full life in May of 1775.

The product of this germination was the Mecklenburg Declaration of Mecklenburg County, North Carolina. As authors Mark Beliles and Stephen McDowell write in their book *America's Providential History:* "As soon as word of the battle of Lexington reached a convention of delegates in North Carolina, they declared independence from England."

George Bancroft writes: "The first public voice in America for dissolving all connections with Great Britain, came not from the Puritans of New England, the Dutch of New York, nor from the planters of Virginia, but from the Scotch-Irish Presbyterians who were meeting in convention as delegates of Mecklenburg County, North Carolina."[1]

Controversy has surrounded the Mecklenburg Declaration of Independence for more than two centuries, but time has given clarity to history and the declaration of May 31, 1775 is now accepted to be a historical fact. Also, though it is considered a historical fiction, the truth of the Mecklenburg Declaration of May 20th is this: Its words are from the true heart of the Scotch and it has proven itself to express an accurate accounting of the Scotch-Irish contribution to

America. Each of the first four chapters begin with an appropriate quote from this declaration.

The saga of those who first spoke for American independence is a saga of the American spirit. This is the story of three ancestral groups who came together in western North Carolina in eighteenth-century America. The Davidsons are representative of the Scottish Highlanders, the Ewings of the Scottish Lowlanders, and the Brevards of the Huguenots of France. Their journey through the ages, from the Old World to the New, centered on a struggle for freedom.

Chapter 1
Origins

"A free and independent people... self governing... under the control of no power other than that of our God."

The first Scottish settlers arrived by sea from Britain and the Low Countries. They came to the west side of Scotland in dugout canoes and animal hide boats finding safe harbors in the islands there. These early explorers traveled up the rivers and the sea lochs to the inland areas where they traveled overland. They were mainly hunters with some limited agricultural abilities. They occupied the great Midland Valley of the Lowlands and occasionally traveled through the highland region.

The New Stone Age people were the second wave of settlers. They brought grains, domesticated animals, and a farming tradition from Europe. They fabricated pottery for the cooking of foods and they built barns and houses of stone.

The Beaker Folk arrived in about 2500 B.C. They were more sophisticated farmers and stockbreeders than their predecessors and used copper and later bronze. They buried their dead surrounded by ceremonial objects in small stone coffins. They made finely decorated pottery, which was comparable to that made later in Greece. Scotland's Bronze Age lasted from 2000 B.C. to 700 B.C., and during the latter part of this time, a style of sword with bronze blades was developed that remained a Scottish trademark through the eighteenth century (though later it was fabricated with iron).

The Celts migrated from Europe and brought iron to Scotland in 800 B.C. These Celts were contemporaries of the Greeks, who thought of them as barbarians, a viewpoint supported by their constant intertribal warfare. By the first century A.D., however, they had become more cultured. In addition, they became skilled at iron working, lived in fortified hill towns, and became successful at agriculture, especially in the fertile midland region. Their advancements would make them ready to stand up against the Romans who would invade Scotland in the later part of the first century A.D.

The Picts were the most warlike group of Celts and lived in the northern highlands of Scotland. (The Romans called them Caledonians.) Other less fierce Celtic tribes farmed the lower midland valleys. Led by Julius Caesar, the Romans invaded Britain during the middle of the first century B.C. but were forced to retreat. They returned one century later and finished the conquest of Britain, then marched into Scotland. In 83 A.D. the Roman commander Agricola invaded the Highlands and defeated the Caledonians. The victory was short-lived, however, because Agricola could not hold the territory he had won. The Scottish Caledonians learned that guerrilla warfare was effective against the Roman camps, and they gradually pushed the Romans out of Scotland. By the end of the second century A.D., the Caledonians (Picts) controlled all of Scotland, and the Romans were not a factor north of Hadrian's wall in Britain, which had been built in 122 A.D. The Caledonians' control of Scotland was unchallenged for a time, but by the late 300s the Scotti of Ireland began attacking the Scottish and British coasts and captured men and women by the thousands, whom they transported back to Ireland by boat to enslave them.

One Roman citizen who was captured by the Scotti in the early fifth century was named Patrick. He was raised in a Christian family and lived on the west coast of Britain. In Patrick's own words: "In years I was then almost sixteen. For I was ignorant of the true God, and I was led to Ireland in captivity with so many thousands of men...

and dispersed us among many
gentiles even as far as the furthest part of the land,
where now my insignificance is seen
to be among members of a strange race.
And there the Lord opened the
conscious of my belief
so that, perhaps late, I might
remember my delicts,
and that I might turn with a whole
heart to the Lord my God
Who turned his gaze round on my lowliness
and took pity on my adolescence and ignorance
and kept watch over me before
I knew him
and before I was wise or distinguished
between good and bad,
and he fortified me
and consoled me as a father
(consoles) a son."[1]

As a slave Patrick lived in isolation herding his master's flock of sheep. His circumstances were grim as to food and shelter and "like many another in impossible circumstances, he began to pray."

Thomas Cahill writes: "Patrick endured six years of this woeful isolation and by the end of it he had grown from a careless boy to something he would surely never otherwise have become—a holy man, indeed a visionary for whom there was no longer any rigid separation between this world and the next. On his last night as Millucc's slave, he received his first otherworldly experience. A mysterious voice said to him. 'Your hungers are rewarded: you are going home.' "[2]

After a perilous journey across Ireland, the Irish Sea, and Britain, he indeed arrives at the home of his parents. He is unable to put the Irish out of his mind and in a vision they call to him: "We request you holy boy that you come and walk further among us."[3]

According to Cahill: "The visions increase, and Christ begins to speak within him: 'He who gave his life for you, he it is who speaks within you.' Patrick the escaped slave is about to be drafted once more—as Saint Patrick, Apostle to the Irish nation."

Patrick again leaves his family to receive a theological education and is in time ordained as a priest and a bishop, only then to return to Ireland as a missionary. In his lifetime, Ireland was "transformed by his teaching. With the Irish—even with the Kings—he succeeded beyond measure... Within his lifetime or soon after his death, the Irish slave trade came to a halt, and other forms of violence, such as murder and intertribal warfare, decreased."

"The greatness of Patrick is beyond dispute: the first human being in the history of the world to speak out unequivocally against slavery. Nor will any voice as strong as his be heard again till the seventeenth century."[4]

According to Kathleen Hughs: "However obscure are his life and career, his writings are unique in the vivid impression they give of a personality. He knew none better, his inadequacies, his lack of learning and education, his youth in exile and slavery, his unworthiness, his sin; but he was absolutely certain that it was God who had called him, given him to the Irish to serve them 'for the duration of my life, I was like a stone lying in deep mire,' he says 'and he that is mighty came and in his mercy lifted me up... Who was it that roused me up, fool that I am, from the midst of those who in the eyes of men are wise?... He inspired me.' And it is because of this summons that he preaches, that regardless of danger he must make known the gift of God."[5]

Saint Patrick spent the remainder of his life in Ireland, but "Patrick's relations with his British brothers" became unhappy when British kings such as Coroticus began descending on the "now peaceful coast of northern Ireland" and carried off thousands of Patrick's converts to enslave them in Britain.[6] At this time the Roman legions had been pushed out of Britain and the Germanic tribes of the east were invading its borders.

By the fifth century, Scotland was divided among four peoples. The Celtic Picts occupied the north, the British Celts the south, the Scotti Celts the west, and the Germanic Angles the east. The Angles attempted to conquer all of Scotland but were decisively defeated by the Picts at Nechansmere in 685 A.D. Brude, the victorious leader of the Picts, was possibly a descendent of the earlier Pict leader Brude, who received St. Columba in the previous century.

In the fifth century, some attempts were made by the British Celtic Christians of the south to evangelize the Picts, but they met with little success. The monk Columba set out early in the sixth century with his 12 disciples from the Church of St. Patrick in Ireland and landed on the northwest coast of Scotland. They built a monastery on the island of Iona, and over a period of years the faith spread and was widely accepted by the Picts. The Pictish King Brude received Columba at his capital at Inverness and welcomed him and his mission. St. Columba died at Iona in 597, the same year that the Italian Church began its mission to the southern region of Scotland. By the end of the seventh century, Scotland was converted.

By the middle of the ninth century, Scotland was becoming a unified country. Most of its people practiced the Christian religion and the Viking threat provided a common foe for the people to resist in unity. In 843 Kenneth became the first king of the United Kingdom of Scotland. He and his descendents resisted the Viking plunderers, and eventually the Vikings intermarried and settled into the Scottish communities.

When David inherited the Kingdom of Scotland in 1124, he established the feudal system. "In theory, all of the land in a kingdom belonged to the king. He had responsibility for providing protection and justice throughout his kingdom. He could grant small estates to knights who formed a royal army... The feudal system originated to provide a measure of security in troubled times; a specialized class of warriors protected the farmers and artisans in exchange for food, clothing and labor."[7]

Through the succeeding monarchies Scotland came under greater English control. In the late thirteenth century, Edward of England attacked Scotland and captured its key fortresses. "The

English were blind as well as arrogant if they imagined that a great and proud people like Scots would tolerate foreign domination so tamely and without opposition."[8]

"The country was already in an uproar when William Wallace, the son of a Clydesdale Knight, killed the English sheriff of Lanarke in May 1292. Wallace rallied the people against the hated conquerors, and the Scottish Wars for Independence began."[9]

"Soon he had gathered about him a small but tough and determined band of warriors dedicated to the task of driving all the English, military and civilian out of Scotland."[10] They recaptured many of the castles, and "in 1297 he caught the English Army at Sterling Bridge, and massacred it, infantry defeating mounted knights"[11] In response, King Edward of England marched to Scotland with considerable forces and defeated Wallace and his warriors in 1298.

Later Wallace was hanged by the English, which only increased the Scottish desire to overthrow the English. As a martyr, William Wallace became Scotland's greatest hero.

In 1314 Robert Bruce led the Scottish forces to victory over the English at Bannock Burn, which eventually led to Scottish independence. In 1320 the Lords and Bishops of Scotland wrote the Declaration of Arbroath, a letter to Pope John XXII insisting on Scottish independence from England.

"Because so long as a hundred of us remain alive we will never be subject to the English, since it is not for riches, or honours, or glory that we fight, but for liberty alone, which no worthy man loses save with his life."[12]

In 1324 the Pope finally recognized Robert's title and Scottish independence. For the next 200 years, Scotland continued to fight for autonomy separate from England. Through battles, wars, various leaders, and different alliances, the struggle continued, leading through the Renaissance and to the Reformation.

Martin Luther began the Reformation in Germany in the sixteenth century and it spread throughout the Christian world. It was a call for "a return to the simplicity of the New Testament" and specifically, that "the word of God is the message of redemption through Christ Jesus our Lord without any merit on our part, and that we are saved solely through heartfelt acceptance in faith."[13] Luther was joined by John Knox, John Calvin, and others to lead the Protestant movement away from the established church because of its numerous abuses that had grown intolerable over the centuries.

In Scotland the Reformation "turned Scotland from a Catholic to a Protestant nation." From the beginning, the Scottish church "was largely independent of Roman authority" due to the distance from Rome and the difficulty of enforcing Roman rules and "because Christianity had arrived in Scotland through missionaries who came not from Rome but from Ireland."[14]

Early in the seventeenth century, conflict between Protestants and Catholics led to the ouster of the Catholics from Ulster, Northern Ireland—a regrettable chapter of history. After eliminating the Catholics in this region, the English invited Scotch and Irish Protestants to farm here as tenants. This area became known as the Ulster Plantation, and between 1606 and 1618 approximately 40,000 Scottish emigrants arrived here.[15] Many of these people were Scottish Presbyterians who had been victims of harassment and religious intolerance in their homeland and were seeking religious liberties in Ulster as well as new economic opportunities.

In the Lowlands

One legend describes the early beginnings of Clan Ewing as a group of Celts who settled along the shore of Lake Lamond in Scotland before the Christian era. According to myth, these Celts were shepherds and originally called themselves the Eagle Wing Clan, later dropping all the letters in Eagle except the E, making their name E-wing.

The Ewing Clan was allied with the Campbells and resided on the River Forth, inland from the McCauleys. This location was in the vicinity of Loch Lamond, near Sterling Castle, in the lowlands.

This clan fought the fight for Scottish independence from the era of the Romans to the time of Wallace and beyond.[16] Because of religious persecution in the mid 1600s, they first moved to the Isle of

Bute in Scotland and then settled at or near Coleraine County Londonderry, of Ulster, to the north of Ireland.

In the Highlands

The Clan Chatton was an ancient and loose federation originally composed of some 17 clans that claimed Pictish origins. The main constituent members were the Clans Davidson south of Inverness in the highlands north of Clan Robertson.

The Davidsons' ancestors were likely of the early converts to Christianity by Columba, Saint Patrick's missionary, in the sixth century. As Picts they fought for centuries to maintain their independence against the Romans, Angles, Saxons, and Vikings. As a united Scotch people, they are believed to have fought under Robert Bruce for Scottish independence from England at the Battle of Bannock Burn.[17] The victory here won Scottish independence for a time and led to the famous Declaration of Arbroath of 1320.

Some members of the Davidson Clan joined the seventeenth-century migration to Ireland and resided in County Derry, Northern Ireland.[18] This clan, along with others that carried highland names, formed a small minority among the Scotch in Ireland. They became a part of the culture of the Ulster plantation and, at some point, left their highland traditions behind.

Before joining the Scots in this migration to Ireland, the Brevards' ancestral beginning was in France.

In France

By 700 B.C. the Celtic tribes were sweeping through France and replacing the earlier cultures. These Celts were called Gauls and from the fifth century B.C. they led France through the Bronze Age and into the Iron Age. This Iron Age culture had distinctive styles of pottery, jewelry, and weaponry.

Caesar noted in his *Gallic Wars* that at one time the Gauls had been more warlike than the Germans. The Gauls fought a united struggle against Rome, but in 52 B.C. they were defeated. Thus

Gaul became a part of the Roman Empire, and in 212 A.D. Emperor Curacalla made all free men within the Empire free citizens.

In 406 A.D. the Franks invaded and established themselves on French soil. With the subsequent fall of Rome, the Frankish rulers dominated. The Franks adopted orthodox Christianity, and by the end of the Middle Ages the country of France was unified, becoming at the same time a European power.

The Reformation, begun by Martin Luther in 1517, fragmented the religious unity of France and led to episodes of civil strife over the ensuing years.

Lucian Fosdick wrote in *The Huguenots:* "The forerunner of the Protestants is found in Joan of Arc. She was a martyr to her faith—as dauntless as any that ever died rather than deny and recant religious belief. The same spirit was in Joan of Arc that moved Calvin and Coligny and the tens of thousands of brave and noble French who were willing to suffer, to leave homes and possessions, to endure exile, but would not surrender their rights of conscience and their religious liberty."

Early in the fifteenth century, France was losing a war with England. Paris had fallen into English hands and it was probable that Orleans would be the next city to be lost. "At this junction there came to the French commander a volunteer, declaring that she had a commission from God to restore to the King of France his kingdom."

Joan was born in 1412. She was a country girl who helped her mother spin and knit and her brothers shepherd their herds. She was deeply religious and lived life close to God. When Joan was 17 in 1429, she believed that God had called her to command the French Army. "St. Michael appeared to her in a flood of light and told her to go to the help of the King and restore him to his realm." She reported to the French commander who was at first skeptical, but he "was at last so stirred by her spirit and story, and by something in her personality which he could not fathom, that he decided to send her with armed escort to the King." The King was in dire straits and Joan's confidence eventually won over his reluctance to believe her. "Asked what signs she had she replied 'give me some men at arms and lead me to Orleans and I will show you signs. The sign I am to give you is to raise the siege of Orleans'… the King placed her in command of the army."

She led an army of 10,000 to Orleans. "She seemed supernatural to the soldiers, as she led them forward against the English who held Orleans in siege. Her enthusiasm and fearlessness were electrifying. Under such leadership the French were irresistible, and the maid's prediction that she would deliver Orleans and restore to the King of France his kingdom was fulfilled."

Joan of Arc briefly enjoyed the high honor that was hers, but tragically she was betrayed and captured by the English, who put her to trial and sentenced her to death, by fire as a heretic. During the inquisition she suffered the threat of torture but replied: "Even if you tear me from limb to limb and even if you kill me I will not tell you anything further. And even if I were forced to do so, I should afterward declare that it was only because of the torture that I had spoken differently."

"The fire was kindled. Her last words were 'Jesus—Jesus!' Then her head fell on her breast and her pure spirit went to paradise."

Joan of Arc was a Protestant before the Reformation and her spirit was to live again in the Huguenots.

"The Huguenot Church was the reformed church of France. From about the year 1560 French Protestants were known as Huguenots."[19] From this time began a period of religious wars that lasted for about 30 years between the established church and the reforming Huguenots. This war continued until with "the famous Edict of Nantes (1598), a settlement was proclaimed which secured definite rights for the Huguenots, and gave securities that those rights would be respected."[20]

Before the Reformation "there was no translation of the Bible into French, and as the popular education of that day did not include Greek or Hebrew, the Gospels remained safely hidden from the people."

"During the Reformation in France, the reading of the Bible by the people was followed by an immediate reaction against the superstition, indifferentism and impiety which generally prevailed. There was a sudden awakening to new religious life."[21]

"Suddenly it was clear for all to see that ecclesiastical abuses, such as the sale of indulgences and the wealth of the clergy and monks, had no biblical authority. The seeds of the Reformation— and those of the sanguinary struggles that were to follow in its wake had been sown."

The Edict of Nantes gave the Huguenots a privileged position and for a short time they "were in absolute possession of 150 strongholds scattered over the country, each one of which was in a position to defy royal authority."[22] At this time the Huguenots numbered about 1 million in a population of 15 million. The established church was determined to repeal the Edict of Nantes. Through Cardinal Richelieu's efforts in 1629, the Huguenots— though they maintained their religious and civil rights—lost all other rights. Through the ensuing years, the Huguenots experienced increasing persecution. "The final blow came in 1685 when Louis revoked the Edict of Nantes. All Protestant churches were to be demolished."[23] Left with no choice, many Huguenots were forced into an exodus from their homeland.

In James G. Leyburn's words: "Historians estimate that some half million of these Protestants left France as a result of the revocation of the Edict, to the benefit of the industry of the countries to which they migrated. Many of them came to Ulster and since they too were Calvinists, for the most part they joined the Presbyterian Church and soon became a part of the Scottish communities. Their thrift and industry were beneficial; but their particular contribution was an improvement of the methods of manufacturing linen, for which the colony was already noted. Ulster's trade thereafter took another leap forward."

Leyburn provides the following description of the Ulster Plantation of Ireland: "The hope entertained by King James that the settlement of northern Ireland would prosper materially, had by 1700 been realized." In Leyburn's book, Green asserts: "In its material result the Plantation of Ulster was undoubtedly a brilliant success. Farms and homesteads, churches and mills, rose fast amid the desolate wilds of Tyrone."

The contentment of the inhabitants of Ulster would be short-lived, however, as measures taken by the English would harass and eventually drive many Scotch-Irish to the New World. "The English Parliament began to grow alarmed by the competition of Irish goods with English ones and to impose restrictive measures that caused great distress (economic) to Ulster."

In 1703 the Test Act was passed, which required all officeholders in Ireland to be members of the established church (the Protestant Anglican Church of England). This political act was then used to turn the Presbyterian ministers out of their churches. In 1717 the Great Migration of the Scotch-Irish to America began. This migration was prompted by economic and religious dissatisfaction. By the time of the Revolutionary War, "some quarter of a million Ulster men had arrived in America."[24]

These emigrants wanted relief from the difficulties they had endured, and they seemed to find the most relief where they found the most freedom—at the edge of the American frontier. Their Scotch-Irish progeny would continue to seek out the frontier, and those with the names Jackson, Houston, and Crockett would in time become symbols of American freedom.

Chapter 2
Independence

"That we the citizens of Mecklenburg County do hereby dissolve the political bands which have connected us to the Mother Country."

The first Scotch-Irish in America settled in the Susquehanna and Cumberland Valleys of Pennsylvania. Subsequent waves of emigration continued and many followed the Great Valley into Virginia and the Carolinas. "Word had spread abroad that land in the Carolinas was available in hundreds of thousands of acres. The colonies south of Virginia eagerly welcomed settlers, and first reports on soil, climate, and religious liberties were highly favorable. The mainstream of movement therefore flowed toward the Carolina Piedmont."[1]

Governor Dobbs' words in 1755 describe 75 families who had settled on land he owned in North Carolina. "They are a colony from Pennsylvania of what we call Scotch-Irish Presbyterians who with others in the neighboring tracts had settled together in order to have a teacher, i.e. a minister of their own opinion and choice."[2] In 1760, Dobbs, the royal governor of North Carolina, "appealed to the King to strengthen his hand so he could more effectively 'oppose and suppress a republican spirit of Independency rising in this Colony.' "[3]

North Carolinians actively opposed the British Stamp Act in 1766 and later joined the revolutionary Non-Importation Association, which opposed British trade. The "committees of correspondence" were begun in 1773 by the 13 colonies to join together in the common cause of opposing British policies, which led to the formation of the Continental Congress in 1774. Royal Governor Martin of North Carolina (who replaced Dobbs) attempted to prevent North Carolina's representation in the Second Continental Congress, but failing to do so, he "dissolved the assembly on April 8, 1775, and a Royal Assembly never met again in North Carolina."[4] The Battle of Lexington occurred on April 19, 1775, and the news of this battle arrived in Mecklenburg County one month later.

Concerning the Battle of Lexington, Thomas Jefferson would write on May 7, 1775, that "This accident has cut off our last hopes of reconciliation, and a frenzy of revenge seems to have seized all ranks of people."[5] The news of Lexington swept across the country and it is possible to place its arrival in Mecklenburg County on May 19, as John McKnitt Alexander, who was present, reported in his notes. Specifically, Alexander stated, "and soon afterwards we smelt and felt the blood and carnage of Lexington which raised all the passions into fury and revenge which was the immediate cause of abjuring Great Britain on May 19, 1775."[6]

John Davidson was the last surviving member of the convention that met in Mecklenburg County during May 1775. In 1830 he provided the following recollection: "When the members met, and were properly organiz'd for business, a motion was made to declare ourselves Independent of the Crown of Great Britain, which was carried by a large majority. Then Doctor Brevard was appointed to give us a sketch of the Declaration of Independence, which he did. Then James Jack was appointed to take it on to the American Congress, then sitting in Philadelphia, with particular instructions to deliver it to the North Carolina delegation in Congress (Hooper & Caswell). When Jack returned, he stated that the Declaration was presented to Congress, & the reply was that they highly esteemed the patriotism of the citizens of Mecklenburg but they thought the measure too premature. I am confident that the Declaration of Independence by the people of Mecklenburg was made publick at least twelve months before that of the Congress of the United States."[7]

Earlier, in 1819, Captain Jack recalled the following: "When the resolutions were finally agreed on, they were publicly proclaimed from the court-house door in the town of Charlotte, and received with every demonstration of joy by the inhabitants. I was then solicited to be the bearer of the proceeding to Congress. I set out the following month, say June, and in passing through Salisbury, the General Court was sitting. At the request of the court I handed a copy of the resolutions to Col. Kennon, an attorney, and they were read aloud in open court. Major William Davidson, and Mr. Avery, an attorney, called on me at my lodgings the evening after, and observed, that they heard of but one person, but approved of them. I then proceeded on to Philadelphia, and delivered the Mecklenburg Declaration of Independence of May, 1775, to Richard Caswell and William Hooper, the Delegates to Congress from the state of North Carolina."[8]

The reply from the delegates to Mecklenburg County indicated that any move toward independence was premature, but they urged the people of North Carolina "to arm and organize themselves into a militia, against further eventualities."[9]

Pursuant to the instructions from the North Carolina delegation, the committees of safety stepped up their action. In the meantime, Royal Governor Martin had fled from North Carolina, fearing that he would be captured by the local committee of safety. In August of 1775, the North Carolina Provincial Congress met at Hillsborough and "laid the foundations for an army, provided for its organization and support, and began forming continental regiments in the state."[10] The journal of minutes from Rowan County (adjacent to Mecklenburg County) illustrate the subsequent steps being taken by the Rowan County Committee of Safety on November 8, 1775: "Resolved, That Mr. John Brevard, John Dickey, Moses Winsley and Hugh Brevard, or any of them, attend at Capt. William Davidson's on the 20th instant, to see that the company of minute men, whom he has enlisted, are embodied, and able effective men and make report to the next committee."[11]

By December, North Carolina was prepared to send troops to aid Virginia in "driving Lord Dunmore, the royal governor of that colony out of Norfolk."[12] At this time Governor Martin, with British help, was planning a campaign to reestablish royal rule in North Carolina. However, his loyalist forces were defeated by the patriots at the Battle of Moore's Creek Bridge, and the revolutionary cause gained new enthusiasm.

At the Provincial Congress that met at Halifax, North Carolina, on April 12, 1776, a resolution for independence was passed. "This document, the Halifax Resolves, was the first official state action for independence, and it was not a declaration for North Carolina alone, but a recommendation to the Continental Congress that independence should be declared by all the colonies through their representatives in the Continental Congress."[13] On May 15, 1776, Virginia was the first colony to follow through and order its delegates to propose independence. This set the stage for the national Declaration of Independence to follow.

Thomas Jefferson was drafted to write the Declaration. Jefferson adopted two preexisting texts to form its basis. One was the draft preamble to the Virginia Constitution, which he had written and was adapted from the English Declaration of Rights. The second was a version of the Virginia Declaration of Rights, which was written by George Mason. Jefferson stated in 1823 that he "did not consider it part of my charge to invent new ideas altogether, and to offer no sentiment which had never been expressed before."[14] The issue of the Mecklenburg Declaration's authenticity and whether it was used as a text by Thomas Jefferson for the Declaration of Independence first came to light in 1819.

William Hoyte would write in 1907: "During the winter of 1818–19, when the subject was a topic of conversation at Washington among members of Congress, the assertion was there made that the people of Mecklenburg county, in North Carolina, formally declared themselves independent of Great Britain before the Fourth of July, 1776."

"The statement was apparently received with incredulity." This statement became more credible when the following article appeared in the April 30, 1819, issue of the *Raleigh Register and North Carolina Gazette:* "It is not probably known to many of our readers, that the citizens of Mecklenburg County, in this state made a Declaration of Independence more than a year before Congress made theirs. The following document on the subject has lately come into the hands of the Editor from unquestionable authority and is published that it may go down to posterity." It would be dated May 20, 1775, and was expressed in the following language: "whosoever… countenanced the unchartered and dangerous invasion of our rights… is an enemy to this Country—to America— and to the inherent and inalienable rights of man… that we the citizens of Mecklenburg County do hereby dissolve the political bands which have connected us to the Mother Country… that we declare ourselves a free and independent people… self-governing… under the control of no power other than that of our God… to the maintenance of which independence we solemnly pledge… our mutual cooperation, our lives, our fortunes, and our most sacred honor… and to use every exertion to spread the love of country and fire of freedom throughout America."[15]

This article was copied by other American newspapers and came to the attention of John Adams, who wrote: "The genuine sense of America at that moment was never so well expressed before, nor since." Adams also wrote: "I was struck with so much astonishment on reading this document that I could not help enclosing it immediately to Mr. Jefferson, who must have seen it, in the time of it, for he has copied the spirit, the sense, and the expressions of it verbatim into his Declaration of the Fourth of July, 1776."[16]

Hoyte continues: "Unlike Adams, Jefferson was not ready to accept the paper of Mecklenburg. He was doubtless as much annoyed as Adams anticipated. 'And you seem to think it genuine,' he wrote to Adams. 'I believe it is spurious… I must not be understood,' said Jefferson, 'as suggesting any doubtfulness in the state of North Carolina. No State was more fixed or forward. Nor do I affirm, positively, that this paper is a fabrication; because the proof of a negative can only be presumptive. But I shall believe it such until positive and solemn proof of its authenticity shall be produced.' "[17]

Adams, in reply, indicated that Jefferson's letter "has entirely convinced me that the Mecklenburg Resolutions are a fiction."[18]

In North Carolina there was a different temperament. Hoyte states: "There was no question in North Carolina about the genuineness of the resolutions. The Mecklenburg Declaration's anniversary was first celebrated at Charlotte on May 20, 1825, and a large number of Revolutionary worthies attended. Thus the matter remained until Jefferson's letter to Adams, discrediting the authenticity of the document, was published in 1829."

In response, "To give the world the 'positive and solemn proof' that Jefferson demanded, the legislature of North Carolina, at its session in 1830–31, appointed a committee 'to examine, collate, and arrange' all documentary evidence that could be obtained. The committee affirmed the genuineness and authenticity of the Mecklenburg resolutions."[19]

Soon after the committee's report was published, archivist Peter Force discovered a proclamation issued by Royal Governor Josiah Martin on August 8, 1775. In it, the governor said that he had "seen a most infamous publication in the *Cape Fear-Mercury* importing to be resolves of a set of people styling themselves a committee for the county of Mecklenburg, most traitorously declaring the entire dissolution of the laws, government, and constitution of this country, and setting up a system of rule and regulation repugnant to the laws and subversive of his majesty's government."[20]

In 1838 Force would discover a set of resolutions from Charlotte Town, North Carolina, dated May 31, 1775, published in the *Massachusetts Spy* of July 12, 1775, which he believed "answer very well to the description given by Governor Martin." He soon afterwards found these same resolutions published in abbreviated form in the *New York Journal* of June 29, 1775. In 1847 a complete version of these resolutions was discovered in the June 13, 1775, issue of the *South Carolina Gazette and Country Journal.* George Bancroft would find a copy of the same resolutions in London a few days later.

The resolutions of May 31, 1775, were clearly a different document than the declaration of May 20, 1775. William Hoyte explains: "Those who had doubted the genuineness of the May 20th resolutions and many others outside of North Carolina, concluded with Mr. Force that the paper of the 31st was the 'Mecklenburg Declaration of Independence'... Their position was fortified by a certificate, dated September 3, 1800, appended by John McKnitt Alexander to the copy of the May 20th resolutions that he gave to Gen. W. R. Davie, from which it was learned that those resolutions were written from memory, after the destruction of the records in Alexander's house in April, 1800."[21] Thus, it is most likely that the Declaration of May 20, 1775, was written in an attempt to resurrect by memory the original resolves that were lost in the fire. It follows that the Resolves of May 31, 1775, were in fact the true Mecklenburg Declaration.

Hoyte continues: "It will be observed that the Mecklenburg Resolves of May 31, 1775, constitute a virtual declaration of independence. They declare that all civil and military commissions granted by the crown are null and void, and the constitution of each colony wholly suspended; that legislative and executive powers are vested solely in the Provincial Congress of each colony; that the people of Mecklenburg should therefore form certain regulations for the government of the county; that county military officers, when chosen by the people, shall exercise their powers by virtue of such popular choice, and 'independent of the crown of Great Britain and former constitution of this province';... and that these resolves shall be 'in full force and virtue until instructions from the Provincial Congress regulating the jurisprudence shall provide otherwise, or the legislative body of Great Britain resign its unjust and arbitrary pretention with respect to America.' By declaring British authority and British forms of government to be wholly suspended in all the colonies and all legislative and executive powers to be vested in the Provincial Congresses, the people of Mecklenburg took a more advanced step in the direction of independence than any other organized body of their compatriots had taken... In effect, Mecklenburg County declared independence subject to a contingent limitation."[22]

On June 30, 1775, Governor Martin wrote to the Earl of Dartmouth, the British Secretary of State for the American Department: "The Resolves of the Committee of Mecklenburgh, which your Lordship will find in the enclosed Newspaper, surpass all the horrid and treasonable publications that the inflammatory spirits of this Continent have yet produced, and your Lordship may depend its Authors and Abettors will not escape my due notice whenever my hands are sufficiently strengthened to attempt the recovery of the lost authority of Government. A copy of these Resolves I am informed were sent off by express to the Congress at Philadelphia as soon as they were passed in the Committee."[23]

The Resolves of May 31, 1775, were published under the signature of Ephraim Brevard as clerk of the committee. There is no historical certainty as to the authorship of the resolves, though Hoyte would write that "Brevard was a graduate of Princeton, an able writer, and the acknowledged draftsman of the Mecklenburg Resolves of May 31, 1775."[24] The significance of the Resolves of May 31, 1775, deserve a greater contemporary appreciation than they have thus far received.

The American Revolution began, just as the British Revolution of the seventeenth century had begun, by the process of petition. The right to petition the King or Parliament for the redress of grievances was the basic right of British citizens. When the Continental Congress of 1774 was convened, its purpose was to address the King concerning the grievances created by the British invasion of the Colonists' rights. The address to the King stated, "we cheerfully consent to the operation of such acts of the British Parliament, as are bonna fide, restrained to the regulation of our external commerce, for the purpose of securing the commercial advantages of the whole empire with the mother country, and the commercial benefits of its respective members; excluding every idea of taxation, internal or external for raising a revenue on the subjects in America, without their consent." To back up their petition, the Colonists enacted their Plan of the Association with an embargo on British goods (non-importation, non-consumption, and non-exportation). Congress agreed on October 22, 1774, to reconvene if the desired redress of grievances had not occurred by May 10, 1775. During the winter of 1774-75, the King refused to redress the grievances of the petition, but his statement concerning the Plan of the Association follows: "The New England governments," he said, "are now in a state of rebellion; blows must decide whether they are to be subject to this country or independent."[25]

Though the Battle of Lexington provided the tinder, the Mecklenburg Resolves of May 31, 1775, were written in response to Parliament's address to King George III, given in February of 1775. As Hoyte put it, Parliament declared the American Colonies "to be in a state of actual rebellion," leading the Mecklenburg committee to write thusly: "we conceive that all laws and commissions confirmed by or derived from the authority of the king or Parliament are annulled and vacated and the former civil constitution of these colonies, for the present, wholly suspended." The Scotch-Irish of Mecklenburg County eagerly awaited a spirited response from the Second Continental Congress (which had reconvened on May 10, 1775) concerning the resolves, sent via Captain Jack, but they would receive only disappointment.

The Congress was drafting the second petition (the "Olive Branch") to King George III promising that America was seeking reconciliation and not independence. Accordingly, it was necessary to suppress the Resolves of Mecklenburg County in Philadelphia, as they proposed independence for all the colonies unless Britain "resign its unjust pretentions." By July the "Olive Branch" Petition was on its way to London, though some members of the Second Continental Congress (John Adams included) believed that a second petition to their unresponsive king was not required nor desired. In the end King George refused, once again, to respond.[26]

Although the daybreak of the revolution had not yet arrived in Philadelphia during the summer of 1775, at that moment it was well past sunrise in Mecklenburg County. Perhaps if Congress had employed the tactics suggested by Mecklenburg, they might have at least confronted the King with a fighting spirit before his back turned on them for the second and final time.

Repeating Royal Governor Martin's response to the Resolves of May 31st: "its Authors and Abettors will not escape my due notice whenever my hands are sufficiently strengthened to attempt the recovery of the lost authority of government."[27] A previous treasonable incident in North Carolina had resulted in six hangings. Ephraim Brevard's life was clearly at risk. Martin, however, did not regain his position. The royal government never met again in North Carolina and despite the conditional independence of the Mecklenburg Resolves, North Carolina remained independent of Great Britain from May 1775 on. As Brevard was the only signer of the Resolves as published, Ephraim Brevard's sole signature stood for independence in America from shortly after the Battle of Lexington until the en masse signing of the Declaration of Independence on August 2, 1776. The names of these signers would not be made public until January 18, 1777, after Washington's victories at Trenton and Princeton gave the cautious American cause a fighting chance.

The Declaration of July 4th would actually be the final American response to the King's refusal of the two congressional petitions. It stated the Colonists' rights in the language of the Enlightenment, the grievances against the King that infringed on these rights, and the final and solemn act of unconditional independence. Of the 56 signers of the Declaration of Independence, five were captured by the British as traitors and tortured before they died, and nine died from wounds or hardship during the Revolutionary War.

Although Brevard's signature was on a different document of independence, he was equally a martyr for liberty as he was captured and placed on a British prison ship after the fall of Charleston, South Carolina, on May 12, 1780. After his release he was elected to the Continental Congress for the state of North Carolina on July 12, 1781. Due to the illness attributed to his confinement on the prison ship, he was unable to travel to Philadelphia to take his seat at the Continental Congress of 1781 and he died soon after.

Although it is of no historical value, historical interest leads us back to the Mecklenburg Declaration of May 20th, the declaration of John McKnitt Alexander, written after the fire in 1800. Though his text included some of the famous words of the Declaration of Independence of July 4th, it is an irony that these familiar and famous words were actually not original to Jefferson's declaration either but were first written and spoken in Scotland during the years leading up to the American Revolution (an earlier version of some originated with John Locke in England).

According to historian Garry Wills: "In the forties and fifties of the [18th] Century, Scotland had a constellation of original thinkers not to be equaled anywhere in Europe—not only Hume and Smith, Kames and Hutcheson, but Adam Ferguson, Thomas Reid, and the young Dugald Stewart… The leadership that had been taken fifty years earlier by the Royal Society in London, and which would pass to France when the Encyclopedia began appearing, was held by Scotland in just those years when Jefferson was laying his own intellectual foundation, under the guidance of a typical product of the Scottish efflorescence, William Small."[28]

Jefferson was born on April 13, 1743, into a family of wealthy planters who had pioneered the settlement of the Virginia Piedmont. Jefferson's early schooling was under the local clergyman, an Anglican minister, where he received a classical education. He received religious training and was a student of the Bible, "but he treated it as a work of history rather than the word of God." When Thomas was 14 years old, his father died, leaving him the bulk of the Jefferson estate, and at age 17 he left home to attend William and Mary College in Williamsburg, Virginia. At William and Mary, Jefferson was trained by Dr. William Small, who had recently arrived from Scotland, where a new enlightenment of rational thought was born.

"Small, who taught mathematics, philosophy, and history as well as logic, ethics and rhetoric, imbued Jefferson with this rationalistic thought."[29] After college Jefferson studied law under George Wythe, who would later help him reform Virginia's legal code.

At the time of his drafting of the Declaration of Independence, Jefferson was preoccupied with the creation of the Virginia Constitution. "In truth Jefferson had not wanted to serve on the drafting committee. The Virginia convention was in the process of adopting a state constitution that summer and that project seemed more important to Jefferson." He submitted his proposals to the Virginia convention, but they were all rejected except for the preamble, which contained his indictment of the King.[30]

"Ephraim Brevard, author of the Mecklenburg Declaration of Independence, physician, teacher, soldier, and patriot, was born in Maryland in 1744. When about four years of age he came to North Carolina with his parents, who settled a few miles east of Mount Mourne, Iredell County. He was the son of John Brevard, and his mother was a sister of the Rev. Alexander McWhorter, president of Queen's College of Charlotte.

"He took an interest in the advancement of learning and aided in the establishment of Queen's College of Charlotte, which was chartered by the colonial legislatures of 1770 and 1771 (both of which were repealed by the King) and by the General Assembly of 1777 under the name of Liberty Hall Academy. For a time he served the institution as a member of its faculty. When the first meeting of the new board of trustees was held on June 3, 1778, Ephraim Brevard, Isaac Alexander, and Rev. Thomas H. McCaule were appointed to frame a system of laws for the government of the institution, and a few months later he was appointed a member of the committee to elect a president."[31]

Ephraim Brevard's father, John, was a delegate to the convention that met at Halifax, North Carolina, on November 17, 1776, and that framed the first state constitution for North Carolina. At the North Carolina Congress, "a committee was appointed to prepare a declaration of rights and a constitution."

"The constitution provided for a legislature of two houses, a senate and a house of commons; a judiciary consisting of a supreme court, an admiralty court, and county courts; an executive department to be composed of a governor, a council and whatever other administrative officers might be needed."[32] This design of government was formulated by John Adams of Massachusetts after a careful and thorough study of the classical governments of Greece and Rome and the more contemporary eighteenth-century governments of Europe. The North Carolina constitutional committee requested Adams' advice and this, their final result, was similar to most of the other states in closely following Adams' model for government.

This same model of government would be used by James Madison, the father of the U.S. Constitution, at the National Constitutional Convention of 1787. Ephraim Brevard had graduated from Princeton College three years before James Madison was to graduate from there. Brevard's qualifications to serve as the author of the Mecklenburg Resolves are largely attributed to his educational background at Princeton.

"At its start, Princeton, like other early American colleges, was a child of the church." "The College of New Jersey, as Princeton was originally known, sprang from a split in the Colonial Presbyterian Church. In what historians called the Great Awakening, evangelists from England and the Netherlands preached a fiery and freewheeling style of religion, intense and personal and based more on inner experience than the accepted doctrines of the church." The founders of Princeton were supporters of the awakening and were "expelled for their beliefs from the synod of Philadelphia. They were less bound to existing authority and more tolerant of differing views than others of their generation."[33] With this background, Princeton would produce the radicals our country needed to set it on a new course.

"Before it [Princeton] had rounded its fifth decade, despite the untimely deaths of many of its leaders, despite financial losses and the ravages of war, it had become a powerful influence for good in the country. Its purpose was to train men for the pulpit, the bench, the bar, the seats of legislation, the schools, the founders had said from the beginning, and now the careers of their graduates as preachers and teachers, as leaders in the revolution, as members of Congress, as framers of the Constitution of the United States, as eminent jurists, physicians, merchants, scientists, soldiers showed how successful these purposes had been attained.

"…More than half of the graduates under Dickinson and Burr entered the ministry. Imbued with the spirit of Whitefield and Tennent, they went forth to keep burning the fires of the Great Awakening and preach the gospel of the religion of experience."[34]

The tours of George Whitefield and Gilbert Tennant marked the culmination of the Great Awakening in America. "The Great Awakening transformed the culture of Colonial America touching its inhabitants with the spark of promised redemption, and daring them to challenge orthodox assumptions and institutions. It set the stage for the American Revolution."

William Tennant Sr. and his family (including son Gilbert) were Scotch-Irish and in Northern Ireland had worshipped in "prayer societies" and large "field meetings" as was the custom there (this tradition was the ancestor of the American revival meeting). The Tennants moved to America in 1718 and were "probably the single most important clerical force in the progress of the Great Awakening."

In Pennsylvania, Rev. William Tennant Sr. "had far more Ulster Scot parishioners than he could deal with and far fewer trained clergy than he counted on," so he opened his own school of theology called the Log College next to his church.[35] Later the Tennants and their allies created a new Presbyterian college in New Jersey that would eventually be called Princeton, and "certain historians have contended that the College of New Jersey grew directly out of the Log College…"[36]

Benjamin Rush would graduate from Princeton in 1760, and "he was the first of a succession of Americans for whom a Scottish education was the transforming event of their lives." In 1767, Rush traveled to Edinburgh, Scotland, to study medicine and while there he was enlisted to persuade John Witherspoon of Glasgow to become the new president of Princeton College in America.

On February 4, 1768, Witherspoon informed Rush that he would accept the position and he wrote Rush to "Pray that it may be for the glory of God and the publick interest…"

"Witherspoon saw education not as a form of indoctrination, or of reinforcing a religious orthodoxy, but as a broadening and deepening of the mind and spirit—and the idea of freedom was fundamental to that process."

"Some of this was in place even before Witherspoon arrived. Samuel Blair, one of Princeton's Ulster Scot founders had said the school's curriculum should 'cherish a spirit of liberty and free inquiry' so that every religious denomination, not just Presbyterians, enjoyed full freedom of conscience."[37]

"[John] Witherspoon's inaugural address as Princeton's president, declaimed in Latin at commencement exercises in September 1768 was on 'the Connection & mutual influences of Learning & Piety' ... He saw no contradiction between faith and reason; he preached from the pulpit twice each Sunday and during the week taught history, rhetoric and French as well as 'moral philosophy.' He was a devotee of the scientific method of testing theory by experience and firmly believed in common sense as the test of any proposition."[38]

Although the words of the Enlightenment did not appear in the Resolves, they would have been familiar to a Princeton graduate. "Dr. Witherspoon, when he arrived to take charge of his infant college [Princeton] in the 'wilds of America,' was no doubt surprised to find that the course of study was not less advanced and up-to-date than in some of his Scottish Universities."[39]

What his Scottish Universities taught was the philosophy of the Scottish Enlightenment. Francis Hutcheson, a Scotch-Irishman from Ulster, is considered the father of the Scottish Enlightenment. This Enlightenment philosophy would form the backbone of the Declaration of Independence of July 4th.

According to Garry Wills: "[Francis] Hutcheson was the author on the central topic of philosophy as it was taught at Philadelphia and Princeton and New York. What was true elsewhere was doubly true of William and Mary in Dr. Small's time there."[40]

Ephraim Brevard graduated from Princeton, and Thomas Jefferson from William and Mary, nonetheless, they had studied the same ideas and philosophies of the Enlightenment. Not only were Brevard and Jefferson familiar with Hutcheson and the Scottish Enlightenment, but they had plenty of company. Bailyn states: "the Scottish philosopher, Francis Hutcheson" was a figure "the colonists knew and cited" in the mid-eighteenth century.[41] "Himself a Presbyterian minister, Hutcheson was for absolute freedom of conscience and of public religious exercise."[42]

Francis Hutcheson would popularize the expression "unalienable rights." His complete statement on unalienable rights is as follows: "All human power or authority must consist in a right transferred to any person or counsel to dispose of the alienable rights of others. Consequently, there can be no government so absolute as to have even an external right to do or command everything. For whenever any invasion is made upon unalienable rights, there must arise either a perfect or external right to resistance... Unalienable rights are essential limitations in all governments."[43]

In Garry Wills' words: "Francis Hutcheson called the moral faculty of man 'uniform in its influence' and to say that men are equal in their exercise of this faculty is to define them as essentially equal." David Hume, a Scottish philosopher, would write about equality in the essay entitled "Of the Original Contract." Hume wrote: "When we consider how nearly equal all men are in their bodily force, and even in their mental powers and faculties, till cultivated by education, we must necessarily allow that nothing but their own consent could at first associate them together and subject them to any authority..."

Wills writes: "In his draft instructions for the Virginia delegation to 1774's Continental Congress (A Summary View) Jefferson wrote: 'Can any one reason be assigned why 160,000 electors in the island of Great Britain should give law to four millions in the states of America, every individual of whom is equal to every individual of them in virtue, in understanding and in bodily strength.' (papers 1:126) That is a very literal reading of equality, at least as between the island British and the continental British."[44]

When Thomas Jefferson wrote that "all men are created equal," he was asserting equal rights for the colonists, respecting Parliament's political power. Jefferson's words were of bold significance for the colonial cause, but of no relevance to those of his peers who were female or black. For these "unequals," the balance of liberty would eventually become just, through the sweat, pain, and tears of later generations. Francis Hutcheson was opposed to slavery and believed that equality was for all and not a matter of gender. This was a more enlightened direction than Jefferson and his fellow colonists were ready to follow.

Also incidental to *A Summary View,* which Jefferson submitted to the Virginia Delegation to the Continental Congress of 1774, is the following recounting. Although rejected by the delegation, this document contained Jefferson's most significant political statements, made prior to the Declaration of Independence. An important theme of *A Summary View* was the contention that America, as a "new habitation" separate from Britain, had a natural right "of there establishing new societies." This was called an expatriation.[45]

The Continental Congress was seeking to provide a proper legal case to support the revolution and Thomas Jefferson's theory was deemed to have no valid basis in this regard. In fact, Jefferson provided no precedent or statute to support this concept. In much the same way, he would later establish the doctrine of nullification, which upheld the right of a state to declare null and void within its boundaries, any act of the federal government. Nullification would eventually be used by the South to justify secession and a civil war would be required to confirm it as unconstitutional.

As to expatriation, in 1831 John Quincy would state: "The argument of Mr. Jefferson that the emigration of the first Colonists from Great Britain which came to America was an expatriation, dissolving their allegiance and constituting them independent sovereignties, was doubtful in theory and unfounded in fact. The original colonists came out with charters from the King, with the rights and duties of British Subjects. They were entitled to the protection of the King, and owed him allegiance."[46]

The Mecklenburg Resolves of May 31, 1775, would declare in the preamble a sound legal case to justify America's revolution— namely that when Parliament, in February 1775, declared the colonies to be "in a state of actual rebellion," calling for forceful measures against them (they in effect placed the colonies outside the protection of the King), thus all laws deriving from the King or Parliament were rightfully "annulled and vacated."[47]

According to the philosophy of Francis Hutcheson as described by Garry Wills: "Life and liberty are the principle rights in Hutcheson's scheme of things. He asserts the right of liberty 'as nature has implanted in each man a desire of his own happiness.' " The "bands of political union" originated with the Scottish philosopher Adam Ferguson.[48] Thomas Jefferson stated his sources for the Declaration of Independence as being "the harmonizing sentiments of the day…" those of political theorists to be found "in conversation, in letters, in printed essays, or in the elementary books of public right."[49] An important point is that the Declaration of Independence of July 4 did not so much lead America to a new vision (at that time) but, rather, expressed very well the ideas that Americans were already thinking by the summer of 1776. In reference to the Declaration of July 4th, John Adams would state: "there was not an idea in it what had been hackneyed about by Congress for two years before."[50]

Thomas Jefferson's place in history as the draftsman of the Declaration of Independence is secure, though this high position, for Jefferson, has included the trials and tribulations of historical scrutiny. As a result, the Jefferson myth's once smooth patina continues with age to reveal the rough edges of reality.

Though the Mecklenburg Resolves of May 31, 1775, are authentic, the Declaration of May 20th must be considered a fiction. It was apparently, however, considered very good fiction by John Adams, for whatever Adams' intent may have been, his description of the Mecklenburg Declaration is worth repeating: "The genuine sense of America at that moment was never so well expressed before, nor since."[51] A radical frenzy of revenge may have occurred on May 20, 1775 in Mecklenburg County, but whatever this event may have been, it can not be considered more than myth or legend. Though the Declaration of May 20th has no historical value, as myth it expresses a resurrection of Scottish Enlightenment ideals, reminding us that Americans were influenced by these ideals well before July 4, 1776. As to its importance and meaning, the value of myth "is not in its factual accuracy of an event, but in its power to suggest larger truths."[52] The truth of the Mecklenburg Declaration of

May 20th is this: Its words are from the true heart of the Scotch and it has proven itself to express an accurate accounting of the Scotch-Irish contribution to America.

The fact remains that North Carolina spoke first for independence in a process that may have in some way begun on May 20th, but with certainty, was signed, sealed, and delivered on May 31, 1775. In addition, the torch that was passed from Lexington to burn brightly for independence in Mecklenburg County during the war for independence, and which continued to spread the fire of freedom throughout America afterward, was in the steady grip of the Scotch-Irish.

On July 2, 1776, Richard Henry Lee proclaimed in Congress that we "are and of a right ought to be free and independent states."[53] Our country was now unified, with one voice of independence, and the Revolutionary War was officially under way.

Chapter 3
Pledge

"...to the maintenance of which independence, we solemnly pledge to each other our mutual co-operation, our lives, our fortunes and our most sacred honor"

According to historian Edmond Cody Burnett: "With the passage of the Declaration of Independence, Congress became, to borrow a phrase of John Adams, 'high charged' with a new and strong purpose… The Declaration of Independence was scarcely a week old when the chief of the heralded peace commission, Admiral Lord Howe, whom the Americans held in affectionate esteem, arrived with authority to endeavor to effect a reconciliation between the mother country and her disgruntled daughters." Congress sent a committee to confer with Howe. "The committee, on its part, represented to his lordship that Congress had adopted the Declaration of Independence 'after long and great reluctance in obedience to the positive instructions of their constituents' and that it was now not in the power of Congress to undo that act… John Penn of North Carolina was confident the people would now realize that 'we have no alternative for our safety but our spirit as soldiers…' Thus had independence passed through its first ordeal and came forth with increased vigor."[1]

Edmund S. Morgan writes: "Many ordeals would follow but providence would bless America. The Americans' "greatest asset was their desire to be free." Though about 20 percent of Americans remained loyal to Britain, nowhere "were they strong enough to enable the royal government to survive." This desire for freedom supported by most Americans still would not ensure an American victory.

Washington throughout the war would be in constant struggle with the Continental Congress for supplies, arms, and men, in addition to leading his less experienced troops against the well-trained British. "The local militia were good at harassing the British, but they were the least reliable part of the American forces when it came to pitched battles, and they could never be kept in the field for more than a short time."

At the Battle of Long Island on August 26, 1776, Washington would learn how ineffective his militia forces could be against the well-trained Red Coats. His army was pushed across New Jersey in a continuing series of defeats.

"There now began to appear however two factors which were to weigh heavily in determining the outcome of the war. One was the mediocrity of the commanders England sent to subdue the colonists… Washington and his subordinates meanwhile were learning about war the hard way. The fact that he and they had the talent to learn was a second factor working toward American success."

On the night of December 25, 1776, Washington and his men crossed the Delaware and "hit the British hard at Trenton. It was not a battle of great importance in itself, but it showed which commander had the daring and the initiative to win a war, and it restored to the Americans some of the assurance they had begun to lose."

"On October 17, 1777, at Saratoga, Burgoyne surrendered to them [Americans]. Saratoga was a great turning point of the war, because it won for Americans the foreign assistance [French] which was the last element needed for victory."

"It never the less took more than three painful years after the French entrance into the war for Washington to find the opportunity for a decisive battle." After Saratoga, General Howe was replaced by General Henry Clinton, whose orders were to move the British offensive to the south.

Morgan continues: "Clinton was able to subject the American coastal towns to heavy raids and at the same time to mount an offensive against Georgia and South Carolina. Clinton was a more energetic commander than Howe. During 1779 he recovered Georgia and by May of 1780 had taken Charleston, South Carolina, and its garrison of 5,000 men. Leaving Lord Cornwallis in command of an army of 8,000 to continue the southern campaign, he departed for the north to take care of a French expedition against Newport, Rhode Island, which the British had occupied since 1776.

"Cornwallis' continuing to move northward with greater haste than Clinton had anticipated, was initially successful and inflicted another crushing defeat on the Americans at Camden, South Carolina (August 16, 1780)."[2]

In *The Road to Guilford Courthouse,* John Buchanan writes: "Although George Washington had preferred Nathanial Green," Congress in June 1780 had given Horatio Gates command of the Southern Department of the American Forces. At Camden, Gates was to make a series of faulty decisions that would lead to disaster. Gates elected to take the direct route to Camden against the advice of Major General DeKalb and Deputy Adjutant Ortho Holland Williams. "It had been DeKalb's intention to strike west, where there was a better possibility of securing supplies among a friendly population, and to approach Camden in a rough semicircle and operate in the general vicinity of the strongly rebel Mecklenburg County, North Carolina."

In late July 1780, Gates sent Frances Marion (of French Huguenot ancestry) to the interior of South Carolina for intelligence purposes, depriving his army of the one who "had not yet earned the name of the swamp fox." The militia of the Williamsburg District of Charleston had asked that a Continental officer be sent to lead them. He (Marion) rode off at the head of his men and boys, white and black, a legend in the making!" Before departing "Gates made a decision that further clouded his generalship." He dismissed most of his cavalry after concluding cavalry would be of no use in the South. When the battle occurred, Gates' leadership was nonexistent and the Americans were routed by the formidable British force.

Buchanan continues: "And what of Horatio Gates? What role did he play in the debacle once it began? None, sad to say… Can we possibly imagine Lord Cornwallis behaving in such a manner? Or George Washington? One hates to call any man a coward, and the history of war is full of tales of men who ran one day and performed acts of gallantry the next. But we are entitled to expect of officers that they never shirk, never run.

"…In an age where generals commonly exposed themselves to inspire their troops and often paid with their lives, Major General Horatio Gates was conspicuously absent from the battles at Saratoga and rode far and fast from Camden's terrible field."[3]

In North Carolina

Author Archibald Henderson writes: "The American drive against Cornwallis having ended in catastrophe, North Carolina became the first and almost the only line of defense as the invaders prepared to sweep northward. But it was not until September 25—more than a month after Camden—that the British Army marched into Charlotte. Meanwhile, with Rutherford a prisoner, Davidson, having recovered from his wounds at Colson's Mill, was on August 31, 1780, appointed brigadier general of militia in the Salisbury district. Caswell on retreating from Camden had ordered out all the available militia of Mecklenburg, Rowan, and Lincoln Counties. Three other regiments from the eastern part of the state were ordered to Ramsay's Mill in Chatham County, where they were organized into a brigade under Jethro Sumner. On September 5, 1780, Davie was appointed colonel of cavalry of the Western District, and under him was a small company of horsemen commanded by Joseph Graham.

With Sumner, Davidson, and Davie concentrating their forces, the march of Cornwallis was not to be unimpeded. Fragments of other commands at Hillsboro, Halifax, and elsewhere were being recruited. Portions of the Maryland brigade that had survived Camden remained, and its commander, General William Smallwood, was appointed to the general command of the North Carolina militia, whereupon Richard Caswell resigned and retired to private life. General Muhlenburg with 500 Virginia regulars was also expected to arrive soon.

North Carolina was resolved, in the words of one of its officials to put up a "stout defense."[4]

Despite the failure of the Americans in large-scale pitched battles, in the South, partisan or guerrilla-type warfare would continue to be successful and would be ably supported by the "rebel stronghold of Mecklenburg County." William Davie, "in conjunction with General William Davidson of the North Carolina militia, would effectively control the countryside of Mecklenburg County. British foraging parties could count on being harried and ambushed every time they rode out from Cornwallis's lines, and British couriers probably had the most dangerous job in the army. A lone courier was a dead man."

Thus while in Charlotte, "Lord Cornwallis had an uncertain line of communication with his commanders at Charleston and the strong points throughout South Carolina. This state of affairs became even more ominous when he decided to deal with the Back Country warriors on his western flank." Major Patrick Ferguson was elated at the mission given to him by Cornwallis. "Ferguson's critical task was to protect Cornwallis's left flank, to move forward into the far Back Country, parallel with the main army as it thrust into North Carolina."

Ferguson had to deal with the Back Country rebels on the east slope of the Appalachians, as well as the Over Mountain People.

According to Buchanan: "The Over Mountain People were largely Scotch-Irish," and "they lived in the extreme northeastern corner of what is now Tennessee" on the western side of the Appalachians where they "were squatters on Cherokee land… The Over Mountain Man, hardened by the toil of pioneering, was further hardened by Indian fighting. His life could be short, nasty and brutal. But if he survived falling trees, fever, snake bites, drowning, disease, backbreaking labor, blood poisoning and the scalping knife, he rode into a fight a warrior for the ages."

Buchanan characterized Patrick Ferguson as misjudging his opposition when he sent a message to the Over Mountain Men stating that if they did not desist from their opposition to the British arms, he would "march over the Mountains, hang their leaders, and lay their country waste with fire and sword."

In response, rebel Isaac Shelby recommended "that a volunteer army from both sides of the Mountains be raised to deal with Ferguson."

"No time was wasted," according to Buchanan, and the Over Mountain Men were ready. "But first befitting a time and a community in which religion played a major role, with leaders of the expedition being Presbyterian Elders, a stern preacher, thirty-one-year-old Reverend Samual Doak, of Ulster descent, Virginia born, Princeton graduate, sent the men on their way with a sermon taken from Gideon and the Midianites, ending it with a rousing cry. 'The sword of the Lord and of Gideon!' To which the Over Mountain Men responded with a ringing shout, 'The sword of our Lord and of our Gideons!' Then 1,040 strong, they rode out to catch Major Patrick Ferguson."

"In common with the Back Country Militia who joined them on the other side of the Mountain, these frontier fighters neither had nor needed an administrative structure," such was their self-sufficiency. "Across the pommels of their saddles rested their principle weapon, for which they were famous on two continents— the American rifle."

At King's Mountain, the Over Mountain Men and the Back Country Militia overtook and destroyed Ferguson and his Tory militia. "When the first reports of the battle reached General William Davidson in North Carolina his reaction expressed it for all 'Ferguson the great partizen has miscarried.'

"The dramatic victory of the Over Mountain Men and their Back Country allies at King's Mountain forced Lord Cornwallis to set aside for the time being his plan to invade North Carolina." The Tories to his west had "been smashed," and Marion and his men were terrorizing the Tories to his east. "Nor could the army remain where it was, for the countryside surrounding Charlotte indeed all

Mecklenburg County, harbored inveterate partisan foes brilliantly led by Major William Richardson Davie under the overall command of General William Lee Davidson."[5]

According to historian Chalmers G. Davidson, King's Mountain "was one of the momentous victories of the war, not only in cutting off Cornwallis's Tory support and forcing him from North Carolina, but in proving to the frontiersmen that their own troops could win triumphs as complete as the continentals. After King's Mountain the Loyalists of the upcountry were content to profess their good will to the king and practice staying at home.

"As Davidson was general of Salisbury District, whose militia constituted the majority of the battle force, he received the first report of the event. He wrote immediately to General Sumner, who sent a copy of his letter posthaste to Gates at Hillsboro. The latter dispatched a messenger with Davidson's communication to Governor Jefferson of Virginia and requested that it be speeded to the President of Congress. 'This instant,' Gates wrote, 'I received the great and glorious news contained in the enclosed letter from Brigadier General Davidson to General Summer… We are now more than even with the enemy!' Camden was forgotten. The letter was published in Philadelphia by order of the Continental Congress and quickly copied both in America and England."[6]

According to Robert Leckie in *George Washington's War:* "The Battle of King's Mountain had lasted exactly an hour. Except for the 200 men Ferguson had sent foraging in the morning, every one of his soldiers was killed, wounded or captured… The less seriously wounded were included among the 698 who surrendered. Rebel losses were 28 killed and 62 wounded."

"The prisoners were entrusted to Cleveland's North Carolina troops, who eventually marched them to Gates at Hillsboro. Gates asked Thomas Jefferson what to do with them, but this dedicated pacifist, who spent the war in his Williamsburg snuggery, made the absurd recommendation of turning them over to the civil governments of the Carolinas, when, in fact, Cornwallis had effectively destroyed both. So they were eventually loosely guarded, and within a few months, all but sixty escaped. Yet those who returned to their homes brought with them a dire tale of death and defeat so chilling that the Battle of King's Mountain, small as it might have been in numbers and brief as it was in duration, had an enormous effect on Cornwallis's campaign in the South, if it did not effectually wreck it. It instantly halted—like a sluice gate suddenly raised—the flow of Loyalists to the cause of the Crown."[7]

Archibald Henderson writes: "Nearly a week passed before the news of King's Mountain reached Cornwallis at Charlotte. That delay was an indication of the extraordinary activity of the men under Davidson and Davie in intercepting messages, cutting off scouting parties, capturing supply trains, and in many other ways harassing and annoying the invaders. Charlotte ever after remained a rankling memory with Cornwallis and his fellow officers. From their experience 'Hornets Nest' was an accurate description."[8]

According to C. G. Davidson: "After such unmistakable proof of the venom of the uplanders, it was suicide to remain longer in their environs. No provisions or local reinforcements, on which the Earl had fondly counted, were forthcoming. His army was half-sick and disheartened. Apprehensive that Ninety-Six in South Carolina would be attacked and being without supplies, he determined to fall back immediately. Shortly after noon on the 12th of October, the British began leaving Charlotte Town."

"Cornwallis had failed to place the Old North State beside her sister to the South. Instead of marching on the heels of a fleeing foe, the Earl was on his toes to get away. He could obtain only hearsay concerning the movements of Ferguson's conquerors and he was convinced that Charlotte was no fit camp for civilized soldiers. His conquest of the village had only thrown a net over the Scotch-Irish hive. He had captured the drones, but the workers continued to swarm from the woods as long as he retained their citadel. They could not destroy him, but the thin whine of their attacks, the sharpness of their jabs and the elusiveness of their flights maddened him beyond endurance. Davidson's policy had met with entire success and it was to him that the Whig newspapers gave the credit for Cornwallis's failure."[9]

"In December 1780 Washington sent General Nathaniel Green, perhaps his ablest subordinate, to concert the American resistance."[10]

Robert Leckie reports: "Green pressed doggedly deeper into the South until on December 2, 1780, he arrived at Charlotte, to meet Gates and replace him as commander of the Southern Army. The meeting was cordial: Green was respectfully sympathetic, Gates dignified and polite. Leaving Charlotte, Gates returned to his life as a Virginia planter."[11]

Henderson again: "An army estimated at 2,000 but only 800 of them armed and equipped greeted the new commander of the Southern Department, Nathanial Green. Davie, Davidson and Sumner were three North Carolina leaders upon whom Green soon placed special responsibilities. In taking Davie from the field service and making him commissary general, Green possibly deprived this brilliant North Carolinian of an opportunity for further distinction on the battlefield, but there was no duty of greater importance than that involved in 'the service of supply' to Green's fast-moving army. Other celebrated Revolutionary leaders then or soon afterward joined Green's staff, including Marion, Sumter, Pickens and Isaac Huger of South Carolina; Daniel Morgan, William Washington, and 'Light Horse Harry Lee' of Virginia; and the Polish engineer, Kosciuszko. Green was aware that England, because of difficulties at home and in Europe, could not increase her armament in America; that a great French fleet and army were expected on the Atlantic coast almost daily; and that the loyalists of the back country would lose heart unless Cornwallis was steadily on the aggressive. The composition and character of the officers and men in Green's army prompted a plan of campaign, which would avoid general engagements. The object was rather to discourage loyalist activity, to harass and delay every extended movement on the part of Cornwallis, and behind this screen of small-scale offensive operations build up a military organization which in time could meet the enemy on even terms.

"At the beginning of 1781 Greene could put in the field little more than 2,000 men. About half of them under Huger, he moved into the Cheraw section on the Pedee River, and was thus in a position to obstruct any attempt on the part of Lord Rawdon to advance his forces from Camden toward the Cape Fear loyalists. The leader of the other division was Daniel Morgan, who was sent to the western side of the Catawba."[12]

According to C. G. Davidson: "Morgan crossed the Catawba and encamped on the Pacolet River in South Carolina on the 25th of December. A week later, he wrote from this camp to Greene, that General Davidson had brought 120 men and had returned to bring forward a draft of 500 more. Colonel Andrew Pickens of South Carolina had joined him with sixty men. 'When I shall have collected my expected force,' said Morgan, 'I shall be at a loss how to act. Could a diversion be made in my favor by the main army, I should wish to march into Georgia.' He had consulted Davidson and Pickens as to whether a safe retreat could be secured if they were pushed by a superior force. The militia Commanders believed it could.

"Davidson in Charlotte was using all his powers of persuasion to bring in the militia. This, in the piedmont, was the time that tried men's souls. Not only had the county troops served repeatedly and with scant remuneration, but also their farms were neglected and exposed. It was a choice in many cases between family and country, and often the more intimate tie won. Both Greene and Morgan counted heavily on Davidson's influence. Complete control of the militia was in his hands, as Smallwood had gone. There was not a busier man in his state than the Brigadier-general of Salisbury District.

"... In the midst of mustering the farmers, rangers and hunters, the General probably took a day off on January 2nd to canter up to Centre, for on that date his namesake and last child was born. From this contracted projection of himself came the realization of many of Davidson's fondest hopes. Would that clairvoyance had been given the father to see the future respected citizen of an independent and peaceful country and the first benefactor of the successor to Queens College, which was to bear the General's name! Perhaps for the seventh time, William Lee Senior did envision some happy predestination.

"The American maneuvers convinced Cornwallis that winter quarters at Winnsboro were untenable. With Marion marauding below him and Morgan and Green menacing his flanks, the Earl's surest defense was offensive action. His army was now rested, and reinforcements had arrived from Charlestown. His posts at Ninety-Six and Camden were both well guarded. The British could not relinquish the delusion that a large number of North Carolina Loyalists would flock to their standard when they entered the state. At the end of the first week in January, Cornwallis began to move slowly toward the Catawba. He dispatched Tarleton with his legion to ride ahead and embroil Daniel Morgan.

"In his designs Tarleton was all too effective. Morgan, fearful of a surprise and lacking confidence in his numbers, wrote Greene on January 15th, requesting that he be recalled with his detachment. 'General Davidson and Col. Pickens may be left with the militia of North Carolina and South Carolina and Georgia. They will not be so much the object of the enemy's attention, and will be capable of being a check on the dissaffected, which is all I can effect.'

"Greene replied with a soothing letter to let Morgan march into Georgia as he had wished (though Greene's correspondence with Sumter implies that he saw no object in so doing), but declining to recall him if it could be avoided, 'but I would rather recall you by far,' he added, 'then expose you to the hazard of a surprise.' If Morgan marched into Georgia, Greene suggested that Sumter, recovering from his wound, and Davidson take his place on the Catawba (their 'hazard of surprise' being apparently not so great); but the commander preferred, if possible, a combined attack by Morgan, Davidson and Sumter upon one of the divisions of Cornwallis's army.

"Davidson sent calls for militia from Dan to Beersheba. Although the men were ordered in 'very pressing terms,' said the Brigadier, to rendezvous at Charlotte on the 10th, they did not begin to come in until about the 16th. Since Cornwallis was veering toward Mecklenburg, Davidson was uncertain whether he should establish a camp in Charlotte or continue to send reinforcements to Morgan. 'Upon learning of the enemies movement,' he wrote

Greene, 'I have issued orders for half of the Militia of Rowan & Mecklenburg Counties to join me on or before the 22nd instant with six days provision—I expect a considerable number & wish to receive your orders by that time—I have received no official accts. from Genl. Morgan for several days.' Davidson understood that Cornwallis had between five and seven hundred, but his past experience with his Lordship was sufficient security against his own hazard of surprise.

"For several days neither Davidson nor Greene heard of Morgan's maneuvers. On January 19th, the Commander-in-chief replied to Davidson's letter. 'I don't apprehend the enemy have any intention of penetrating the country upon the upper route & wish you not to keep a greater force on foot than is necessary to give cover to the lower country. Avoid coming to general actions unless you catch the enemy in a divided state.' As for joining Davidson's force with Morgan's, Greene would leave that to Morgan, Sumter and Davidson to decide. Morgan had about 900 and seemed disposed to make 'a diversion into Georgia.' If that were agreed to, Sumter and Davidson were to remain to front the British.

"Meanwhile on the 17th, Morgan, despite his fears, had fallen in with Tarleton at Cowpens near the Pacolet and thoroughly worsted him."[13]

On January 16th, the night before the battle, Morgan's preparations had been completed.

Buchanan explains: "At Cowpens the little army settled down and lighted cooking fires. Lieutenant Colonel John Howard recalled the arrival of large numbers of Militia. 'Some militia joined us in the march, but Pickens, with its principal force, did not join us until the evening before the battle of the Cowpens.' Howard stated that Morgan decided to fight when Pickens arrived with the main Militia force." The militia and regulars would be under the command of Brigadier General Daniel Morgan. Daniel Morgan, along with Benedict Arnold, had been responsible for the American victory at Saratoga in 1777 and he led his corps into battle then as he would at Cowpens with "imagination and the extraordinary coolness under fire that always marked his battlefield performances."

"The profession of arms does not often attract innovative minds. Good generals do what has been done before them better than run-of-the-mill generals, and great generals do it far better. On rare occasions, however, the uncommon man appears who solves a serious problem with a method untried yet on the face of it so simple that afterward others wonder why it took so long to discover. Daniel Morgan was one of those rare individuals. This untutored son of the frontier was the only general in the American Revolution, on either side, to produce a significant original tactical thought. As I have written before he had no illusions about the behavior of militia in formal battle. But the use of militia was vital to the cause because there were rarely enough Continentals to face the British alone. The unanswered question until Cowpens was how best to use them when their presence was required in orthodox eighteenth-century combat. Morgan answered the question. He would not try to get militia to do what they were not meant to do. For he knew them. He came from them, those country people and backwoodsmen, knew their faults and virtues, their capabilities, and failings, knew as did William Moultrie that 'the militia are brave men, and will fight if you let them come to action in their own way.'

"Put the militia in the front ranks, said Morgan. But don't expect them to stand fast as Generals before him had insisted… He neither expected nor wanted the militia in the two first lines to stand their ground before a British bayonet charge… All he would ask for were two volleys at fifty yards, with special attention paid to officers and sergeants. Then Pickens militia would fall back across the left front of Howard's left to be held as a reserve. If necessary during their withdrawal Washington's cavalry would come to their assistance."

Thomas Young describes the night before the battle of Cowpens: "It was upon this occasion that I was more perfectly convinced of General Daniel Morgan's qualifications to command militia that I had ever before been. He went among the volunteers, helped them fix their swords, joked with them about their sweethearts, told them to keep in good spirits, and the day would be ours. And long after I laid down he was going about among the soldiers encouraging them and telling them that the old wagoneer would crack his whip over Ben in the morning, as sure as they lived. 'Just hold up your heads, boys, three fires' he would say 'and you are free, and when you return to your homes, how the old folks will bless you, and the girls kiss you for your gallant conduct.' "

At the Cowpens Daniel Morgan proved once again that he was "a battle captain for the ages."[14] The front line consisted of Major McDowell of North Carolina, "with about 60 picked men of his command, and Major Cunningham with a like number of Georgians, all having been selected with reference to their courage and their skill as marksmen."[15] His regulars and militia supported each other as planned and under Morgan's confident leadership, Tarleton and his brash corps were stopped in their tracks and routed.

As C. G. Davidson wrote: "The victory warmed the backwoods like a religious revival. The whole country praised the heroes of Cowpens. In some respects, Morgan had achieved the most brilliant coup of the Revolution." Under his leadership, the militia would prove its worth to the Continental Army. (McDowell and his North Carolinians, after successfully initiating the fight, would later perform a delaying action that ensured the victory.[16]) Since their uncourageous confusion under Rutherford at Camden, the frontiersmen had imbibed a new spirit. At King's Mountain they silenced the Tories, at Cowpens they conquered a Royal legion.

"Davidson once more missed the opportunity of participating in a momentous encounter. While Davie slaved at the Commissary's desk and Davidson built an army man by man, other commanders reaped the rewards of conquests. The Brigadier's disappointment was keen, the volunteers were his own followers, but he gave Morgan his wholehearted applause. 'You'l pleas to accept my warmest congratulations on your late glorious victory,' he wrote. 'You have in my opinion paved the way for the Salvation of this Country. I hope Major McDowell and the volunteers answered the character I gave you of them.' "[17]

Henderson wrote: "The Cowpens, like King's Mountain, was a blow to British prestige in the backcountry, and Cornwallis with his main army at Winnsboro could not let the defeat go unpunished. When the British commander set his troops in motion to pursue

Morgan there began 'that thrilling series of military movements which was continued with the activity of a steeplechase for quite two months,' and which military critics have generally acclaimed as a retreat equivalent in moral and materials to a victory. Greene's problem was to keep the two wings of his army about parallel fighting back at every favorable opportunity, yet never getting into a situation where Cornwallis's larger numbers could strike a decisive blow. Leaving the Cheraw after ordering Huger to retire toward Salisbury, Greene hurried across country to join Morgan."[18]

In Leckie's words: "He [Greene] had to reach Morgan as soon as possible to discuss with him his own plan for a daring game of martial cat and mouse that would lure Cornwallis farther and farther away from his base in South Carolina, while drawing him closer to Greene's base in Virginia. Traveling light, he could be on the Catawba in two or three days."

"Greene reached Morgan in an incredible two-day ride. He astonished the Old Wagoner by his boundless enthusiasm, and when he heard that Cornwallis had destroyed his baggage and was marching north in pursuit, he cried aloud in joy: 'Then he is ours.'

"He would lure His Lordship north, ever northward, until at last they were in Virginia, with Greene close to his own supplies and reinforcements and Cornwallis out of reach of his. Marching north, Cornwallis would have to cross many small streams and four major rivers: the Catawba, Yadkin, Deep and Dan. Where he could, Greene would oppose him at the fords, hoping to whittle him, to douse his ardor and drown his dreams. The Old Wagoner shook his head. It was a plan born of desperation, too bold, too risky—too frought with danger and unhappy circumstance. If it were attempted, he, Morgan, could not answer for the outcome. 'Neither will you!' Greene cried. 'For I shall take the matter upon myself.' "[19]

On January 31, 1781, General Greene met with Daniel Morgan, William Davidson, and William Washington at Beatie's Ford on the Catawba River.

"While they conferred, a sizeable party of British horsemen appeared on the right bank of the Catawba, and an officer they assumed to be Cornwallis raised a spyglass and studied the

American defenses. Greene and his officers saw the situation as critical. It took Greene and his officers only twenty minutes to come to the obvious conclusion… Davidson and his men would contest Cornwallis's crossing with no expectation of stopping him permanently but to delay him long enough to give the regulars a good start on the way to Salisbury and their rendezvous with Huger's column coming from the Great Pee Dee. Then Davidson would execute a quick get away. It was well that Morgan had decided to move that afternoon to evacuate the continentals, for Lord Cornwallis had also come to a decision. He would move out the next morning and force the Catawba."

"Nathaniel Greene and his party took the main road to Salisbury, to the farm of David Carr, from where Greene planned to direct Davidson's retreat after Cornwallis crossed the river. It was sixteen miles from Beatty's Ford. Morgan and Washington went another way that would take them to Howard and the Continentals. Behind them General William Lee Davidson of North Carolina, who had served in the North as a Continental officer in George Washington's Army, prepared to defend the Catawba with his 800 militiamen against Cornwallis's 2,500 stripped down regulars."[20]

Of Davidson's men Leckie says: "About three hundred held the likeliest crossing at Beatie's, while a lesser number was posted at the more difficult Cowan's or McCowan's Ford. Cornwallis's plan was to feint at Beatie's with a small force under Lieutenant Colonel James Webster, while he and General Charles O'Hara took the main body across Cowan's to turn the Yankee flank. It was Cornwallis's favorite maneuver, and with the river falling, he was ready to execute it.

"What his Lordship did not know was that Cowan's Ford, about five hundred yards wide and in that great width not exactly an easy crossing, also had a peculiarity of splitting in two about halfway across the river. The straight course, used by the wagons, was about three or four feet deep and swift and turbulent over a rocky bottom. The one diverging to the right, used by horsemen, was shallower and smoother, although longer. It reached the east bank about a quarter mile below the wagon course. Here Davidson had posted most of his remaining guard, with only twenty-five pickets opposite the wagon course. Cornwallis's Tory guide knew of these divergent courses, but no one else did—least of all the gallant Colonel Hall, who was to lead the spearhead crossing there.

"Just before dawn of a dark and rainswept morning, General O'Hara ordered his advance guards into the wagon course of Cowan's Crossing. In waist-deep icy water, their cartridge boxes high above their heads, they struggled four-abreast through the swirling black water. They had advanced a hundred yards before the smaller rebel force became aware of them, opening fire. Their bullets took a terrible toll among Colonel Hall's first three ranks, and the column halted. Then the men struggled forward again, taking more hits, stumbling over the rocky bottom, some soldiers being swept downstream—but still advancing. At this point the Tory guide took fright and fled—without warning Hall of the easier horse course to the right. So the British column splashed doggedly through the uneven, deeper wagon course. Now men and horses were swept off their feet. Hall's horse was shot from under him. Cornwallis's horse was wounded, but did not fall until it reached the farther bank. Both Leslie and O'Hara were unhorsed. Still the British advanced, now clearly visible as the thin light of dawn crept across the swirling black water.

"Down at the horse course General Davidson heard the firing above him and rushed with his men toward the sound. He arrived in time to take a bullet in the heart from the sodden redcoats, who had routed the American pickets, loaded their muskets and opened fire. With Davidson's death, the American defenders broke, but not before Colonel Hall was killed as he rode ashore."[21]

Davidson continues the story: "In the opinion of 'Light-Horse Harry Lee,' 'The loss of Brigadier Davidson would have been felt in any stage of the war. It was particularly detrimental in its effect at this period, for he was the chief instrument relied upon by Greene for the assemblage of the militia, an event all important at this crisis and anxiously desired by the American general.' Greene and Morgan had hoped that their forces might be united and sufficiently augmented to stop the British at the Yadkin. But on February 3rd,

Greene, still retreating, wrote to Sumter, 'We have been oblidged to retire over the Yadkin... The loss of General Davidson is a great misfortune at this time. I stayed at one of the places of rendezvous the night after the enemy crossed until midnight, but not a man appeared, nor has there a single man joined us except a few belonging to South Carolina...' And Cornwallis, close behind, reported to the colonial Secretary of State in Britain that the events of February 1st had 'so effectively dispirited the militia that we met with no further opposition in our march to the Yadkin, through one of the most rebellious tracts in America.'[22]

Leckie goes on: "It had been a costly crossing for Cornwallis, and it gained little more than the death of Davidson—for Morgan and his division had broken camp marching all night until they were thirty miles away on the road to Trading Ford on the Yadkin. Continued rain made the roads impassable for pursuit. Drenched like his soldiers by rain and river, mounted uncomfortably on a strange horse, his wig plastered against his flesh, Lord Cornwallis stared glumly north, where as he well knew, another probably difficult and defended river had to be crossed.

"Meanwhile Nathaniel Greene, in whose innovative brain just such discomfiture had been planned, had narrowly escaped capture. After Morgan departed, he had remained behind near Salisbury to arrange for Davidson's militia to join him and follow Morgan once their ford duty was done. Below him as he sat on his horse, he heard the sound of musketry. It was Tarleton's cavalry scattering mounted Tar Heels at Tarrant's Tavern. Greene stayed where he was, still waiting for Davidson—until a messenger arrived to tell him that the general was dead and Cornwallis was over the Catawba. Dismayed, Greene rode on alone to Steele's Tavern in Salisbury. There a friendly voice came out of the darkness: 'What? Alone, Greene?'

'Yes' he replied softly, 'alone, tired, hungry and penniless.' Then he went inside, where Mrs. Steele prepared him a hearty breakfast. As he ate, she came to his table bearing two little bags of hard money.

'You need them more than I do,' she said, placing them in his hands. Greene looked up at her with tears of gratitude shining in his eyes. He had come to her hungry, penniless and forlorn but now he had been fed, and in his hands he held—a pittance though it might be—the renewed war chest of the Grand Army of the Southern Department of the Continental Army."[23]

With his spirit also renewed, Greene continued to strike at Cornwallis, "in a damaging series of quick, sharp jabs, relying on speedy attack and withdrawl to prevent his opponent from using full force."[24]

Leckie goes on: "For all practical purposes, Nathanael Greene, because of the vast distances between himself and Washington in New Jersey, was completely on his own. Every tactic, every maneuver, line of march or order of battle sprang from his own brain, just as he chose every position on which to attack or defend. In a sense, while being his own strategist and tactician, he was also his own quartermaster, for he had to supply the necessary logistics—food, clothing, shelter and arms—for his own troops.

"And the troops, again, in their endurance, doggedness and loyalty were a kind of soldier perhaps unrivaled in military history. They could be beaten, of course, and were, for they were up against the splendidly trained and equipped and equally brave British Redcoats with their German allies. But they were nevertheless unconquerable. A lost battle to them was a familiar reverse from which they made the likewise-customary rapid recovery."

"His [Greene's] modest report to La Luzerne—'We fight, get beat, rise and fight again'—would forever be cherished as a motto of the United States Army to be. More important, he forced Lord Cornwallis to take the fatal step of invading Virginia."[25]

In Virginia

Thomas Jefferson did not seek the office of governor in May 1779, but he "accepted the office out of a sense of duty, with a realization that a wartime executive faces uncommon burdens." The office of governor had limited powers, and the legislative assembly "kept control of military and commercial affairs through a board of war and a board of trade, which produced much confusion and delay in decision-making."[26] For this Jefferson himself was responsible. He distrusted executive authority and helped write the Virginia laws that placed the real political power in the assembly and not in the office of governor.[27]

On May 10, 1779, a British fleet landed at Portsmith, Virginia, and terrorized the surrounding area before departing two weeks later. Virginia was virtually defenseless as her troops were stationed in New York and South Carolina. On January 2, 1781, the traitor Benedict Arnold landed by ship near Richmond with 1,500 Redcoats and succeeded in his mission to disrupt Greene's supply lines and damage Virginia's morale before retreating to Portsmith. Jefferson attempted to coordinate a defense with the militia but was unsuccessful. In February, Washington sent a force to Virginia under the command of Lafayette to coordinate with the Virginia militia in an operation designed to drive Benedict Arnold from Portsmith. Before this plan could be enacted, Cornwallis, who had fought Greene at Guildford Courthouse, North Carolina, in March, invaded Virginia.

On May 20, 1781, Cornwallis was joined by a British landing force and would control the state of Virginia with little resistance throughout the summer. During this time Virginia's pride was destroyed, and although Jefferson's term as governor expired on June 2, he was made the 'scapegoat' by the Virginia Assembly for Virginia's failure to defend herself. These would be the darkest moments of his political career.

In September 1781, Washington's army, along with the French Naval Squadron, arrived and eventually forced Cornwallis's surrender; but for Jefferson the censure by the Virginia Assembly, though later reversed, would "follow him the rest of his life and into the history books."[28]

When Cornwallis pressed on to Virginia in 1781, Greene shifted his raiding farther south, "where he not only prevented the British from coming to the aid of Cornwallis but made them fight hard to retain the coastal cities of Savannah and Charleston.

"As a result Washington had the chance to isolate Cornwallis. With the aid of French forces exceeding the American by two to one, he closed in on Yorktown from land and sea simultaneously. The French fleet under DeGrasse achieved temporary superiority in the area; the French and American soldiers outnumbered the British, and together they forced Cornwallis to surrender his entire army (which still amounted to more than seven thousand men) on October 17, 1781."[29]

The Brevard Family

The following are brief sketches of the Brevard Family condensed from Wheeler's *Historical Sketches.*

"At the commencement of the Revolutionary War, John Brevard, then an old and infirm man, had eight sons and four daughters. He was a well-known and influential Whig, and early instilled his patriotic principles into the minds of his children.

"Mary, the eldest daughter of John Brevard, married Gen. Davidson, who was killed at Cowan's Ford on the Catawba River.

"Nancy married John Davidson. They were both killed by the Indians at the head of the Catawba River.

"Jane married Ephraim, a brother of John Davidson. Though very young, he was sent by Gen. Davidson, on the night before the skirmish at Cowan's Ford, with an express to Col. Morgan, warning him of the approach of the British Forces.

"John Brevard, Jr. served in the Continental Army with the commission of Lieutenant.

"Hugh Brevard, with several brothers, was at the battle of Ramsour's Mill. Early in the war he was appointed a Colonel of the militia, and was present at the defeat of General Ashe at Brier Creek.

"Adam Brevard first served one year in the Northern Army under General Washington. He then came South, and was present at the battle of Ramsour's Mill.

"Alexander Brevard first joined the army as a cadet. He then received the commission of Lieutenant, and soon afterward that of Captain in the Continental Army. He was engaged in the battles of White Plains, Trenton, Princeton, Brandywine, Monmouth, and Germantown, and remained in the Northern Army under General Washington until some time in 1779. He joined the Southern Army under General Gates and later served under General Greene in his battles. Thus, he was in active service from the beginning to the end of the war.

"Joseph Brevard also served as a Continental Officer."[30]

John Brevard's brother-in-law was the Reverend Alexander MacWhorter of Newark, New Jersey. His family was of Scotch-Irish ancestry and his parents had been linen merchants in Ireland before migrating to America. Alexander's sister Jane married John Brevard some time after their families arrived in North Carolina in 1748.[31] In the fall of 1775, Rev. Alexander MacWhorter was appointed by the Continental Congress to travel to North Carolina to convert the loyalists there to the patriotic cause. But he met with little success (reality unfortunately mirrored the less than optimistic prediction that MacWhorter had made to Benjamin Franklin before leaving on this mission).[32] Rev. MacWhorter was known as one of the "fighting parsons" of New Jersey and was a mighty force in stiffening the militant resolve of the New Jersey patriots, especially in the winter of 1776-1777. He would inspire George Washington's troops with a sermon on December 7, 1776,[33] would act as an advisor to Washington on the strategic situation in New Jersey circa 1776, and was present at the council that recommended the crossing of the Delaware. MacWhorter would cross the Delaware with Washington and was with the troops at the battles of Trenton and Princeton before returning to Morristown in January of 1777.[34]

Previously on June 25, 1775, George Washington had passed through Newark on his way to Cambridge to assume the command of the Continental Army. It is believed that he consulted with Rev. MacWhorter at that time to gauge the feelings of the local populace on the cause of independence.[35]

"The day after he assumed command of the army, Washington had issued an order: The General requests and expects of all officers and soldiers not engaged on actual duty, a punctual attendance in divine service, to implore the blessing of heaven upon the means used for our safety and defense."

Later in the war, Washington would write to the church members of Raritan, New Jersey, where his winter camp of 1778-1779 was located:

Gentlemen:

To meet the approbation of good men cannot but be agreeable. Your affectionate expressions make it still more so. In quartering my army and supplying its wants, distress and inconvenience will often occur to the citizen. I feel myself happy in the consciousness that these have been strictly limited by necessity, and in your opinion of my attention to the rights of my fellow citizens. I thank you, gentlemen, sincerely for the sense you entertain of the conduct of the army, and for the interest you take in my welfare. I trust the goodness of the cause, and the exertions of the people, under Divine protection, will give us that honorable peace for which we are contending. Suffer me, gentlemen to wish the Reformed Church at Raritan a long continuance of its present minister and consistory, and all the blessings which flow from piety and religion.[36]

William Lee Davidson

William Lee Davidson would spend a portion of the Revolutionary War camped at Rocky River near Charlotte, North Carolina. "The camp at Rocky River was only about 20 miles from Centre (Davidson's church). For the past four years, Reverend Thomas Harris McCaule had kept the faith for God and country in that congregation. He was frequently in the camp utilizing his Princeton learning to write dispatches for the Salisbury Brigadier... Parson McCaule, as Davidson called him, was good for camp spirit... In the pulpit and in the field, he was ardent in assistance to his church's outstanding soldier."[37]

Davidson would receive the news of the American victory at King's Mountain while camped at Rocky River.

The Ewing Family

Rev. John Ewing of Philadelphia declared that he would offer no prayers for King George III after the signing of the Declaration of Independence occurred in 1776. As a result, his church, the Old Pine Street Presbyterian Church, would be desecrated by British troops during their occupation of Philadelphia in 1777. It survived, however, and became known as "The Church of the Patriots." Today it is the only pre-Revolutionary Presbyterian structure still standing in Philadelphia.

In 1773, Rev. John Ewing had traveled to Scotland to receive a Doctor of Divinity degree from the University of Edinburgh. Dr. William Robertson, a principal of the Scottish Enlightenment, presented the award. Dr. Ewing was made provost of the University of Pennsylvania in 1777.[38]

Prestley Kittredge Ewing, in his genealogy of the Ewing family, writes of George Ewing: "[He] was a Commissary under appointment of Colonel Ephraim Blaine to purchase for the Army, and under this appointment he bought and sold goods, upon his own personal responsibility, to Washington's army at Valley Forge, in the winter of 1777. The Government being unable to pay the debts he thus incurred, his individual property was sold to satisfy them, leaving him and his family destitute; he died, and the family was taken to Fayette County, Pennsylvania in 1786 by his son-in-law."

Of Nathaniel Ewing, Mr. Ewing writes, that he was "of or near Charlotte, North Carolina, was a soldier of the war of the Revolution, a member of Capt. Houston's Company, and engaged in the battle of Ramsour's Mill, King's Mountain, and Cowpens."[39]

Thomas Jefferson

Thomas Jefferson served in the Virginia legislature from 1776-1779. He spent most of these three years at Monticello with a lesser portion of each year in residence at the capital city of Williamsburg. While many Americans were sacrificing and contributing to the war effort during this time, Jefferson lived an idyllic life at home: writing and revising Virginia laws in the comfort of his personal library, enjoying his gardens, building an elaborate addition to his house, and entertaining Hessian prisoners of war, captured at Saratoga, whom he considered a welcome addition to his social circle.[40]

Andrew Jackson

Andrew Jackson was of Scotch-Irish ancestry. From the *History of Davidson County, Tennessee,* W. W. Clayton writes: "When the Revolution had reached that part of South Carolina where young Jackson resided, he was a youth of thirteen years of age. Robert was too young to be a soldier, but his oldest brother, Hugh, had two years before joined the army under Col. Davie, had fought at the battle of Stono, and died after the action from heat and fatigue. After the terrible havoc of the 29th of May, 1780, by Tarleton's dragoons in the Waxhaw settlement, Robert and Andrew assisted their mother in taking care of the wounded in the old wooden church of the neighborhood. Upon the great disaster of the war in the South, the defeat of Gen. Gates, Aug. 10, 1780, the boys and their mother abandoned their home for a safer retreat north of the scene of war.

"In February, 1781, Mrs. Jackson and her sons and many of the neighbors returned to the ravaged homes at Waxhaw. The desultory war between Whigs and Tories was soon renewed in that section. Robert and Andrew were taken prisoners at the house of their cousin, Lieut. Thomas Crawford, who lay ill from a wound received the day before from a party of dragoons. Before the family had suspicion of danger, the house was surrounded and the doors secured. Regardless of the fact that the house was occupied by the defenseless wife and young children of a wounded soldier, the dragoons, brutalized by mean partisan warfare, began to destroy with wild riot and noise the contents of the house. Crockery, glass, and furniture were dashed to pieces, beds emptied, the clothing of the family torn to rags, even the clothes of the infant, which Mrs. Crawford carried in her arms, were not spared. While this destruction was going on, the officer in command of the party ordered Andrew to clean his high jack-boots, which were well splashed and crusted with mud. The reply, which the boy made, was worthy of a prince: 'Sir, I am a prisoner of war, and claim to be treated as such.' "

W. W. Clayton continues: "The fate of the brothers was next to suffer as prisoners at Camden. The wounded Lieut. Crawford, the Jacksons, and some two hundred and fifty other prisoners, were confined in a contracted enclosure around the Camden jail; no beds of any description, no medical attendance, nor means of dressing their wounds; their only food a scanty supply of bad bread. They were even robbed of part of their clothing. The three relatives were separated as soon as their relationship was discovered. Miserable among the miserable, gaunt, yellow, hungry, and sick, robbed of his jacket and socks, ignorant of his brother's fate, chafing with suppressed fury—Andrew passed now some of the most wretched days of his life. Ere long the smallpox broke out among the prisoners, and raged unchecked by medicine. Thus they remained, the sick, the dying, and the dead together. Andrew for some time escaped the contagion. While in this prison camp, he took his first lesson in reconnoitering an army on the field of battle. Gen. Greene, having arrived with a force superior to that of Lord Rawdon's, which occupied Camden, encamped on a slight eminence in front of the jail-yard, which was only hidden from full view of the prisoners by a high board-fence that surrounded the enclosure. All the prisoners were overjoyed with the prospect of being speedily released from their sufferings, as the news of Gen. Greene's arrival spread among them. Andrew looked for a crevice in the board-fence, thorough which he might feast his longing eyes on the camp of the soldiers, but he could find none. In the course of the night, however, he managed, with the aid of an old razor blade, which had been generously bestowed upon the prisoners as a meat-knife, to hack out a knot from the fence. The morning light found him spying out the American position with eager eye. What he saw that morning through the knothole of his prison was his second lesson in the art of war. An impressive lesson it proved, and one he never forgot. There was the American encampment spread out in full view before him at the distance of a mile. Gen. Greene, being well assured of Rawdon's weakness, and anticipating nothing so little as an attack from a man whom he supposed to be trembling for his own safety, neglected precautions against surprise. At ten in the morning, when Rawdon led out his nine hundred men to the attack, Andrew, made with vexation, saw Greene's men scattered over the hill, cleaning their arms, washing their clothes, and playing games, totally unprepared to resist. Rawdon, by taking a circuitous route, was enabled to break upon Greene's left with all the effect of a surprise. From his knot-hole the excited youth saw the sudden smoke of musketry, the rush of the Americans for their arms, the hasty falling-in, the opening of Greene's fire, the fine dash of American horse upon Rawdon's rear, the wild flight of horses running riderless about the hill, the fire slackening, and, alas! receding, till Rawdon's army swept over the hill and vanished on the other side, Greene in full retreat before him. The prisoners were in despair. Andrew's spirits sank under this accumulation of miseries, and he began to sicken with the first symptoms of the smallpox. Robert was in a condition still worse. The wound in his head had never been dressed, and had not healed. He, too, reduced as he was, began to shiver and burn with the fever that announces the dread disease. Another week of prison-life would have probably consigned both boys to the grave. But they had a friend outside—their mother—who at this crisis of their fate strove with the might of love for their deliverance. Learning of their forlorn condition, this heroic woman went to Camden and succeeded, after a time, in effecting an exchange of prisoners between a Waxhaw captain and a British general. The Whig captain gave up thirteen soldiers, whom he had captured in the rear of the British Army, and received in return the two sons of Mrs. Jackson and five of her neighbors. Through forty miles of lonely wilderness the little company made their way home, Robert Jackson being supported on a horse by one of the exchanged prisoners, and Andrew, bare-headed, bare-footed, and without a jacket, the fever of the smallpox raging in his veins, dragged himself wearily along on foot. Part of their journey was through a cold, drizzling rain, which aggravated the disease. In two days after they reached home Robert was a corpse, and Andrew was raving in delirium. He remained an invalid for several months. Andrew was no sooner out of danger than his brave mother resolved to go to Charleston to minister to the sufferings of her sister's sons, who were prisoners on the loathsome prison-ships in that harbor. She made the journey, one hundred and sixty miles, probably on horseback, with two or three other women bound on a like mission, ministered to the prisoners, and was seized with the ship fever, of which she died shortly after at the house of a relative, William Barton, a few miles out of Charleston."[41]

Ephraim Brevard

Withers writes of Ephraim Brevard: "While engaged as a teacher in Queen's College, Ephraim Brevard raised a company from the young men of that institution to assist in putting down the Tories assembled on the Cape Fear. They marched in the direction of Cross Creek (Fayetteville), but upon hearing of the dispersion of the Tories, returned home. This was in February, after his return from the 'Snow campaign' with General Rutherford in December 1775. In 1776, in his professional capacity, he joined the expedition of General Rutherford during the Cherokee campaign. In 1780 he entered the Southern Army under General Lincoln as assistant surgeon. He was captured at the surrender of Charleston on May 12th, and during his confinement there as a prisoner of war he suffered so much on the prison ship that his health gave way. He died at the home of his old friend and fellow patriot, John McKnitt Alexander."[42]

William Davidson

General Henry Lee would describe William L. Davidson as follows: "Devoted to the profession of arms, and to the great cause for which he fought, his future usefulness may be inferred from his former conduct. The Congress of the United States in gratitude for his services and in commemoration of their sense of his worth, passed the following resolution:

" 'Resolved, That the governor and council of the state of North Carolina be desired to erect a monument at the expense of the United States not to exceed five hundred dollars, to the memory of the late Brigadier-General Davidson, who commanded the militia of the district of Salisbury, in the state of North Carolina, and was killed on the first day of February last, fighting gallantly in the defence of the liberty and independence of these states.' "[43]

Thomas Jefferson

Lee would also describe Thomas Jefferson. Henry Lee (also known as Light Horse Harry Lee) was the father of the Civil War's Robert E. Lee and the commander of Lee's Legion in the Southern states during the Revolutionary War. At that time he had won the favor of the commander of the Southern Department, Nathanael Greene, and the commander of the Continental Army, George Washington. Henry Lee's *Memoirs of the War in The Southern Department of the United States* was published in 1812.

Charles Royster writes: "As he contemplated writing his memoirs, thinking about the lesson he wished to teach, as well as the story he could tell, Lee's mind fixed on Thomas Jefferson. In 1809 while Lee faced bankruptcy, Jefferson was retiring to Monticello after having served two terms as president of the United States. Lee deplored Jefferson's policies. He had tried to prevent Jefferson's election. The Republicans led by Jefferson, not content with defeating Lee and other Federalists in elections, claimed also to be the true heirs of the American Revolution—the real patriots who saved the republic. They called the Federalists 'tories' and 'monarchists.' Amid the ruin of his fortunes Lee believed that Jefferson had tried to rob him of his greatest distinction—his achievements as a patriotic fighter on behalf of American independence and self-government.

"Thomas Jefferson served as governor of Virginia during the British Army's incursions into the state in 1779, 1780, and 1781. Lee fought in South Carolina and North Carolina, as Lord Cornwallis moved his British force northward into Virginia. Lee did not witness Jefferson's conduct but in his *Memoirs* he wrote about it.

"... If his narrative could demonstrate that Governor Jefferson had fled Richmond rather than confront the traitor Benedict Arnold and a detachment of British troops, and then had run away from Monticello to escape Banastre Tarleton and a British raiding party, Lee could fix in his reader's mind a conviction that Jefferson—for all the good words in the Declaration of Independence and elsewhere—lacked courage. [Fortunately, Jefferson had the courage to successfully escape capture during these two British invasions of Virginia. It would be his strategic military dependence on last-minute ineffective militia call-ups that led to these stinging defeats.]

"Lee's account of the British invasions of Virginia made Thomas Jefferson angry for the last fourteen years of his life. Jefferson encouraged and assisted rival accounts: Louis Girardin's history of Virginia during the war years and William Johnson's biography of Nathanael Greene. During the last week of his life Thomas Jefferson was still working to prove Lee wrong."[44]

Despite these efforts, some twentieth-century historians continue to echo Lee's words. In this quotation, respected historians Henry Steele Commager and Richard B. Morris write: "Washington had long before warned Governor Jefferson that Virginia must prepare to defend itself. But Jefferson was strangely inert. Virginia was apathetic and its governor had no talent for leadership in a war emergency. The defense was a travesty."[45]

Jefferson accepted the governorship out of a sense of duty and may have done the best he was equipped to do, but in reality, the real patriots of the American Revolution would be those who followed the sacred pledge.

Chapter 4
Freedom

"To use every exertion to spread the love of country, and fire of freedom throughout America."

From the late 1700s to the early 1800s, Daniel Boone's example would set the standard for westward expansion—a pattern that would be followed by his contemporary Americans and their descendants. The route through the Cumberland Gap from the East into Kentucky, Tennessee, Missouri, and later to the far West would be traveled by many. Daniel Boone did not discover the Cumberland Gap, but he, as leader, along with "thirty-two axemen and Indian fighters… hewed through the woods and thickets… the Wilderness Road, the first road across the mountains into Kentucky."[1]

Margaret Davidson, along with her mother and family, migrated west after the end of the Revolutionary War to reside in the county named after her father. Late in her life she recalled the shock, sadness, and heartbreak she felt when, as a little girl, she was told that her father had been killed and would never return home. The Davidson family's new home would be the frontier town of Nashville, Tennessee.

Harriet Simpson Arnow writes: "The long, rough, and dangerous route through Cumberland Gap and across Kentucky" was bypassed by those bound for Tennessee by taking a "much shorter route, that of Tollunteeskee's Trail across the Plateau… Rough as it was dangerous, this route formed the basis of future roads across the Plateau that tied the two parts of Tennessee together. The first party of around a hundred people protected by Colonel Kaspar Mansker and other guards came over it in late 1787, more than a year before the official opening, September 25, 1788. The following November there came another large group of emigrants that included Judge John McNairy, Prosecutor Andrew Jackson, and the widow of General William Davidson, for whom Davidson County was named."[2]

According to W. W. Clayton: "Davidson County was erected into a civil municipality by an act of the Legislature of North Carolina, approved Oct. 6, 1783.

"The area included in these boundries embraced between eleven and twelve thousand square miles, lying along the northern line of the State from Cumberland Gap to the Tennessee River, and southward about fifty-six miles to the old military line run by the Commissioners of North Carolina. It embraced more than three-fourths of Middle Tennessee.

"This county, like the other three west of the Appalachian Mountains, received its name from an officer of the army of the Revolution, Gen. William Davidson, of Mecklinburg Co., N.C. He was a native of that part of the State which had early exhibited an enthusiastic devotion to independence."[3]

Margaret Davidson grew to maturity in Davidson County and married Finis Ewing in 1793. Ewing had moved to the edge of the frontier in Tennessee after his parents had died in Virginia. He would later become the Reverend Finis Ewing, and he founded the Cumberland Presbyterian Church.

R. C. Ewing writes of Finis Ewing: "At the time of their marriage Mr. Ewing was in his twenty first year and Miss Davidson in her nineteenth… At this time neither Mr. Ewing or his wife knew anything of experimental religion.

"… The truth is that the Presbyterian Church, at that time and in that region, is acknowledged to have been in a lamentably lukewarm and almost lifeless state: its ministers were formal and cold; and but few of its members, as it became manifest, knew anything of experimental religion. Much was heard from the pulpit about the 'elect of God,' but little or nothing about 'born of the spirit'.

"… Ewing and his wife were now the united head of a family and moved from Tennessee just across the border into Kentucky."[4] Finis Ewing would serve as a deputy sheriff before joining the ministry there. It was said that when the Ewings came to Kentucky they brought the law and the gospel with them.

According to Dr. Cossitt: "They settled in Logan County, near the town of Russellville and near the Red River Meeting House. The congregation which worshiped at this church was under the pastoral care of Rev. James McGready and afterward became famous as the initial point of the great revival of 1800.

"Mr. McGready was one of the most remarkable men of his day. As the original and most efficient promoter of that great religious awakening above mentioned, he will always occupy a conspicuous place in the religious history of that period. His biography has been written and sketches of his life by different authors have frequently appeared in the religious literature of this country. It will, therefore, suffice to say but a single word about him in this connection.

"Mr. McGready's great forte and special mission seemed to be to unsettle the foundations of those who had built upon the sand, to disturb the peace of those who had no adequate grounds for their security, to awaken those who were dead in their tresspasses and in sins; to arouse to a sense of their danger, those who were sleeping on the very verge of ruin, and to point out with inimitable precision and directness the way of escape. The testimony is also that he was a very earnest man, that he had great faith in the promises of the gospel and could successfully infuse that spirit into the minds of his church, that under his tremendous preaching the leaden dullness and the icy coldness that lay as a fatal incubus upon the spiritual life of the church, was broken up, and a new era in the history of Christianity on this continent was inaugurated through the revival of 1800.

"The results to the general church of Christ in this country, and to the good of mankind generally, that legitimately follow from that great religious awakening, cannot be comprehended by finite minds and will only be known fully in the last great day.

"His method was heart-searching and soul stirring, powerful to detect the hypocrite and alarm the formalist, to sweep away sandy foundations, to cause men to build anew on the rock Christ Jesus.

"The sermons of Mr. McGready soon awakened in the minds of both Ewing and his wife new thoughts and anxieties with regard to their spiritual condition. They heard nothing to which their minds could remain indifferent, or over which their consciences could slumber. The whole system of religion seemed to be presented to their view in an unusual form and invested with a different character; but whether their past or their present instructions were the more scriptural and worthy of their regard, was a question they were not prepared to decide. It was an absorbing question, however, which occupied their thoughts and investigations during their waking hours. The soul's concerns and the minds exercises were not with them, as with too many professors of religion at that time, prohibited. They had been taught that saving faith consisted in the belief that Jesus Christ is the Son of God; but their present pastor made a clear distinction 'between a mere historical and a true saving faith.' When doctors differ, what shall the learners do? The subject appeared intricate and full of mystery: it conflicted with all their previous instructions and settled opinions; and to their grief and consternation, it struck at the very foundation of their hopes.

"Knowing that God desired 'truth in the inward parts'; and praying that he might 'make them know wisdom,' long and carefully did they investigate this subject.

"But this state of things did not last long. After a few days, as Mr. Ewing was returning from the grove where he had been praying for the conversion of one so dear to his affections as his wife, she met him, her countenance beaming with joy and her heart glowing with love to God. She too had found a kneeling place, where her savior had designed to meet her and speak pardon and peace to her soul.

"Now the love of Christ, which passeth knowledge, had come to that house; and the peace of God, which passeth all understanding, was to keep those hearts and minds through Jesus Christ."[5]

John Vant Stephens writes: "The Rev. James McGready was the leader of the Revival Party. He was born in North Carolina, in 1763, of Scotch-Irish descent. After becoming a candidate for the ministry, he removed to western Pennsylvania, where he was under the tuition of Rev. John McMillan, later the founder of Jefferson College. He served a congregation in Orange County, North Carolina. While in that state he became a noted revivalist. In 1796 he removed to Logan County, Kentucky, in the Green River section, the northern part of the Cumberland Country. He took charge of three small country churches, Gasper River, Red River, and Muddy River. These churches showed very little spirituality. Mr. McGready drew up a 'Preamble and Covenant,' which he and some of his people signed. They pledged themselves 'to observe the third Saturday of each month, for one year, as a day of fasting and prayer, for the conversion of sinners in Logan County and throughout the world' and 'to spend one-half-hour every Saturday evening at the setting of the sun, and one-half-hour every Sabbath morning, at the rising of the sun, in pleading with God to revive his work.'

"In this letter Mr. McGready told his own story. In part it reads as follows: 'On the fourth Sabbath in July, at the administration of the sacrament in Gasper River Congregation, the Lord appeared in majesty and power. On Monday multitudes were solemnly awakened; some in almost every family throughout the congregation. The following week, the impressions were so deep, that little or no business was attended to.

'On the first Sabbath in September following, the sacrament was administered in Muddy River Church, another congregation under my charge. This was also a glorious time The Lord poured out his Spirit in a very remarkable manner. About this time the work spread into many infant churches that were forming in this country, and many souls were savingly brought to Christ.

'In June 1800, the most glorious time commenced that my eyes ever beheld. At the sacrament at Red River, on Monday after preaching, the people broke out in a general outcry over the whole assembly. About ten persons were hopefully converted. About a month after at Gasper River large multitudes attended. The work began on Sunday evening, and continued until Tuesday morning. Many persons from Sumter County, in the state of Tennessee, came out of curiosity, and the Lord graciously converted some of them. They carried home the divine flame, and spread it through the greater part of the Cumberland sections.

'In my narrative, I have confined myself to the sacramental times, as there were the most remarkable seasons. But very wonderful circumstances have occurred at private meetings, and praying societies, which I must pass over. Instances have been of a whole neighborhood meeting together, without any previous appointment, and joining in prayer, and the power of God descending among them. At one such accidental meeting nine persons out of sixteen professed to experience religion before they parted. At one society, the power of God came among the people and they continued from Tuesday evening to Thursday evening when ten persons were converted.

'The glorious work has disseminated a principle of love through the hearts of all Christians. Bigotry and prejudice have received a death wound; names, parties, and divisions seem to subside totally. Presbyterians and Methodists love one another. They preach together, and commune together, and mutually rejoice to see the work of the Lord go on.' "[6]

This revival became known as the Second Great Awakening and it spread throughout the United States to affect the lives of many Americans.

Margaret and Finis Ewing enjoyed a friendship with Rachel and Andrew Jackson during the time of the Great Revival.[7] Missouri's first senator, Thomas Hart Benton, described Andrew Jackson in the following manner: "There was a deep-seated vein of piety in him, unaffectedly showing itself in his reverence for divine worship, respect for the ministers of the gospel their hospitable reception in his house, and constant encouragement of all the pious tendencies of Mrs. Jackson. And when they both afterwards became members of a church, it was the natural and regular result of their early and cherished feelings.

"He was attached to his friends, and to his country, and never believed any report to the discredit of either, until compelled by proof.

"He never gave up a friend in a doubtful case, or from policy or calculation. He was a firm believer in the goodness of a superintending Providence, and in the eventual right judgement and justice of the people. I have seen him at the most desperate part of his fortune, and never saw him waver in the belief that all would come right in the end."[8]

Andrew Jackson would be elected president in November 1828. In a letter dated October 14, 1828, Finis Ewing wrote to Andrew Jackson as follows:

"And Sir I am proud to tell you that, not withstanding there are three prefers to one against you here, you are sure of the state of Missouri as you are of Tennessee.

"…The foul efforts to tarnish your reputation especially the attack on your lady has had just the contrary effect, from what was intended. Mrs. Ewing who is a retired, pious woman was compelled to speak when those efforts were made."[9]

In *The Life of Andrew Jackson,* R. V. Remini writes: "As the presidential campaign gained momentum in 1827 and as a swelling army of political managers appeared on the scene to direct a vigorous demonstration of support for Old Hickory, Jackson was hard pressed to meet all the obligations they placed on him: their call for information; the plea for clarification; the necessity of explaining his behavior in connection with one event or another… But perhaps the most devastating charge leveled at Jackson, as the campaign swung into full operation, involved the circumstances of his marriage to Rachael… Jackson was visibly shaken by the widespread broadcast in the newspapers of the circumstances of his marriage… The contemptible tactics of the coalition, stormed Jackson, in dredging up the details of his marriage in this campaign was another example of their moral and political bankruptcy."[10] (The controversy concerned the legitimacy of Rachael's divorce from her first husband before her marriage to Andrew Jackson.)

In a letter from the Hermitage dated November 17, 1828, Andrew Jackson replies to Finis Ewing: "... Mrs. J. and myself have often heard from your amicable Lady and her sister & were always gratified to learn that they were the Defenders of Mrs. J and my reputations..."[11]

Rachael died one month after Andrew Jackson was elected to the presidency of the United States. Rachael Jackson was buried on Christmas Eve in the garden of the Hermitage. Robert V. Remini writes: "During the rites Jackson himself broke down. For the first time since her death tears ran freely down his cheeks... To the day he died Andrew Jackson grieved over the loss of his wife. Becoming President meant little to him at this moment. 'A loss so great,' he said 'can be compensated by no earthly gift.' "

Before Rachael's death Jackson had promised her that he would join the church, but he postponed it until he retired from the Presidency to avoid any perceived political overtones. Before joining "he consulted with the Reverend James Smith who officiated at the Hermitage Church, which Jackson had built for Rachael in 1823."[12]

The Rev. James Smith was born in Scotland and as a young man emigrated to the United States. He moved to southern Indiana in 1824 where he taught school. "A confirmed Deist, he enjoyed discussing religion and attending camp meetings to make fun of the preachers."[13] When he heard Rev. James Blackwell preach the religion of experience and subsequently had an encounter with God's presence, he could no longer deny reality. After his conversion, he was licensed to preach by the Logan Presbytery of the Cumberland Presbyterian Church in Kentucky.

In 1831 he moved to Nashville, Tennessee, where he was associated with the Hermitage Church as well as editing the Cumberland Presbyterian newsletter *The Revivalist.* He edited the works of the Rev. James McGready and wrote a history of the Cumberland Presbyterian Church, which was founded by Finis Ewing and two others on February 4, 1810.

James Smith wrote a book entitled *The Christians Defense* in 1843 based on his lengthy debate with a skeptic who opposed Smith's defense of the Christian faith. In 1844 Smith would join the regular Presbyterian Church and transfer to Springfield, Illinois, for a later meeting that some might call a divine appointment. While still with the Cumberland Presbyterians in 1838 James Smith wrote to Finis Ewing that Andrew Jackson felt more "identified with the Presbyterian Church than any other."

On July 15, 1838 the Hermitage Church "was jammed with parishioners" when Jackson formally joined and "for the remainder of his life General Jackson conducted himself as a true believer."

Shortly before his death Jackson stated: "I am in the hands of a merciful God, I have full confidence in his goodness and mercy… the Bible is true… I have tried to conform to its spirit as nearly as possible. Upon this sacred volume I rest my hope for eternal salvation through the merit and blood of our blessed Lord and Savior, Jesus Christ." To his servants and loved ones, he said: "God will take care of you for me. I am my God's. I belong to him. I go but a short time before you, and I want to meet you all in heaven, both white and black."[14]

In *The History of Davidson County* W. W. Clayton goes on: "Gen. Jackson's life belongs to our national history, yet, in a restricted sense, it is a part, and a very important part, of the history of Davidson County. His home was here from early manhood; from this county emanated those military campaigns which were supported with such singular unanimity by his countrymen… here at Nashville and in Tennessee, he founded a new political dynasty, which rose rapidly into ascendancy, and for many years controlled the politics of the nation.

"Andrew Jackson was of humble birth, but in his veins flowed the blood of a long line of ancestors noted for their independence, their personal energy and courage, their restlessness under political and ecclesiastical restraint, and their great sincerity and earnestness in their convictions."

Clayton also gives the background of James K. Polk: "James Knox Polk, eleventh President of the United States, was of Scotch-Irish ancestry. His progenitors, Col. Thomas Polk and Ezekiel Polk, the latter of whom was his grandfather, were among the early settlers of Mecklenburg County, North Carolina, in 1735 and took a prominent part in the Mecklenburg Declaration…

Ezekiel Polk's son, Samuel, who married Jane Knox, and was a farmer of Mecklenburg County, was the father of the subject of the memoir. The latter was the eldest son of a family of six sons and four daughters, and was born in Mecklenburg Co. on the 2d of November, 1795.

"In 1806, Samuel Polk, with his wife and children and soon after followed by most of the members of the Polk family, emigrated to the wilderness of Tennessee, and settled in what is now Maury County. Here in the hard toil of a new farm James K. Polk spent the early years of his childhood and youth.

"He entered the office of Hon. Felix Grundy, at Nashville, as a student-at-law. Here the intimate acquaintance grew up between him and Gen. Jackson which ripened into the life-long friendship known to have existed between these two truly great men. The politics in which he had been educated, his father being an earnest Jeffersonian, had prepared him to sympathize heartily with the views and principles of which Gen. Jackson became the great leading exponent; and to these he adhered steadily throughout life."[15]

During the years between Jackson's presidency and Polk's presidency, the road to the Civil War would become more certain. Before that time there would be a second war with Great Britain— the War of 1812.

Hubbard Cobb, in *American Battlefields,* writes: "There was no single crisis that drove the United States to declare war on Great Britain on June 18, 1812, but rather, it was years of frustration over unsuccessful efforts to maintain its honor and national economic interests. These imperatives became tangled up in the war between Great Britain and Napoleon's France. In 1792 these two countries began a war that lasted with a few brief interruptions until Napoleon's final defeat at Waterloo in 1815."

"Portions of the country, especially New England, were not in favor of war… many believed the nation was unprepared for such a conflict in spite of Clay's claim that the Kentucky militia alone could conquer Canada. There were also those who felt that the real enemy was not Britain but France. But the warhawks prevailed, and war against Britain was declared on June 18, 1812.

"In the first two or so years of the war most of the battles took place along the northern frontier, which adjoined British territory in North America, including the sparsely settled areas on and around Lakes Erie and Ontario, the Niagara River, and western parts of the St. Lawrence River. By the summer of 1813, Great Britain was receiving help in its war with Napoleon from Russia, Prussia, and Austria, allowing it to send more troops and warships to fight in America.

"In 1814, Britain launched a major counteroffensive, which resulted in the significant battles of the war fought at Plattsburg, New York; Washington, D.C.; Baltimore; and New Orleans."

Washington, D.C., was attacked first. Cobb continues the story: "Washington had no defenses, not even an army. Secretary of War John Armstrong and his military leaders had been too involved dreaming up impractical plans to invade Canada to pay attention to the defense of the capitol or other major coastal towns." At last a "makeshift force of 4,000 was organized," but no defensive fortifications were put in place.[16] The Americans were put on the run and Washington was destroyed and burned by the British. America's first lady, Dolly Madison, proved the hero of the day: "Alone in a practically deserted Washington, she went to work loading a wagon with the White House Silver and China, cabinet papers, and Gilbert Stewart's famous portrait of George Washington and then drove to join her husband in Virginia."[17]

When the War of 1812 renewed the conflict between America and Great Britain, Young Ewing formed a mounted militia to help defend the state of Kentucky.[18] Young Ewing led the four hundred soldiers of the Ewing Regiment, which was involved with Indian conflicts during the war. Young Ewing and William Ewing served with the Kentucky Militia led by Isaac Shelby (the rebel leader of King's Mountain who was now 66 years old), which marched from Kentucky to Lake Erie in 1813.[19]

After Commodore Perry defeated the British fleet and gained naval control of Lake Erie, the Kentucky Militia joined Henry Harrison in a successful invasion of Canada and defeated the British at the battle of Thames. They soon were to march home to Kentucky as the United States was now in control of the Lake Erie region.

Late in the war other regiments of the Kentucky Militia would travel to New Orleans to reinforce Andrew Jackson's forces there.

General Andrew Jackson

In a letter to Gen. Andrew Jackson dated November 24, 1813, Rev. Finis Ewing stated: "Divine providence has given you almost unexampled success for the time your army has been in motion. I hope by his blessings that you may soon teach the British allies in the South as impressive or more impressive lesson than they have been recently taught in the North. It is surely the prayer, the ardent prayer of all good men, that heaven may prosper you in your future cause."[20]

The final battle of the War of 1812 was the battle of New Orleans led by Andrew Jackson. Although a peace treaty had already been signed, this news had not yet reached New Orleans.

Jackson "regarded Sir William Wallace as 'the best model for a young man… We find in him the truly undaunted courage, always ready to brave any dangers, for the relief of his country or his friend.' Small wonder he admired Wallace, the virtues Jackson ascribed to Wallace were precisely his own."[21]

In New Orleans, "Jackson set about improving the city's defenses." Trees were felled to block passages and fortifications were improved. "The British invasion army consisted of about 8,000 regulars," and Jackson had "a force of about 5,700."[22] The battle was violent, short, and a disaster for the British. "General Jackson stared at the scene in front of him in disbelief" when the fighting had ended. "The British later admitted to casualties totaling 2,037. Jackson received a report which claimed a total of 13 Americans killed, 39 wounded and 19 missing in action… It was the greatest feat of American arms up to that time. Andrew Jackson's role made him a popular and beloved hero for the remainder of his life… He restored to the American People their pride and self-confidence and they never forgot it… The battle of New Orleans created the Nation's first military hero. And because of that victory and what it produced, the history of the American Nation was permanently altered."[23]

The ensuing peace brought the opportunity for Americans to seek new frontiers. Finis Ewing and his family would migrate to a state created by congressional compromise. For the Republic of Texas, though, statehood would only be possible through a war of independence from Mexico. The story of Texas's independence begins with Sam Houston.

Sam Houston

The following narrative on Sam Houston is taken from *The History of Davidson County,* Tennessee by W. W. Clayton.

"The following interesting sketch of one of the most remarkable men of our day is copied from the *Washington Sunday Gazette*. It was written by Col. Willoughby Williams, late of Nashville, an intimate personal friend, who was better acquainted with the illustrious hero than perhaps any other living man. As Col. Williams begins his sketch with his first recollections of Gen. Houston in 1811, we will precede his narrative with a few facts relating to his early life and parentage.

"Gen. Houston was born in Rockbridge Co., Va., on the 2nd of March, 1793. He was descended from a Scotch-Irish family, who emigrated from the north of Ireland to Pennsylvania, and thence to Virginia, towards the close of the last century. His father served in the Revolutionary War, where he was a brigade inspector, and upon his death, in 1807, his widow removed with her family to Blount Co., Tenn. Sam was then a lad of fourteen years of age, and about this time was adopted into the Cherokee Nation and became clerk to a trader.

"Col. Williams' sketch proceeds as follows: 'My earliest recollections of Gen. Houston date back to 1811, at Kingston, Roane Co., Tenn. He was a clerk at the time in the store of Mr. Sheffy. My mother, in her widowhood, was living about three miles from Kingston. I was thirteen years of age, and Mr. Houston was five years my senior. He was especially kind to me and much of my time was spent in his company. He remained in the capacity of clerk until after the declaration of the war of 1812. At that time the United

States were recruiting troops at Kingston for the war. The whole population had caught the war fever, and intense interest prevailed.

"The manner of enlisting at that day was to parade the streets with drum and fife, with a sergeant in command. Silver dollars were placed on the head of the drum, and, as a token of enlistment, the volunteer stepped up and took a dollar, which was his bounty; he was then forthwith marched to the barracks and uniformed. The late Robert H. M'Ewen, of Nashville, cousin to Gen. Houston, and myself were standing together on the street, and saw Houston take his dollar from the drum and enlist as a private in the year 1813. He was taken immediately to the barracks, dressed as a soldier, and appointed the same day as a sergeant. (He was ordered to the Creek war and fought in the battle of the Horseshoe).

"At that battle he mounted the Indian defenses with colors in hand, and was wounded by a barbed arrow in the thigh. A soldier, whom he ordered to extract it by main force, made several ineffectual efforts, and only succeeded under a threat by Houston to kill him unless he pulled it out. He was carried back, suffering intensely from the wound, which had been much lacerated. His indomitable will led him immediately back into the fight, when he was soon wounded by two balls in his right shoulder. His intrepid spirit displayed on this occasion won for him the lasting regard of Gen. Jackson. Disabled from further service, he was sent back to Kingston with the sick and wounded."[24]

"Houston afterwards became an Indian agent among the Cherokee, while reading law. Admitted to the bar in Tennessee, he rose rapidly, not in the least due to the sponsorship of Andrew Jackson, the state's most famous son. Houston soon acquired a considerable reputation, became a major general of militia, and was elected to Congress in 1823 and again in 1825. In 1827 he was elected governor of Tennessee." A scandal surrounded his short-lived marriage of four months, which was never explained. "He soon resigned his governorship and headed west. Houston settled among the Cherokee in Arkansas, where they had recently been 'removed.'

"Meanwhile, the pressures for Indian 'removal' were again at work and in 1832 Houston went to Washington to see what his old friend Andrew Jackson, now President, could do to protect the Cherokee. In Washington he got nowhere, since Jackson was a strong backer of Indian removal. While Jackson was unwilling to do anything for the Cherokee, he suggested that Houston go to Texas to negotiate with various Indians who were raiding into the United States. Houston, who had recently made several trips to Texas, and had even attempted to secure funding for a venture there, took up the assignment and headed west. For the rest of his life he was closely identified with Texas.

"Houston was made a major general and commander of the Revolutionary Army in 1835. Shortly after Texas declared its independence from Mexico on 2 March, 1836, his birthday, Houston led the Revolutionary Army to victory at San Jacinto (21 April 1836)" where he was wounded by enemy fire.[25]

In his book *Sam Houston,* John Hoyt Williams picks up the story: "Houston's wound, though treated by army surgeon Alexander Ewing, continued to cause him acute pain and became seriously infected. Because he lacked adequate medical facilities, Ewing urged the general to depart immediately for New Orleans or risk death from infection.

"As Houston was preparing to leave, Santa Anna signed an armistice. Moreover, he indicated a willingness to negotiate a 'permanent' treaty with Texas to recognize its independence as 'fait accompli.'[26]

"Three months later he [Houston] was elected President of the Republic of Texas. Houston served two terms as President of Texas. When Texas was admitted to the Union… Houston was elected to the United States Senate, serving until 1859, when he was elected governor of Texas, becoming the only man in American history to have been the governor of two states."[27]

Davy Crockett

During the time that Sam Houston was the governor of Tennessee, Davy Crockett was elected to Congress for that state. Crockett's family members had fought in the Revolutionary War as Scotch-Irish patriots in the Battle of King's Mountain. While serving in Congress, Crockett was present in Philadelphia on the Fourth of July, 1834.

James Atkins Shackford writes: "Finally the big day arrived for which David was waiting—Independence Day in Independence City, the Fourth of July in Philadelphia! In the company of Senators Daniel Webster, Poindexter, Mangum, Ewing, Robbins, and Representative Denny, he went early in the day to the Music Fund Hall, where, in the wake of the other speakers, he gave a rousing oration about tyranny, sword, and purse, despotism, and independence."[28]

After a falling out with his old friend President Andrew Jackson, Crockett lost his congressional seat in the fall election of 1835. Crockett packed up and with several friends and rode to Texas, where he intended to fight for its independence. Crockett and his Tennessee Mounted Volunteers arrived at the Alamo to a rousing welcome—he responded with a speech that stirred up a great cheer. However, Davy Crockett's presence could not overcome the fact that the defenders of the Alamo were vastly outnumbered by Santa Anna's troops. James Ewing died with Crockett, but George Ewing and the others with Sam Houston "remembered the Alamo" and won the fight for Texas's independence.

Texas, however, would soon be mired in a difficult road to statehood, as Missouri had been in 1820, due to the slavery issue.

The Slavery Issue

What to do about slavery and Missouri became a troublesome issue for Thomas Jefferson. Pauline Maier writes: "More than anything else he had done, writing the Declaration of Independence came to justify his life and helped save Jefferson from an acute despair he experienced during the Missouri Controversy of 1819-20, which seemed to jeopardize all that he and his generation had accomplished... 'I regret now that I am to die in the belief,' he wrote in April 1820, 'that the useless sacrifice of themselves by the generation of 1776, to acquire self-government and happiness to their country, is to be thrown away by the unwise and unworthy passions of their sons.' "[29]

Thomas Jefferson was morally opposed to slavery, but the dilemma of how to willingly solve the slavery question was as perplexing in his personal life as it was for his country, and he continued to hold slaves on his Virginia plantations at his passing on July 4, 1826—the 50th anniversary of the Declaration of Independence.

Thomas Jefferson understood the depravity that was inherent in the practice of slavery: "There must doubtless be an unhappy influence on the manners of our people produced by the existence of slavery among us... The man must be a prodigy who can retain his manners and morals undepraved by such circumstances."[30]

An incident that involved Jefferson's nephews, Lilburne and Isham, slaveholders in western Kentucky, would bear the fruit of slavery's dark nature. On the night of December 15, 1811, an episode began that would be reminiscent of an Old Testament reading. In a drunken rage, Lilburne and Isham would kill a slave with an axe after he had dropped and broken a water pitcher. They ordered his body dismembered by other slaves, and the body parts were placed in a large kitchen fireplace with the intent of cremating them.

At 2:15 a.m. on December 16, the New Madrid (Missouri) earthquake, one of the greatest earthquakes of known history, began, which caused the brick fireplace to collapse onto the fire, putting it out before the evidence of the crime could be destroyed.

Lilburne and Isham were later arrested, and the local population would be outraged by their crime. The brothers were brought to trial and the continued earthquakes and aftershocks would mirror the convulsions of the gruesome courtroom testimony. The natural tumult would subside shortly after Lilburne committed suicide on April 10, 1812.

Isham was found guilty and sentenced to hang, but he escaped and was never again seen in Kentucky. Shortly after this incident, Young Ewing of Christian County was one of two state senators in western Kentucky who voted to increase the penalties to slaveholders for acts of cruelty against their human property. The measure failed to pass, however, due to the apathy of senators from other parts of the state that were not as intimately affected by this incident.

Two years later, Lilburne's lawyer, Henry F. Delany, professed religion at a camp meeting under the preaching of Rev. Finis Ewing. He was apparently so affected by the murder that he subsequently joined the ministry of the Cumberland Presbyterian Church and became a major force in the church against the evils of excessive alcohol consumption. Although he owned 20 slaves at his death, in his will he urged his remaining family members to move to a state where slavery was not tolerated.[31]

As for Thomas Jefferson: "The answer is unclear to as basic a question as how many slaves Jefferson possessed at the end of his life. According to the *Farm Book,* by 1822 he seems to have had upwards of 260. The advertisement for the November 3, 1826 sale of his personal property said that about 200 Negroes would be offered. This should not have included the five he wanted to set free."[32]

Before his death Jefferson compared himself to Jesus: "I am a Materialist; He takes the side of Spiritualism. He preaches the efficacy of repentance towards forgiveness of sin; I require a counterpoise of good works to redeem it etc., etc."[33]

This viewpoint may reflect Jefferson's inner feelings about the meaning of his own life expressed in another letter at about the same time: "My business is to beguile the wearisomeness of declining life, as I endeavor to do, by the delights of classical reading and of mathematical truths, and by the consolations of a sound philosophy, equally indifferent to hope and fear."[34]

Margaret Davidson Ewing

Thomas Jefferson's views contrast vividly with those of Margaret Davidson Ewing. Margaret Davidson Ewing was the daughter of William L. Davidson, the niece of Ephraim Brevard, the wife of Finis Ewing, and the mother of twelve children. A brief sketch by one of her sons follows: "The features of the religious life of Mrs. Ewing are deserving especial remark. Religion to her was a sublime and living reality—a real experience, derived from an abiding trust and faith in the great Author of her salvation. The very mental constitution and temperament of the woman demanded an experience that could not be doubted, and an actual realization of its joys and consolations.

"It was her great happiness to enjoy a large share of the comforts of religion. It was her unfailing resource in all the trials and afflictions that beset her pathway in life. It was her constant practice to refer all her difficulties to her Heavenly Father, and to ask his guidance and direction on all occasions. A favorite idea of hers—and she so expressed herself very often—was to live very near the Saviour, and to realize constantly that the Holy Spirit was in communion with her own spirit. Some persons will scout this as idle enthusiasm; but it was a living and sensible condition to her, especially in the later years of her life, when no business or worldly cares were upon her hands. If it were enthusiasm, it was a blessed one, and brought infinite happiness to the subject of it."[35]

Margaret and Finis Ewing settled in Missouri in 1820 at an outpost of the Cumberland Presbyterian Church establishing a seminary in the promised land of Thomas Jefferson's Louisiana Purchase (Jefferson's vision for the Louisiana Territory would be fulfilled by those with the courage to claim it). "Webster's dictionary defines a seminary as an 'institution for the training of candidates for the priesthood or ministry.' This was what Rev. Finis Ewing and Rev. Robert D. Morrow founded at New Lebanon [Missouri] in 1821. This 'pioneer theological seminary' was, as far as is known, the first established west of the Mississippi River." It was later called the "School of the Prophets."[36]

Some of the issues in the Rev. Finis Ewing's personal life are revealed in a letter to his brother dated May 22, 1822, concerning finances, his eldest daughter Winifred, and camp meetings.

"I am much embarrassed for money, Winifred, a weakly girl, has no Negro woman to help her nor won't perhaps till I get money, but I know you will do what you can for me.

"After these glooms I want to make your heart glad & will make it glad, when I tell you we had a good camp meeting at the above mentioned place. There was but a small assembly & considering the size of the Assembly take it all together, I am sure I never saw such a meeting in all my life! There were thirty two souls hopefully converted to God! Among the number were a sister in law, a niece & two nephews (by marriage) of the President of the United States [James Monroe]!!… I must enter on the arduous business of writing Divinity, now since King etc. has come to help us, but O how can I stay away from those blessed (of God), camp meetings… Give my love to all, tell all to pray for us O Lord carry on thy work, humble our hearts."[37]

"The Rev. Finis Ewing owned slaves, but slavery came to be distasteful to him."[38]

In the words of Joseph J. Ellis: "Perhaps it was inevitable, even preferable, that slavery as a national problem be moved from the Congress to the churches, where it could come under scrutiny as a sin requiring national purging, rather than as a social dilemma requiring a political solution. That in any event is what happened."[39]

Dr. Cossitt wrote of one such example: "At some period in Mr. Ewing's life, but the precise period is not known, his mind became exercised on the subject of slavery. In 1835 he published a sermon in the Cumberland Presbyterian Pulpit, in which he took strong ground against at least some of the evils of slavery. The public mind was not so easily inflamed on the subject at that time as it has been since, and he expressed himself, to what has since been denominated a slaveholding church, with great freedom. In the progress of the sermon he gives the following as his own experiences and purposes in relation to his slaves: 'I think it proper to state in this place, that after a long, painful and prayerful investigation of the subject, I have determined not to hold, nor to give, nor to sell nor to buy any slave for life, mainly from the influence of that passage of God's word, which says, "Masters, give unto your servants that which is just and equal." ' "[40]

According to historian Eugene Allen Cordry: "The 1830 census for Cooper County shows fourteen slaves in the household of Finis Ewing… He made exertions to qualify them for freedom. Some of the younger servants were instructed to read; and provision was made for the comfort and support of the older ones."[41]

When Finis Ewing died on July 4, 1841, the 65th anniversary of the Declaration of Independence, all his slaves received their independence.[42]

Once while discussing slavery in a sermon, Ewing used the expression "physician heal thyself" in relating this issue to himself. In the years ahead for the state of Missouri and for the union, healing would eventually occur, but it was to be a long and painful process.

Finis Ewing's eldest son carried his grandfather's name and was a resident of Illinois, the land of Lincoln.

"William Lee Davidson Ewing, early lawyer and politician, was born in Kentucky in 1795, and came to Illinois at an early day, first settling at Shawneetown. He was Brigadier General of the State militia at an early day, Colonel of the 'Spy Battalion' during the Black Hawk War, and as Indian Agent, superintended the removal of the Sacs and Foxes west of the Mississippi." He was a "Representative from the counties composing the Vandalia District in the Seventh General Assembly (1830-1831), when he also became Speaker of the House."[43]

It was during the political campaign of 1830 that Abraham Lincoln gave his first political speech. After hearing the speech W.L.D. Ewing would call Lincoln "a bright one." In 1837 Ewing opposed Lincoln's successful effort to move the Illinois state capitol from Vandalia to Springfield. W.L.D. Ewing was by this time a former U.S. senator and a formidable opponent. "Lincoln's brave and effective response to Ewing did more than help preserve the seat of government for Springfield, it exposed a further dimension of his abilities and earned him a new measure of respect."[44]

In his *Reminiscences of the Early Bench and Bar of Illinois*, Usher Linder wrote: "…this was the first time that I began to conceive a very high opinion of the talent and personal courage of Abraham Lincoln."[45] Ewing "was returned to the House of Representatives from his old district in 1838, as he was again in 1840, at each session being chosen Speaker over Abraham Lincoln, who was the Whig candidate."[46]

Abe Lincoln used to tell the funny story of how he and Ewing came to a farmhouse to win the vote, but the husband was gone and the wife said she was too busy to listen to them. She had to milk the cow. William Lee Davidson Ewing offered to milk the cow for her. When he had finished, the lady thanked him because if he hadn't, she wouldn't have had a delightful chat with Mr. Lincoln.[47]

Chapter 5
Equality

All are created equal. The cornerstone of what the
Declaration of Independence would become...

"Masters give unto your servants
that which is just and equal"
Colossians 4:1 (King James)

Abraham Lincoln was known as a good storyteller, but more importantly, he exhibited great perseverance. This last quality allowed him to overcome many early defeats to eventually win the presidency and in addition a great victory for our country.

To win this victory, he utilized the Declaration of Independence in a way that had not been envisioned by its creators, to end the practice of slavery in the United States and in the process, to save the Union.

Pauline Maier writes: "Before the 1850's, however, Lincoln seems to have had relatively little interest in the Declaration of Independence. Then suddenly, that document, and above all its assertion that all men are created equal became his 'ancient faith,' the 'father of all moral principles,' an 'axiom of free society'... His understanding of the document became in time that of the nation."

Lincoln's stand on the Declaration was well publicized during his debates with Stephen Douglas during the 1858 Senate race in Illinois. During the debates Lincoln would rely on several documents for reference, including a quote from Henry Clay in which "Clay described the phrase 'all men are created equal' as a 'great fundamental principle' of significance both 'in the original construction of society and in organized societies.' "[1]

In the coming years, Lincoln would rely also on the principles of the Holy Bible. In *Abraham Lincoln: From Skeptic to Prophet,* Wayne C. Temple writes: "To explain his position on religion, Lincoln issued a handbill to the voters of the Seventh Congressional District on July 31, 1846. 'Fellow citizens,' he began, 'a charge having got into circulation in some of the neighborhoods of this District, in substance that I am an open scoffer at Christianity, I have by the advice of some friends concluded to notice the subject in this form... That I am not a member of any Christian Church, is true,' Lincoln admitted; 'but I have never denied the truth of the Scriptures; and I have never spoken with intentional disrespect of religion in general or of any denomination of Christians in particular.' "

In 1846 Lincoln declined to make a personal commitment to one church, but in 1849 the events during a trip to his wife's hometown of Lexington, Kentucky, would "change his entire religious thinking." Lincoln would discover a copy of *The Christian's Defense* written by Rev. James Smith on his in-laws' library shelf, which he took home with him and began reading. Lincoln later told his friend Thomas Lewis about "finding *The Christian's Defense* while in Lexington and asked if Lewis could introduce him to Dr. Smith. He had partially mastered this study, said Lincoln, and desired to conclude his reading of these volumes and also make the acquaintance of Dr. Smith. Lincoln supposedly declared that the author's argument had forced him to 'change his views about the Christian Religion.' "

Later, when the Lincoln's young son Eddie died on February 1, 1850, the Rev. James Smith provided comfort for the grieving parents. Christian parents were encouraged to find comfort in the resurrection and the kingdom of heaven after the loss of a child. The

Lincolns would engrave "Of such is the Kingdom of Heaven" on Eddie's tombstone, offering the hope of a future reunion in heaven.

In 1851 Lincoln's wife, Mary, "experienced a religious revival in her life—a rebirth of her very soul... In those days the session examined potential members on their 'experimental religion'... Through questioning, the session sought to determine if the candidate had experienced a profound religious encounter."

In contrast to Mary, as late as the Civil War, "President Lincoln had not solved this matter to his own satisfaction. One day he asked a visitor to the White House, 'What constitutes a true religious encounter?' "

In March 1865 Lincoln gave his second Inaugural Address to the nation. Author Wayne C. Temple writes: "With great care, Lincoln had prepared his address. It was quite short and actually read like a sermon with numerous references to God and the Bible. It would appear that Abraham Lincoln's Presbyterian experiences with that particular denomination's theories of religion helped to shape this magnificent oration. It could have been read from one of their pulpits. The President was so familiar with the Scriptures that he often incorporated whole sentences and phrases into his own writings without quotation marks.

"Lincoln explained there was no need for a long speech. Both the North and South deprecated war, Lincoln thought, 'but one of them would *make* war rather than let the nation survive; and the other would *accept* war rather than let it perish. And the war came.' Each side looked 'for an easier triumph, and a result less fundamental and astounding,' admitted the president. Then Lincoln launched into his religious message to the Nation and perhaps the world—each sentence a perfect gem of preparation, experience and thought."

As Lincoln said in his second inaugural address, commenting on the North and the South: "Both read the same Bible, and pray to the same God; and each invokes His aid against the other. It may seem strange that men should dare to ask a just God's assistance in wringing their bread from the sweat of other men's faces [Genesis 3:19]; but let us judge not that we be not judged [Matthew 7:1]. The prayers of both could not be answered; that of neither has been answered fully."

Lincoln continued: "The Almighty has His own purposes [2 Timothy 1:9]. 'Woe unto the world because of offenses! for it must needs be that offenses come; but woe to that man by whom the offense cometh!' [Luke 17:1]. If we shall suppose that American Slavery is one of those offenses which, in the providence of God, must needs come, but which, having continued through His appointed time, He now wills to remove and that He gives to both North and South, this terrible war, as the woe due to those by whom the offense came, shall we discern therein any departure from those divine attributes which the believers in a Living God always ascribe to Him? Fondly do we hope—fervently do we pray—that this mighty scourge of war may speedily pass away. Yet, if God wills that it continue, until all the wealth piled by the bond man's two hundred and fifty years of unrequited toil shall be sunk, and until every drop of blood drawn with the lash, shall be paid by another drawn with the sword, as was said three thousand years ago, so still must be said 'the judgments of the Lord, are true and righteous altogether.' [Psalm 19:0].

"With malice toward none; with charity for all; with firmness in the right, as God gives us to see the right, let us strive on to finish the work we are in; to bind up the nation's wounds; to care for him who will have borne the battle, and for his widow, and his orphan— to do all which may achieve and cherish a just, and a lasting peace, among ourselves, and with all nations."

Temple continues: "If there had been a slight doubt in Lincoln's mind about the effectiveness of his Gettysburg Address, there was absolutely none in regard to his Second Inaugural. Eleven days after delivering his masterpiece at the Capitol, President Lincoln asserted that it would 'wear as well as—perhaps better than any thing I have produced; but I believe it is not immediately popular. Men are not flattered by being shown that there has been a difference of purpose between the Almighty and them. To deny it, however, in this case, is to deny that there is a God governing the world. It is a truth which I thought needed to be told; and as whatever of humiliation there is in it, falls most directly on myself, I thought others might afford for me to tell it.'

"Here, again is Abraham Lincoln's religious creed in writing: God governed the world. And he was God's instrument. Who could still say that Lincoln was not a religious man?"[2]

Maier brings us back to the Declaration: "Lincoln saw the Declaration of Independence's statements on equality and rights as setting a standard for the future, one that demanded the gradual extinction of conflicting practices as that became possible."

In explaining the conflict of the Civil War, Maier continues: "the North fought not only to save the Union, but to save a form of government, as Lincoln told Congress on July 4, 1861, 'whose leading object is to elevate the condition of men; to lift artificial weights from all shoulders—to clear the paths of laudable pursuit for all—to afford all, an unfettered start and a fair chance in the race of life.' The rebellion it opposed was at base an effort 'to overthrow the principle that all men were created equal.' "[3]

In 1819 the rebellion's symptoms had become apparent in the debate over the slavery issue in the Missouri territory. As the national debate over the Missouri Question mounted, Thomas Jefferson began to describe the crisis as "the most portentous one which ever yet threatened our Union" and "the greatest threat to the survival of the American republic since the gloomiest days of the [Revolutionary] war... An old colleague from Presidential days who visited Monticello in 1820 described him as obsessed with the Missouri Question, warning of imminent civil war."[4]

Fortunately, the Missouri Compromise of 1820 eased the tension of the nation for a period of years. It allowed Missouri into the Union as a slave state with the remaining territory of the Louisiana purchase to remain free north of 36° 30' north latitude. Although not part of the compromise, Maine's concurrent admission as a free state made agreement on the compromise possible.

When Senator Stephen Douglas of Illinois successfully steered the Kansas-Nebraska Act through Congress in 1854, the Missouri Compromise was made null and void. John F. Kennedy's words in *Profiles in Courage,* describe Sam Houston's actions on the

Senate Floor: "Sam Houston looked upon the Missouri Compromise, which he had supported in 1820 as a youthful Congressman from Tennessee, as a solemn and sacred compact between North and South, in effect a part of the Constitution when Texas was admitted into the Union...

"With rugged, homely but earnest eloquence, he begged his weary colleagues in an impromptu plea not to plunge the nation into new agitations over the slavery issue."[5] Unfortunately, Houston's efforts to prevent passage of the Kansas-Nebraska Act failed. From now on, all issues of slavery in the new territories would be decided by the settlers themselves. Thomas Jefferson's fears were about to be realized, as the border war between the pro-slavery factions of Missouri and the antislavery factions of Kansas soon began. Kansas was supported by the abolitionists of the Northeast, and Missouri was supported by the pro-slavery South. This border war began in 1855 and continued well into the Civil War, which its fires had helped to ignite.

In 1854 Abraham Lincoln supported those congressmen who opposed the Kansas-Nebraska Bill and was elected to the state legislature of Illinois. In 1856 Lincoln was one of the organizers of the new Republican party in Illinois, which opposed slavery.

In contrast, the Democrats controlled the state of Missouri and were sympathetic to the pro-slavery cause. In 1856 Finis Ewing's youngest son, Ephraim Brevard Ewing, won the office of attorney general on the ticket with Trusten Polk as governor. Ephraim's brother, Robert C. Ewing, opposed Polk and was a close second in the governor's race, with former senator Thomas Hart Benton a distant third.[6]

The election of 1856 effectively ended Thomas Hart Benton's career as a statesman, in which he above all else had stood for the Union. Unfortunately it was the increasing pro-South secessionary sentiments of his constituents in Missouri that led to his final ouster.

Benton's first term as a U.S. senator coincided with Missouri's birth and entry into the Union as a state in 1820. Six years later he faced reelection as described by William Nisbet Chambers: "Meanwhile, Benton canvassed the election situation. In early

September he wrote his ally Finis Ewing that, among the Assemblymen-elect, every engine of intrigue will be put in motion, and every lie told that can make a personal or political enemy.' But by early October, Benton was on the way to the East with his family confident of the outcome.

"The Assembly met toward the end of November, 1826, at the new capital near the center of the state—Jefferson City. One of the members, an ally of Benton's, William Carr Lane of St. Louis, noted that Finis Ewing, General Thomas Smith, Alphonso Wetmore, and others were on hand electioneering for the Colonel... 'He will be elected—the voice of the people demands it. Who dares disobey?' Or, as one citizen put it: 'Benton, right or wrong, is the people's man.' "[7]

Elbert B. Smith writes: "His base of support in Missouri was broad and strong. He had enunciated and served western interests in the best western spirit with a clear-cut philosophy of nationalism in theory and states' rights in application, and all with the accents of education and knowledge. His people understood this and his position in their hearts was secure.

"He had also made or accepted another momentous decision. He had rejoined the cult which surrounded another western hero. Andrew Jackson was preparing to bestow his character and name upon an entire era of American history, and Thomas Benton stood ready to march at his side."[8]

Future President Theodore Roosevelt in his biography of Thomas Hart Benton, written in 1887, comments in these excerpts: "The change of parties in 1800 when the Jefferson Democracy came in altered the policy of government, but not the character of the officials. In that movement, though Jefferson had behind him the mass of the people as the rank and file of his party, yet all his captains were still drawn from among the men of the same social position as himself...

"The Revolutionary War had been fought under the leadership of the colonial gentry; and for years after it was over the people, as a whole, felt that their interests could be safely entrusted to and were identical with those of the descendants of their revolutionary leaders. The classes in which were to be found almost all the learning, the talent, the business activity, and the inherited wealth and refinement of the country, had also hitherto contributed much to the body of its rulers…

"The Jacksonian Democracy stood for the revolt against their rulers; its leaders as well as their followers, all came from the mass of the people. The majority of the voters supported [Andrew] Jackson because they felt he was one of themselves, and because they understood that his election would mean the complete overthrow of the classes in power and their retirement from the control of the government…

"Until 1828 the prominent political chiefs of the nation had either been its presidents, or had been in the cabinets of these presidents. But after Jackson's time they were in the Senate, and it was on this body that public attention was concentrated…

"When the rupture between Calhoun and the Jacksonian Democrats, and the resignation of the former from the vice-presidency took place, three parties developed in the United States Senate. One was composed of the Jacksonian Democrats, with Benton at their head; one was made up of the little band of Nullifiers, led by Calhoun; and the third included the rather loose array of the Whigs under Clay and Webster…

"When the protective tariff bill of 1828 came up, its opponents and supporters were sharply divided by sectional lines…

"Certainly, even if the new tariff laws were ill-advised, unjust, and unequal in their working, yet they did not, in the most remote degree, justify any effort to break up the Union; especially when she herself had joined in laying heavier burdens on the shoulders of New England…

"Complain she did, however; and soon added threats to complaints, and was evidently ready to add acts to threats. Georgia, at first, took the lead in denunciation; but South Carolina soon surpassed her, and finally went to the length of advocating and preparing for separation from the Union; a step that produced a revulsion of feeling even among her fellow anti-tariff states. The South Carolinian states men now proclaimed the doctrine of nullification—that is, proclaimed that if any state deemed a federal law improper, it could proceed to declare that law null and void so far as its own territory was concerned—and, as a corollary, that it had the right forcibly to prevent execution of this void law within its borders. This was proclaimed, not as an exercise of the right of revolution, which in the last resort, belongs, of course, to every community and class, but as a constitutional privilege. Jefferson was quoted as the father of the idea, and the Kentucky Resolutions of 1798–1799, which he drew, were cited as the precedent for the South Carolinian action. In both these last assertions the Nullifiers were correct. Jefferson was the father of nullification, and therefore of secession. He used the word "nullify" in the original draft which he supplied to the Kentucky legislature, and though that body struck it out of the resolutions which they passed in 1798, they inserted it in those of the following year. This was done mainly as an unscrupulous party move on Jefferson's part, and when his side came into power he became a firm upholder of the Union; and, being constitutionally unable to put a proper value on truthfulness, he even denied that his resolutions could be construed to favor nullification—though they could not possibly be construed to mean anything else…

"At this time it is not necessary to discuss nullification as a constitutional dogma; it is an absurdity too great to demand serious refutation. The United States has the same right to protect itself from death by nullification, secession, or rebellion, that a man has to protect himself from death by assassination…

"The feeling in Congress, as a whole, was as strong against the tariff as it was against nullification…

"Beyond question Jackson's firmness, and the way in which he was backed up by Benton, Webster and their followers, was having some effect. (Which led to a compromise settlement which preserved the Union). Without doubt, the honors of the nullification dispute were borne off by Benton and Webster…

"Webster was a high tariff man, and was backed up by all the sectional antipathies of the Northeast in his opposition to the Nullifiers; Benton on the contrary, was a believer in the low tariff, or in one for revenue merely, and his sectional antipathies were the other way. Yet, even when deserted by his chief, and when he was opposed to every senator from south of the Potomac and the Ohio, he did not flinch for a moment from his attitude of aggressive loyalty to the national Union.

"Towards the close of Jackson's administration slavery for the first time made its permanent appearance in national politics; although for some years yet it had little or no influence in shaping the course of political movements. In 1833 the abolition societies of the North came into prominence; they had been started a couple of years previously…

"Hardly was Polk elected [1844] before it became evident to Benton and the other Jacksonians that the days of the old Union or Nationalist Democracy were over, and that the separatist and disunion elements within the party had obtained the upper hand…

"From this time the slavery question dwarfed all others, and was the one with which statesmen had mainly to deal…

"When Calhoun introduced his famous resolutions declaring that Congress had no power to interfere with slavery in the territories and therefore no power to prevent the admission of new states except on the condition of their prohibiting slavery within their limits, Benton promptly and strongly opposed them as being fire brands needlessly thrown to inflame the passions of the extremists, and, moreover, as being disunionist in tendency…

"Meanwhile the Missourian had gained an ally of his own stamp in the Senate. This was Houston, from the new state of Texas, who represented in that state, like Andrew Jackson in Tennessee, and Benton himself in Missouri, the old Nationalist Democracy which held the preservation of the Union dear above all other things…

"[In 1850] Benton had now finished his fifth and last term in the United States Senate. Hitherto Benton had been the undisputed leader of the Democracy, but now proslavery and disunionist Democrats organized a very powerful opposition to him."[9]

Smith writes: "America desperately needed her elder statesmen, but even Thomas Hart Benton could not last forever…" On April 10, 1858 "the long struggle of Benton had ended. The tragedy from which he had labored to save America still lay ahead.

The democracy in which he had believed would stand firm, however, and the nation he had called 'the world's last hope for a free government on earth' would survive. Perhaps the contentment of his final hours rested in part upon the instinctive faith that this would be so."[10]

Chambers takes up the story: "However, in 1860 the outcome of the growing storm over slavery was far from certain. Abraham Lincoln lost the Illinois Senate race to Stephen Douglas in 1858, but the preceding Lincoln-Douglas debates gave Lincoln national prominence. He was elected president in the fall of 1860 and in December, South Carolina seceded from the Union. By Lincoln's inauguration on March 4, 1861, six other southern states had dissolved themselves from the Union with four more to follow. In Missouri the electorate voted to remain in the Union.

"For this result, Benton might have claimed some credit. He had given years of his life to preparing Missouri public opinion to resist disunion. He had labored valiantly to maintain a political organization devoted to resisting slavery extension and maintaining the Union."[11]

John F. Kennedy, who was of Irish descent, describes the Scotch-Irish descendant Thomas Hart Benton in *Profiles in Courage*. Benton's death was "mourned throughout the nation… But even in death and defeat, Thomas Hart Benton was victorious. For his voice from the past on behalf of Union was one of the deciding factors that prevented Missouri from yielding to all the desperate efforts to drive her into succession along with her sister slave states. Fate had borne out the wisdom of Benton's last report to his constituents as Senator: 'I value solid popularity—the esteem of good men for good action. I despise the bubble popularity that is won without merit and lost without crime… I have been Senator 30 years… I sometimes had to act against the preconceived opinions and first impressions of my constituents; but always with full reliance upon their intelligence to understand me and their equity to do me justice—and I have never been disappointed.' "[12]

In spite of Benton's efforts, Thomas Jefferson's earlier prediction had become a reality. The sons of Finis Ewing joined the other sons of the Confederacy and our country became a house divided. Although Missouri remained in the Union, it was a divided state and a microcosm of the greater Civil War.

Ephraim B. Ewing was appointed as a Missouri Supreme Court justice in 1859. When the Civil War began, he refused to take the Test Oath of allegiance to the Union and was forced to resign.[13] Most of the Missouri state leaders also refused to sign and were forced into hiding by the Union Army.

General Sterling Price led the Missouri Confederate forces to solid victories at Wilson's Creek and Lexington in August 1861 and September 1861 respectively. This occurred on the heels of the severe defeat of the Union Army at Bull Run by the Southern Confederates in July 1861.

In the Missouri region, the confidence of the rebels was crushed at the battle of Pea Ridge in Arkansas in March 1862. Many Missouri Confederates had a change in heart and ceased to support the Southern cause after this striking defeat inflicted by the Union Army.[14] Robert C. Ewing, along with two thousand other ex-Confederates, left their war-torn state for the Gold Fields of Montana in the spring of 1862.[15]

In his book *The Civil War on the Western Border,* author Jay Monaghan tells the story: "The Border War reached its most destructive point in the summer of 1863. William Quantrill with several hundred so-called Border Ruffians including Frank James and Cole Younger rode into the Jayhawker stronghold of Lawrence, Kansas, and destroyed it, burning numerous homes and killing many.

"In retaliation General Thomas Ewing of the Union Army issued Order Number Eleven, which evicted all rural residents of Western Missouri from their farms. Many of these farmsteads would be plundered and burned before their owners were allowed to return at war's end. The devastation inflicted by both sides turned the border into a wasteland of gang warfare."

Remnants of the lawlessness of the roving gangs along the border would continue on until Jesse James' death in 1882 in St. Joseph, Missouri.

The Union gained control of the Mississippi with victories at New Orleans in April 1862 and at Vicksburg and Port Hudson in July 1863. In July the Union victory at Gettysburg also took place. Its importance was the overthrow of the South's attempt to carry the war into the Northern states. On November 19, 1863, a cemetery was dedicated on the battlefield, and Lincoln would deliver his Gettysburg masterpiece stating that "government of the people, by the people and for the people shall not perish from the earth."

The year 1864 would be an election year. Monaghan elaborates: "The [Union] victories of 1863 had been stalemated and something must be done or Lincoln would not be nominated for another term. Two plans to split the South and hasten a Northern victory were considered. Lincoln favored cutting Louisiana in half, then marching across Texas to the Gulf. Grant and Sherman preferred to capture Atlanta and then jayhawk across Georgia to the sea. In case Lincoln approved this plan, Sherman promised to give the command of a division to his brother-in-law, Tom Ewing, who was now in charge of the District of St. Louis, which included southeast Missouri." The plan to split Louisiana was tried first and failed due to spring flooding, which interfered with effective troop movements. "Two months before the election, Sherman captured Atlanta and asked final permission to undertake his march to the Sea. At the same time, his brother-in-law Ewing prepared to leave on furlough for Lancaster, Ohio where his wife expected to be confined [to give birth] at about election time or sooner. But before he left St. Louis, he learned that Shelby's horsemen were probing his outposts in the southern part of the state. He had heard rumors since last April that Price planned another invasion, but nothing had come of it. The route ahead of Old Pap (Price), if he attempted it, was twice as long as Sherman's proposed march to the sea. However the white-haired patriarch had become an expert at living off the country on long marches—in fact had taught generals like Sherman that it could be done successfully. Now if Sherman dared cross Georgia to Savannah, Price might disconcert him by marching north to take St. Louis. The South's strategy to foil Sherman was plain enough. Did Sherman dare take such a chance, at least before election?

"The problem of stopping Price in southeast Missouri devolved on Rosencran's district commander, Tom Ewing." Ewing's furlough was cancelled, and "Gray haired Pap Price rode exultantly north on his gray-haired horse Bucephalus, hoping to counteract Sherman's victories in the Southeast."

Price and Ewing fought to a draw at Pilot Knob, Missouri. Ewing retreated but prevented Price from invading St. Louis.

Price and his remaining Missouri Confederates rode west, were unable to capture Jefferson City (Missouri's capital), lost the battle of Westport in 1864, and retreated from the state of Missouri into the western territory.

Sherman's march to the sea was successful and Abraham Lincoln was reelected. Grant defeated Lee's army in Virginia the following spring, and Lee's surrender at Appomatox Courthouse on April 9, 1865, effectively ended the war. The 13th Amendment to the U.S. Constitution adopted after the war extinguished slavery in the once again United States.

On July 4, 1865, Sterling Price with Jo Shelby and their five hundred remaining Confederate soldiers crossed the Rio Grande River on their way to Monterrey, Mexico, still having not surrendered. "The veterans tried to farm for a season, but they dreamed always of past battles and read in imported papers the accounts of reconstruction in their native states." Many began returning to Missouri.

"Pap Price also returned to the United States within a year. An old man now at fifty five, broken in spirit and health, he died shortly after his return. Shelby followed him to Missouri living quietly near his old home until the Democrats became respectable under President Cleveland in 1893. Then he was appointed United States Marshal for the western district of Missouri."[16]

Robert C. Ewing, who had also served as a U.S. Marshal before the Civil War, returned to Missouri in 1868. While in Montana he served as president of the first Constitutional Convention for the state of Montana in 1866. After his homecoming he served as a judge in Jackson County, Missouri, in the postwar years. His brother Ephraim B. Ewing was reappointed to the Missouri Supreme Court in 1872.[17]

Missouri, having been a border state, was spared some, but not all, of the postwar trauma. Although life was beginning to return to normal, the prodigal sons of the Confederacy were initially punished for their transgressions. In Missouri, the State Constitution of 1865 denied them the right to vote.[18] In the South the reconstruction policies of the U.S. government were designed to the same effect.

Lincoln's initial plan for reconstruction was very generous to the South and took the position that they had never been out of the Union because they had no legal right to leave it. After Lincoln's death, the radicals in Congress sought to punish the Southern States and President Grant faithfully carried out this vindictive policy.

Gradually Northern public opinion favored a more humane and liberal policy toward the South. All the Southern states were restored to the Union by 1870, and an Amnesty Act was passed in 1872 that pardoned almost all who had taken part in the war against the Union. In Missouri, future Supreme Court Justice Elijah H. Norton was one of the leaders who redrew the Missouri State Constitution in 1875 to reflect the principles of this amnesty for former Missouri confederates.[19]

Equal Under the Law

The quarter-century following the Civil War was the time of *laissez faire* national policy. Thomas Jefferson's minimalist federal government ideal would be, in reality, an unworkable illusion. The result was an excessive concentration of local power, which resulted in an invasion of the rights of many law-abiding citizens. "Machine" politicians controlled the large cities. St. Louis, Missouri, was one such city.

The *Missouri Historical Review* recounts: "It was not until the middle of February 1886, that the *Post-Dispatch* took notice of the contested election suit brought by ex-Mayor William L. Ewing, the defeated Republican candidate in 1885. Claiming that he and not Francis was the rightful mayor, Ewing produced indisputable evidence of fraudulent registrations. He had been battling in the courts for almost a year for permission to examine the actual ballots, which was the only way to prove, in the eyes of the law, that the election frauds had been committed by Democrats.

"The *Post-Dispatch* gave full coverage to Ewing's allegations, and left no doubt in the minds of its readers that the circumstantial evidence was heavily against the Democrats. It emphasized the fact that the illegal registrations were in the boss-controlled Democratic wards, where Francis received his biggest majorities, and that the Democrats unfairly controlled the election machinery in the city. Time and again it called upon Francis to vindicate his honor by agreeing to a recount of the votes, but Francis ignored the challenge. 'Open the ballot-boxes!' the *Post-Dispatch* cried in banner headlines every day, and when Ewing's case seemed hopeless, blocked by a legal technicality, it poured out its wrath upon the mayor in a March 4 editorial:

'We have given Mayor Francis more than ample time to repudiate the exposed and undenied frauds. He does not repudiate them. We have given him opportunity to explain. He has no explanation to make. We have left the door wide open for defense or palliation. No defense or palliation is suggested. We have waited for him to consent that the ballot-boxes should be allowed to tell their own story. He used the Law Department of the city to defend his personal interest in keeping the story hidden and suppressed.'

"From that time on the *Post-Dispatch* rarely missed a chance to expose the links between the Francis administration and the crooked machine politicians who had raised him to power."[20]

Foster R. Dulles recounts the frustration of the postwar years and the eventual resolution: "In the aftermath of war there was a startling letdown in both public and private morals. It was not only in the carpet bag government of the South, that corruption often ran rampant. Throughout the country local political machines, of which the best known was the Tweed Ring in New York, were mulcting the public without let or hindrance.

"The country had fallen on evil days, partly because of the extravagance and speculation that marked the Gilded Age, and there was everywhere severe economic distress."

"The progressive era which may perhaps be dated from that memorable day when [Theodore] Roosevelt took the oath of office [1902] and was to extend to the eve of our entry into World War I, was marked by a shift in popular attitudes that spelled the eclipse of the *laissez faire* philosophy that had dominated national life throughout the nineteenth century.

"The progressive movement was a drive to restore to the people as a whole the political power that had been usurped by the business community. It was an attack on privilege and 'invisible government'—a campaign to control the railroads, the trusts, and the money power in the national interest. Where populism had failed to break through the ramparts of embattled industry, progressivism breasted them successfully. The aims of its leaders were by no means fully realized, but the bases of democracy were strengthened. A broad program of social and economic reform accounted for a very considerable advance along the endless road to social justice." The road to justice in the struggle for civil rights would have to wait through another half century and two world wars.[21]

Woodrow Wilson served as president of the United States on the eve of the First World War. His college education began at Davidson College in Davidson, North Carolina, which had been named in memory of William L. Davidson. Wilson received his degree from Princeton College but returned to Davidson for a visit while president. "Davidson's sense of personal identification with President Wilson grew stronger when he came to Charlotte [Mecklenburg County] in 1916 to speak at the annual May 20 celebration. In the late afternoon he decided unexpectedly to drive up to Davidson and walked briefly around the campus."[22]

Shortly before his election to the presidency in 1912, Wilson wrote: "There are serious times ahead… It daunts me to think of the possibility of my playing an influential part in them. There is no telling what deep waters may be ahead of me. The forces of greed and the forces of justice and humanity are about to grapple for a bout in which men will spend all the life that is in them. God grant I may have strength to count, to tip the balance in the unequal and tremendous struggle!"

"Wilson was determined to be the spokesman both of his party and of the nation and to look for support from neither bosses nor congressman but from the people themselves."[23]

Civil Rights

Certainly the end of slavery was only the beginning chapter in the struggle for equality for blacks in the United States.

A century of injustice would be followed by reform in the post World War II years. In the late 1940s Harry Truman began a civil rights program (aided by administration member Oscar R. Ewing) that Adlai Ewing Stevenson had pledged to support as the Democratic party's nominee for president in 1952 and again in 1956. With Stevenson's defeat in 1952 and 1956, civil rights were put on hold until John F. Kennedy's election in 1960, though strides were made through the court system in the 1950s. Then in 1963 Dr. Martin Luther King, Jr. dared to dream a dream for his people and a dramatic transformation was put in motion.

"The year 1963 was the centennial of the signing of the Emancipation Proclamation. It was truly a momentous year in American history and in the life of Martin Luther King, Jr."

"The nation stood in the brink of racial civil war. It needed a prophet who could help see through the smoke left by gunpowder and bombs. Martin Luther King, Jr. was the prophet of the hour… He delivered *I Have a Dream* before the Lincoln Memorial on August 28, 1963, as the keynote of the March on Washington, D.C., for Civil Rights."[24] Some key excerpts follow: "When the architects of our republic wrote the magnificent words of the

Constitution and the Declaration of Independence, they were signing a promissory note which every American was to fall heir. This note was the promise that all men, yes, black men as well as white men, would be guaranteed the unalienable rights of life, liberty, and the pursuit of happiness.

"It is obvious today that America has defaulted on this promissory note in so far as her citizens of color are concerned...

"We have also come to this hallowed spot to remind America of the fierce urgency of now...

"I have a dream that one day on the red hills of Georgia, sons of former slaves and sons of former slave owners will be able to sit down together at the table of brotherhood...

"I have a dream that my four little children will one day live in a nation where they will not be judged by the color of their skin but by the content of their character. I have a dream today!...

"I have a dream that one day every valley shall be exalted, every hill and mountain shall be made low, the rough places will be made plain, and the crooked places shall be made straight and the glory of the Lord will be revealed and all flesh shall see it together...

"And when we allow freedom to ring, when we let it ring from every village and hamlet, from every state and city, we will be able to speed up that day when all of God's children—black men and white men, Jews and Gentiles, Catholics and Protestants—will be able to join hands and to sing in the words of the old Negro spiritual 'Free at last, free at last; thank God Almighty, we are free at last.' "

In July of 1964 the late President Kennedy's Civil Rights Bill was passed and signed by President Johnson. On December 10, 1964, Dr. King received the Nobel Peace Prize in Oslo, Norway.

Dr. King stated in summary: "Today I come to Oslo as a trustee, inspired and with renewed dedication to humanity. I accept this prize on behalf of all men who love peace and brotherhood."[25]

Today the wounds of racism are healing and "created equal" is moving closer to its ideal. Though there are still many problems, the spirit of the Declaration of Independence seems to be pushing us in the right direction. Dr. Martin Luther King, Jr.'s dream is becoming reality.

Native American Rights

It is a tragic irony that when the European immigrants gained their independence in America, they at the same time destroyed the independence of the Native Americans. With each step of European settlement, the first Americans were pushed to the frontier, which was moving rapidly westward by the 1800s.

During this time Andrew Jackson adopted a Creek Indian boy as his son, but his ruthless policies against the Native Americans were extreme.

Every movement of the frontier westward resulted in conflict with the established Native Americans, and Jackson's solution as president was for them to be dispersed to areas west of the Mississippi. "There can be no question that he [Jackson] believed he had acted in the best interest of the Indian, but to achieve his purpose countless men, women, and children suffered deprivation and death."[26]

Davy Crockett opposed Jackson's treatment of the Indians, and he later lost his seat in Congress because of this opposition to Jackson's policies in general.[27] As a result, Crockett rode west to seek a new challenge.

Many other adventurers were attracted to the frontiers of the West. Finis Young Ewing, a son of Finis and Margaret Ewing, in 1837 traveled to the far Northwest.

Helen Howard writes: "Many, many moons ago, so many moons that not even the oldest people of the tribe could remember, the Nez Perces wandered a free and happy people, over a vast area of mountains, plains, valleys, and sagebrush plateaus. Their hunting and fishing grounds extended throughout what is now north central Idaho, southeastern Washington, and northeastern Oregon.

"As the Great Spirit Above intended they should, these peace-loving and carefree Nez Perces roamed the grassy plateaus and valleys during the spring, summer, and fall, seeking pasturage for their large herds of well-bred horses."

Lewis and Clark were the first whites ever to be seen by the Nez Perces. The oral history of the expedition was passed down to Young Joseph (Chief of the Nez Perces) who said: "All the Nez Perces made friends with Lewis and Clark and agreed let them pass through their country, and never make war on white men. This promise the Nez Perces have never broken. No white man can accuse them of bad faith and speak with a straight tongue."

After Lewis and Clark, "French Canadian trappers came to trade the white man's guns, cloth, metal articles, and trinkets for their pelts of beaver... Later the Hudson's Bay Company "spread a chain of forts and trading posts throughout the Northwest... In 1832 Captain B. L. E. Bonneville's expedition came in contact with the Nez Perces and he found them to be... among the gentlest and least barbarous people of these remote wildernesses... and also some of the most religious. Their piety, according to a well-established account, caused them to send a delegation in 1831 to St. Louis in search of the white man's teachers and Book."

Howard continues the story: "The Nez Perces waited three years for the white men to bring them the teachings of the 'spirit law.' The Methodist Church was the first to respond. That denomination sent out Jason Lee and his associates, among whom was his nephew, Daniel Lee. The party of missionaries traveled into the Northwest with the trading expedition of Nathaniel J. Wyeth and William L. Sublette. Early in July, 1834, they met Lawyer's band of Nez Perces in the vicinity of Fort Hall on Snake River. But Lee and his assistants did not tarry long among these Indians, for they had instructions to make their way to the Willamette Valley in Oregon.

"The next missionaries to arrive were Dr. Marcus Whitman, a physician, and the Reverend Samuel Parker. They came in August of the following year and held a religious council with the Nez Perces at the rendezvous on Green River. So delighted and impressed was Dr. Whitman with these Indians that he returned east to make arrangements for founding a mission, while Parker continued to the settlements on the lower Columbia. Whitman was accompanied to the States by two Nez Perce boys, one the son of a chief. The youths wished to learn the English language...

"The American Board of Commissioners for Foreign Missions, which then included the Presbyterian and Congregational denominations, commissioned Whitman for missionary work among the Nez Perces. In the spring of 1836 he again started west, bringing as his assistant his bride, the former Miss Narcissa Prentiss, the Reverend and Mrs. Henry H. Spalding, and W. H. Gray. A party of Nez Perces met them at the Green River rendezvous in the present state of Wyoming, and some of the Indians accompanied the missionaries to the Columbia River Valley."

The missionaries had converted Chief Joseph to Christianity, but he remained so only temporarily. Young Joseph was his son.

In *Chief Joseph,* Helen Howard continues: "Taken from Lapwai before he received more than a primary education in Spalding's school, little Joseph's knowledge came from lessons taught him by the experiences of his daily life. Under his father's guidance he learned how to hunt the creatures of the forest and to fish the streams for salmon, and how to ride a pony without saddle or bridle. He could imitate the calls of birds and animals, and he acquired an intimate knowledge of their habits. He learned to fashion spears and knives, arrows and quivers, and other weapons of war. From the red fir he made a spear with barbed stone points to be used to hunt the buffalo when he grew older and stronger. He learned to watch for the roots of plants that provided food and medicine. This training developed his senses to a keen alertness, and fitted him for a life of economic self-sufficiency.

"Nor was his spiritual development overlooked. From the tribal myths and legends (akin to the moral lessons of Aesop's *Fables*), little Joseph learned that selfishness and greed were great sins. Under the gentle teaching of his father, he learned to share his food, even to his last morsel, with the poor, and never wantonly to destroy animals nor plants, but to kill only when in need. His father taught him respect for the wisdom of his elders, and always to be thankful for the bounteous gifts of the Great Spirit.

"After he had grown to manhood, Young Joseph said regarding his spiritual training: 'Our fathers gave us many laws, which they had learned from their fathers. These laws were good.

They told us to treat all men as they treated us; that we should never be the first to break a bargain; that it was a disgrace to tell a lie; that we should only tell the truth; that it was a shame for one man to take from another his wife, or his property without paying for it. We were taught to believe that the Great Spirit sees and hears everything, and that he never forgets, that hereafter he will give every man a spirit-home according to his deserts: if he has been a good man he will have a good home; if he has been a bad man, he will have a bad home. This I believe, and all my people believe the same.'

"In this statement of his creed we may recognize the golden-rule philosophy of Christian precept, and the influence on Young Joseph's father of the Reverend Henry Spalding's missionary teaching."[28]

At the summer rendezvous of July 1838, which occurred on the Papo Agie River, just beyond South Pass Wyoming, there was present a diverse mix of humanity, including fortune seekers, mountain men, missionaries, and Native Americans. According to the missionary diary of Myra Sells, Devoto writes, Jim Bridger was present, and Bridger "was trying to raise the status of Christians in his men's eyes. He felt an obligation to them because they were in the same business as Marcus Whitman, who three years ago had removed from his shoulder what Myra calls an Indian spear." Kit Carson joined Bridger as another mountain-man-trapper who was present. John Sutter was also there and would have brought "his fine manners to the tents in the willow grove and, stretched on buffalo robes, spin a vision of his military past and his imperial future."

Devoto writes: "Then on Sunday July 8 a small, confident, and temperately uproarious outfit came in from the west. It was Francis Ermatinger with a Hudson's Bay Company party in territory unquestionably American, and let the trust make something of it if it wanted to. He began to sign up trappers who could see that the American Fur Company was not what it used to be. Also he had letters from Spalding and Whitman with news of the mission."[29]

In Richard Dillon's words: "Ermatinger's companions were an equally interesting lot. There was Jason Lee of the Oregon Methodist Mission, who was on his way back to the States with a gentleman named F. Y. Ewing, the first of a long line of people to go to the Pacific Coast for reasons of health. Having recovered his health, he was returning to civilization. Also with Ermatinger were three half-breed sons of Thomas McKay, the factor at Fort Hall, and two Chinook Indian boys bound for school in the East. While Sutter watched, the westbound and eastbound clergy mingled delightedly, engaging in animated conversation. So excited were his religious trail companions, in fact, that they quite forgot to hold Sunday services that day. Lee passed on the good news that Oregon Missionaries Whitman and Spalding were sending horses and provisions to Fort Hall and Fort Boise to help the reinforcements on the last leg of their journey… Reverend Lee may have been almost as welcome a visitor as Ermatinger. In him, Sutter met an outstanding frontier missionary, a man who had the skill to sow the seeds of civilization in the wilderness. Probably he passed on some of his ideas about transforming Oregon's migratory hunting society into a stable agricultural one. If so, just as he had influenced Marcus Whitman and Henry Spalding at Waiilatpu and Lapwai, so too, he influenced Sutter in planning his Sacramento River settlement."[30]

It is believed that Finis Young Ewing may have visited Ewing Young's homestead in Oregon during the previous winter. Ewing Young had been "one of the most considerable figures of the fur trade of the far west." In 1822 he followed the Santa Fe Trail west from Missouri and led trapping parties beyond it into Arizona and California. "Young's first California expedition, besides being profitable, must be credited with the effective opening of trade with California. It is also notable that Kit Carson served his apprenticeship as a Mountain Man under so experienced a leader as Ewing Young."

Ewing Young's grandfather, Robert Young, had been one of the leading Patriots at the battle of King's Mountain during the Revolution. In 1836 Ewing Young migrated to the Northwest and settled in Oregon. In 1840 a group of the first arrivals on the Oregon trail were struggling to survive.

"They had to turn for help to the Hudson's Bay Company, to the Methodists, and to the few extrapper settlers, notably Ewing Young." It was a hard life and Ewing Young died in 1841 at age 49.[31]

As for the souls at the summer rendezvous of 1838, their destiny would play a large part in the destruction of the independent life of the Native Americans of the West. Ewing Young, as previously mentioned, helped open the Southwest for settlement, as did Jim Bridger in the Northwest. For Bridger the era of the fur trade was in its twilight and he would eventually retire to Missouri. Kit Carson and F. Y. Ewing would later lead trading caravans on the Santa Fe Trail and Carson would guide the pathfinder John C. Fremont west to California. For John Sutter there was yet a material fortune to be gained and lost. In the process there would be a stampede to California. For Jason Lee there would be many souls to save and many settlers that his lectures back East on the fertile Williamette Valley of Oregon would lure west. The site of their camp was adjacent to South Pass, Wyoming, which would become one of the landmarks of the Oregon Trail.

The letter from Rev. Spalding concerned his mission, which was to the Nez Perce and their chief, known as Chief Joseph. Chief Joseph's son would later become the leader of the Nez Perce.

"[Young] Chief Joseph was a leader for peace and tribal liberty, he was destined to see the defeat of his people in the Nez Perce War of 1877 and the loss of all that was important to them— their lands, their horses and their independence."[32] And of course, this was the fate of all the great Native Americans.

In *Touch the Earth,* author T. C. McLuhan writes: "On January 14, 1879, Chief Joseph addressed a large gathering of cabinet members and congressmen. He appealed to President Hayes to allow what was left of his tribe, whose members were dying by the score, to return to their old territory in the Northwest. His appeal was ultimately successful and in 1883, a small party of women and children were allowed to go back to their old home. Joseph was never granted this privilege and spent his remaining days on the Colville Reservation at Nespelim, Washington. He died there September 21, 1904.

'I have shaken hands with a great many friends, but there are some things I want to know which no one seems able to explain. I cannot understand how the Government hands a man out to fight us, as it did General Miles, and then breaks his word. Such a Government has something wrong about it... I do not understand why nothing is done for my people. I have heard talk and talk, but nothing is done. Good words do not last long until they amount to something. Words do not pay for my dead people. They do not pay for my country, now overrun by white men. They do not protect my father's grave. They do not pay for my horses and cattle.

'Good words do not give me back my children. Good words will not make good the promise of your war chief, General Miles. Good words will not give my people good health and stop them from dying. Good words will not get my people a home where they can live in peace and take care of themselves.

'I am tired of talk that comes to nothing. It makes my heart sick when I remember all the good words and all the broken promises. There has been too much talking by men who had no right to talk. Too many misinterpretations have been made; too many misunderstandings have come up between the white men about the Indians.

'If the white man wants to live in peace with the Indian he can live in peace. There need be no trouble. Treat all men alike. Give them all the same law. Give them all an even chance to live and grow... You might as well expect the rivers to run backward as that any man who was born free should be contented penned up and denied liberty to go where he pleases. If you tie a horse to a stake, do you expect he will grow fat? If you pen an Indian up on a small spot of earth and compel him to stay there, he will not be contented nor will he grow and prosper.

'I have asked some of the Great White Chiefs where they get their authority to say to the Indian that he will stay in one place, while he sees white men going where they please. They cannot tell me.

'I only ask of the government to be treated as all other men are treated. If I cannot go to my own home, let me have a home in a country where my people will not die so fast…

'I know that my race must change. We cannot hold our own with the white men as we are. We only ask an even chance to live as other men live. We ask to be recognized as men. We ask that the same law shall work alike on all men. If an Indian breaks the law, punish him by the law. If a white man breaks the law, punish him also.

'Let me be a free man—free to travel, free to stop, free to work, free to trade where I choose, free to choose my own teachers, free to follow the religion of my fathers, free to think and talk and act for myself—and I will obey every law or submit to the penalty.' "[33]

Chief Joseph's request would eventually be honored, but only after many seasons and several generations had passed. Along with the Civil Rights Movement of the early 1960s, the Native Americans were making progress in asserting their rights by the later part of the decade.

In 1968 the American Indian Movement (AIM) was founded in Minneapolis, Minnesota, by Dennis Banks and others. Its purpose, according to Judith Nies, was to "represent urban Indian goals, protect the traditional ways of Indian peoples, hire legal counsel and intervene in cases relating to treaty and aboriginal rights to hunting, fishing, trapping and gathering wild rice." In 1971 the Native American Rights Fund was founded to provide legal assistance to tribes. In 1973 AIM leaders Dennis Banks and Russel Means led protests at Pine Ridge and Wounded Knee, which brought national attention to Native American issues.

The American Indian Religious Freedom Act became law in 1979, stating that Indian religion was protected under the First Amendment. Through the latter two decades of the twentieth century, Native Americans have effectively asserted their unalienable rights through the judicial, legislative, and executive branches of local and federal government.

In 1996 "the white residents of the Wallowa Valley in Oregon, from which Chief Joseph and his Nez Perce were expelled in 1877, have invited the Nez Perce to return... After his 1,500 mile march in which he outwitted the U.S. Army and won 21 separate military encounters [Joseph was actually the spiritual leader of the tribe and other warriors led the battles], Chief Joseph and his band were surprised in the open plain 40 miles from the Canadian border and forced to surrender... It is said that Chief Joseph died of a broken heart."[34]

Just as the Native Americans overcame many broken hearts to seek their rights, the women of America have shown the strength of their hearts by fighting for equality in what was once a male-dominated world.

Women's Rights

With the issue of slavery settled and the issue of civil rights far in the future, the issue of women's suffrage surfaced in St. Louis, Missouri, and made its way through the court system. In 1873 this issue was brought before the Missouri Supreme Court. As previously mentioned, Ephraim B. Ewing was re-appointed as a justice of the Missouri Supreme Court in 1872.

Gerald T. Dunne writes in *The Missouri Supreme Court:* "Among closing reflections in his classic *An American Dilemma* author Gunnar Myrdal explained the choice of the indefinite article for the title of his landmark work. The reason, he said, was that the racial gap between profession and practice of an American ethos that proclaimed equality and opportunity represented only one of many social inconsistencies in which the injustices were successfully and constitutionally perpetuated both by the neurosis of race and the preconceptions of gender. Nowhere was this better shown than in the actions of the Federal Reconstruction, U.S. Congress and the Missouri General Assembly. Both bodies moved to enfranchise ultimately newly freed black men but were singularly unmoved to do anything about the corresponding powerlessness of women. Quite the contrary, the distinction was emphasized in the vocabulary chosen by both legislative bodies in the use of the adjective 'male' in their ameliorative legislation.

"Not that women of Missouri had acquiesced in the arrangement. Rather, during the intermezzo between the state's 1865 and 1875 constitutions (both of which had explicitly limited the vote to the male gender), a gathering of women met on May 8, 1867, in St. Louis's Mercantile Library and petitioned the General Assembly for the right of women to vote. Predictably, their plea lost in Jefferson City, as did their subsequent petition the next year. However, in 1869, a new element in the effort was suggested by a convention in St. Louis of the Woman Suffrage Association, a group including Elizabeth Cady Stanton, Susan B. Anthony, and St. Louis's Virginia Minor. The latter was married to her distant cousin Francis and fortuitously retained her maiden name. She had been the spearhead of the 1867 petition to the General Assembly, as had her husband—a respected lawyer and one-time clerk of the Missouri Supreme Court—who became a fervent convert to the cause of women's voting rights. A new factor appeared when the reformers changed their tactic from importuning the legislature to demands in litigation. 'Failing before the Legislature,' said Mrs. Minor, 'we must turn to the Supreme Court.'

"And she did, taking the first step on October 15, 1872, when she undertook to register with the St. Louis election authorities. Predictably, registrar Reece Happersett refused to enter her name in the rolls. Mrs. Minor, together with her husband (an indispensable party in view of his wife's common law disabilities), responded in December with a lawsuit in the Circuit Court of St. Louis County. They asserted that the voting sections of Missouri's 1865 Constitution that limited voting to males had been nullified by the recently adopted [1868] Fourteenth Amendment to the U.S. Constitution. Joining them was John Brooks Henderson, whose close connection with the Civil War amendments to the U.S. Constitution lent his intervention as a compelling force for persuasiveness. The Fourteenth Amendment forbade any state from impairing the privileges and immunities of citizens of the United States. These, insisted the Minors and Henderson, included the right to vote. Indeed, their suit resurrected the keystone question of *Dred Scott:* who were 'citizens' and what were their rights?

"On February 3, 1873, the circuit court dismissed the Minors' action, and appeal was duly taken to the Missouri Supreme Court. Before the 1873 term was out, the court unanimously sustained Happersett's refusal to register Mrs. Minor. The court's logic was simplicity itself: that under the original understanding of the Constitution, admission to voting was a state matter and, aside from protection of the newly emancipated male slaves, nothing had changed.

"The result of Mrs. Minor's appeal to the U.S. Supreme Court merely underscored the preemptive logic of the Missouri Supreme Court. One of Minor's lawyers on the appeal was John B. Henderson. As noted, Henderson had changed Father Cummings's plea in the Pike County court to save the constitutional issue in the iron-clad oath controversy. He had also written the Thirteenth Amendment (abolishing slavery) and had been a major protagonist of the Fifteenth (forbidding states to use slavery as a disqualification for voting but apparently permitting any other constraint). Henderson must have done his best on the brief, but he was hoist with his own petard. The argument countering his plea for Mrs. Minor asserted that if the Fourteenth Amendment conferred voting rights on all citizens, why was there the need for the Fifteenth? And such was the temper of the Supreme Court during his argument that Justice Field, author of *Cummings,* forced Mr. Minor to admit that if the Fourteenth Amendment conferred voting on all citizens (including women), logically children had that right. As far as the U.S. Reports show, no counsel even appeared to argue against Mrs. Minor so obvious was the question deemed, and the Supreme Court affirmed the state tribunal."[35]

In the days of the Revolutionary War, women had no legal voice and there were no prospects for one, but they did their best under the circumstances.

Edith Patterson Meyer reports: "In February, 1780, the *South Carolina and Georgia Gazette* recorded that the young ladies of the North Carolina counties of Mecklenburg and Rowan had entered into a similar pledge: 'not to receive the attentions of young men who would not volunteer in defense of the country, they being of the opinion that such persons as stay loitering at home, when the important calls of the country demand their military services abroad, must certainly be destitute of the nobleness of sentiment, the brave and manly spirit which would qualify them to be the defenders and guardians of the fair sex."[36]

In *Sketches of Western North Carolina,* C. L. Hunter speculates: "And who were the young ladies of Mecklenburg and Rowan counties then prepared to sign such an association, and willing to bestow their fair hands, and pledge their loving hearts only to those brave soldiers, who, on the calls of duty, fought the battles of their country? Imagination carries us back to that eventful period, and pictures to our admiring view, among others, the following daughters of Western Carolina, as actuated by such patriotic motives:

Miss Elizabeth Alexander, daughter of Abraham Alexander.

Miss Mary Wilson, daughter of Samuel Wilson who married Ezekiel Polk, grandfather of President James K. Polk.

Miss Violet Wilson, sister of the above, who married Major John Davidson.

Miss Jane Morrison, daughter of Neill Morrison, who married Major Thomas Alexander.

Miss Polk, daughter of Colonel Thomas Polk, who married Dr. Ephraim Brevard.

Miss Margaret Polk, sister of the above, who married Nathaniel Alexander, Representative to Congress from 1803 to 1805, and in the latter year, elected Governor of the State.

Miss Jane Brevard, daughter of John Brevard, and sister of the 'seven brothers in the rebel army,' who married General Ephraim Davidson.

Miss Mary Brevard, sister of the above, who married General William Davidson, killed at Cowan's Ford, on February 1, 1781. (That day 'George Templeton of Centre took the sad tidings to Mary Brevard Davidson. She left her month-old baby, mounted her horse and rode fifteen miles through enemy-held territory to see her husband. In the yard of Hopewell meeting-house, a few miles from the ford, the burial took place by torch light.')

Miss Charity Jack, sister of Captain James Jack, the bearer of the Mecklenburg Declaration to Philadelphia.

Miss Hamiah Knox, daughter of Captain Patrick Knox, killed at the battle of Ramsour's Mill, who married Samuel Wilson, a soldier of the Revolution.

"These are the names of a few of the patriotic young ladies, then on the theatre of action, who would be willing to sign such an association, stimulate the 'loitering young men' to a proper sense of their duty, and promote the cause of freedom by all fair means. The reality beyond this pledge was that the war invaded their community. The wives and mothers of Mecklenburg county bore a large share of the trials and dangers of the Revolution."[37]

According to Bernice Kohn: "In 1840, a World Antislavery Convention was held in London. Several very advanced and 'unfeminine' women, including Elizabeth Cady Stanton and Lucretia Mott, attended as delegates, but as in the case of the Temperance Society, they were not permitted to participate in the meetings.

"The women went home, but they went home angry and determined to act. It took them a while, but in 1848, they called a Women's Rights Convention at Seneca Falls, New York. Two hundred and fifty women attended, and they issued a document that was patterned closely on the Declaration of Independence. They called it *The Declaration of Sentiments and Resolutions* and it stated in part:

"The history of mankind is a history of repeated injuries and usurpations on the part of man toward woman, having in direct object the establishment of an absolute tyranny over her. To prove this, let facts be submitted to a candid world.

"He has never permitted her to exercise her inalienable right to the elective franchise.

"He has made her, if married, in the eyes of the law civilly dead.

"He has taken from her all rights to property, even to the wages she earns.

"He has denied her the facilities for obtaining a thorough education—all college being closed against her.

"He has created a false public sentiment, by giving to the world a different code of morals for men and women, by which moral delinquencies which exclude women from society are not only tolerated but deemed of little account in man.

"He has endeavored, in every way that he could, to destroy her confidence in her own powers, to lessen her self-respect, and to make her willing to lead a dependent and abject life.

"Like the Declaration of Independence before it, this powerful statement had no immediate impact; it needed some time."[38]

In 1883 Ephraim B. Ewing's book on rules for the conduct of the Supreme Court of Missouri was published,[39] even though his death had occurred in 1873, during the trial of Mrs. Minor's petition for the women's vote. As would be expected, it did not view women's rights as a legitimate issue.

Eventually the old would give way to the new. In 1920 women won the right to vote and by 1993 things had changed dramatically. The recommendation made that year by the Missouri Task Force on Gender for the conduct of the Missouri Supreme Court was as follows: "A judge shall perform judicial duties without bias or prejudice. A judge shall not, in the performance of judicial duties, by words or conduct manifest bias or prejudice, including but not limited to bias or prejudice based upon race, sex, religion, national origin, disability, age, or socioeconomic status, and shall not permit staff, court officials and others subject to the judge's direction and control to do so." (paraphrased)[40]

Also, "in a history-making event, the Missouri Supreme Court elected Judge Ann K. Covington, the first woman member of the Missouri Supreme Court, to the office of Chief Justice. Judge Covington, who has been a member of the Court since December 1988, assumed her new role on July 1, 1993. The new Chief Justice, a native of West Virginia, is a 1963 graduate of Duke University (Durham, North Carolina) and obtained her law degree from the University of Missouri-Columbia in 1977, the same year she was admitted to the Missouri Bar."[41]

Summary

From the days of the Revolution, to the time of Abraham Lincoln and Elizabeth Cady Stanton, to the recent era of Dr. Martin Luther King, Dennis Banks, Russel Means, and Ann K. Covington, many wrongs have been righted.

Thomas Jefferson embraced the Enlightenment concept of individual freedom, embalmed it into the Declaration of Independence, and offered it to America. But it was a limited freedom, applying only to the chosen. True equality and freedom would eventually become the story of all Americans because they in fact would make it so! Only when the unalienable rights of all were protected, would the promise of the Scottish Enlightenment be fulfilled in America. From its origins, to its creation, and its interpretation, the Declaration of Independence of July 4, 1776, was a mosaic crafted by many. Over time, the Declaration would be resurrected and given new life! Its meaning would be transformed to serve a more universal purpose than originally intended.

Through it, all Americans have become one people, and through their voice, the Declaration calls out to a world in need.

Chapter 6
The Final Chapter

From philosopher to politician, Thomas Jefferson's vision and dedication on behalf of our fledgling nation was exceptional—earning him a place of reverence in the consciousness of twentieth-century America. Jefferson's public image as a revered American icon remains an idealized Thomas Jefferson, symbolizing the Declaration of Independence as we interpret it today. This image overshadows the real Jefferson that historians continue to seek out and reveal.

The real Thomas Jefferson wrote eloquently for freedom, but he was not among those who put their lives on the line, to in fact win America's freedom. The real Thomas Jefferson would leave the office of governor with Virginia in disarray due to the repeated and unopposed British invasions of its borders. He would end his second term as president of the United States with America mired in economic chaos due to his failed Embargo Act of 1807. He would escape to Monticello to recover from each of these political disasters. In time, Jefferson's reputation was gradually restored, as his authorship of the Declaration of Independence was increasingly acknowledged and appreciated by his country. America owes much to the idealism of Thomas Jefferson, but in Jefferson's life itself, reality seemed to stand in his way and was at times, a stumbling block for him.

Thomas Jefferson, himself, most wanted to be remembered as the author of the Declaration of Independence. He requested that the following be inscribed on his tombstone:

Here was buried
Thomas Jefferson
Author of the Declaration of Independence
of the Statutes of Virginia
for Religious Freedom
and
Father of the University of Virginia

Ephraim Brevard's story is a different one. His epitaph is written into the Declaration itself. Before God, on his most sacred honor, he pledged his life as did many others.

When he and his fellow patriots gave their lives in the War for Independence, the Declaration of Independence became their monument. Their deaths made it a legacy of a truth worth fighting for and a cornerstone for future generations.

Throughout its history America has fulfilled this legacy through its continued firm and solemn support of freedom. The public reminders of this tradition are fittingly most apparent in our nation's capital. The city of Washington, D.C., is America's monument to George Washington and it has blossomed over time to become a glorious city of many monuments—a public display of America's heritage.

In the beginning, Kapper relates, Congress "left it to Washington himself to locate the capital city, and he selected 'a situation not excelled for commanding prospect, good water, salubrious air and safe harbor by any of the world'… as to its design President Washington later wrote 'for prosecuting public works and carrying them into effect, [L'Enfant] was better qualified than anyone who had come within my knowledge in this country.' "

L'Enfant was a Frenchman who had followed Lafayette across the Atlantic to fight for the cause of liberty in America.

President Washington and Secretary of State Jefferson wanted a capital that would rival Paris.

"L'Enfant responded with a plan on such a scale as to leave room for that aggrandizement and embellishment which the increase of the wealth of the nation will permit it to pursue at any period however remote. In short, the French visionary set himself the task of designing for the ages."

The Washington Monument was begun in 1848 and completed in 1888 when it was "topped out" at 555 feet.[1] The dome of the Capitol, completed during the Civil War, was made of cast iron and was an engineering marvel in its time. The Washington National Cathedral was chartered in 1893 and completed in 1990.

The two most magnificent memorials, Lincoln's and Jefferson's, were constructed in the 20th century—as L'Enfant desired, they would aggrandize and embellish the surrounding natural beauty of a great city. The waterfront setting and architecture of the Jefferson Memorial is particularly impressive. This monument was approved by President Franklin D. Roosevelt on the eve of World War II. During the planning stages some decisions were required as to what passages from Jefferson's writings would be inscribed on his memorial. In particular, the space available for the Declaration of Independence would require some considerable condensation and editing. The Jefferson Memorial Commission would propose the following version:

We Hold These Truths To Be Self-Evident: That All Men Are Created Equal: That They Are Endowed By Their Creator With Certain Inalienable Rights: That Among These Are Life, Liberty And The Pursuit Of Happiness: That To Secure These Rights Governments Are Instituted Among Men, Deriving Their Just Powers from the Consent Of The Governed. Whenever Any Form Of Government Becomes Destructive Of These Ends It Is the Right Of the People To Alter Or Abolish It.

When this version was sent to President Franklin Roosevelt in May 1941, he suggested some changes and submitted them to the commission.[2] With some further alteration the Commission approved this, the final result:

We Hold These Truths To Be Self-Evident: That All Men Are Created Equal, That They Are Endowed By Their Creator With Certain Inalienable Rights, Among These Are Life, Liberty And The Pursuit of Happiness, That To Secure These Rights Governments Are Instituted Among Men.

[Unalienable and inalienable were used interchangeably during this era. According to author Carl Becker, unalienable was more commonly used during the 18th century.]

This first paragraph was only slightly amended and clearly reveals the influence of the Scottish philosophers, Thomas Reid, David Hume, and Francis Hutcheson.

Francis Hutcheson's *An Inquiry into the Origin of Our Ideas of Beauty and Virtue,* written in 1725, was included in Thomas Jefferson's library that was sold to Congress in 1815. In this work, Hutcheson defines alienable and unalienable rights and distinguishes himself from John Locke in calling property an alienable right. John Locke's scheme of rights consisted of life, liberty and property. Hutcheson's unalienable rights included life, liberty and happiness— the exclusion of property would be a distinguishing factor. David Hume's *Of the Original Contract*, written in 1748, was included in Jefferson's library list recommendations made to Robert Skipworth in 1771. This essay contains Hume's definition of equality, which was apparently a resource for Jefferson. Thomas Reid's *An Inquiry Into the Human Mind* was written in 1764, and was also included in Jefferson's library list of 1771. In this book, Reid described a self-evident truth as an idea (Jefferson's usage was the same). John Locke in *An Essay Concerning Human Understanding* defined a self-evident truth as a maxim of reasoning that could not be used as an idea.

The words of David Hume and Francis Hutcheson were previously discussed. Thomas Reid would add the following: "Moral truths, therefore, may be divided into two classes, to wit: Such as are self-evident to every man whose understanding and moral faculty are ripe, and such as are deduced by reasoning from those that are self-evident..."

Garry Wills writes: "Jefferson was given in Reid's work, a concept of self-evident truths that accords well with his general training, his known reading and recommendations, and the language he used both in and of the Declaration."

Benjamin Franklin may have contributed the words "self evident" to the revised draft of the Declaration; if so, his source would have been the same as Jefferson's. He was a student of the Scottish Enlightenment and an associate of its philosophers during his long pre-Revolutionary War sojourn in the British Isles. Franklin and Jefferson would have been familiar with the philosophy of the Englishman John Locke, who would write about self-evident truths in the late 1600s. But Locke's ideas would be transformed and given new meaning by the Scottish philosophers during the pre-Revolutionary War years.

Wills challenges Carl Becker's basic thesis—that Jefferson found in John Locke "the ideas which he put into the Declaration." When Thomas Jefferson's plantation house burned on February 1, 1770, no lives were lost. "But time would reveal what the world had lost: It had lost a world. Everything Thomas Jefferson had composed to the age of twenty-seven, along with the library he had been assembling with great care and cost for over a decade."

"The ideas expressed by Jefferson in 1776 were first introduced to him, and examined by him, in the prior decade of intense reading and discussion that formed his mind. We have enough evidence of his reading, and of his conclusions from that reading, to establish that the real lost world of Thomas Jefferson was the world of William Small, the invigorating realm of the Scottish Enlightenment at its zenith."[3]

The second paragraph inscribed on the Jefferson Memorial was totally changed by FDR to read:

We Solemnly Publish and Declare, That
These Colonies Are And of Right
Ought to Be Free and Independent
States… And For The Support of This
Declaration, With A Firm Reliance
On The Protection of Divine
Providence, We Mutually Pledge
Our Lives, Our Fortunes And Our
Sacred Honour.

Roosevelt was apparently pleased with the final wording.

Coincidentally, FDR's editing of this second paragraph in effect re-created the third paragraph of the Mecklenburg Declaration of May 20, 1775 (a close match). Thus, as a consolation to the Scotch-Irish of Mecklenburg County, "their words," although only symbolic, were now inscribed in marble—a memorial to those who were true to the sacred pledge.

Their Scottish ancestors at the first Covenant of Scotland in 1557 had set the standard when they separated from the Church of Rome, as they pledged "our health, power, substance, and our very lives to maintain, set forward and establish the Most Blessed Word of God and his Congregation."[4] George Bancroft described the Scotch-Irish as those "who brought to the New World the creed, the spirit of resistance, and the courage of the covenanters."[5]

Banastre Tarleton would give substance to symbol in calling Mecklenburg County more hostile to England than any other county in America.[6]

Postscript 1

The French Connection

The Brevard family was forced to depart their native France due to the loss of their personal rights in 1685. (In Ireland and America, they would intermarry with and become a part of the Scotch-Irish community, but their French identity remained intact.)

Almost a century later, the Mecklenburg Resolves of May 31, 1775 were published under the signature of Ephraim Brevard.

In *The Scotch Irish in America,* Henry Jones Ford writes, "Even were the Mecklenburg Declaration authentic it would possess merely antiquarian interest rather than historical importance for no recognition of such action or mark of its influence appears in the records of the times. There is however recorded action taken by a Mecklenburg County Convention on May 31, 1775, which is of such signal importance as marking the beginning of American independence...

"These resolutions practically constitute a state of political independence. Crown authority is annulled, provincial authority under the direction of Congress is substituted, and it is declared that no other authority is in existence. Such language asserts independence, and the resolutions then go on to make provision for giving practical effect to the decision by arranging for the collection of taxes, the administration of justice and the public defense. Resolutions providing for organized opposition to British policy were abundant at this period, but the Mecklenburg County

Convention was the first to announce independence. The leaders in the meeting were Thomas Polk, an ancestor of President Polk, Abraham Alexander and Ephraim Brevard, and the movement gained its strength from the Scotch-Irish settlers...

"The Mecklenburg Resolves were not only the first to make a virtual declaration of independence but they also indicated the course that had to be followed to gain independence, namely, the setting up of a system of government independent of crown authority. The institutions of colonial government were rooted in Crown authority, and they served as entrenchments for the opposition to independence. As a matter of fact it became necessary to revolutionize colonial government before the Declaration of Independence could be carried through Congress.

The Mecklenburg Resolves were the first step in this direction, and proclaimed a policy that nearly a year later was adopted by Congress. On May 10, 1776, Congress voted: "That it be recommended to the respective assemblies and conventions of the United Colonies, where no government sufficient to the exigencies of their affairs has been hitherto established, to adopt such government as shall in the opinion of the representatives of the people, best conduce to the happiness and safety of their constituents in particular and America in general.

"This action was completed on May 15 by the adoption of a preamble which pursues the same line of argument adopted in the Mecklenburg Resolves, namely, that since the American colonists had been excluded from the protection of the Crown, 'it is necessary that the exercise of every kind of authority under the said Crown should be totally suppressed.' The language differs; the argument is the same."[1]

The stage was now set for Thomas Jefferson's rough draft of the Declaration of Independence which was modified by Congress before its approval on July 4, 1776.

At the end of the Revolutionary War, Jefferson's interest turned to international issues in service to our country. Thomas Jefferson was appointed Minister to France and served there from August 1784 to September 1789. While in France, Jefferson expressed a growing optimism, as the expected revolution in France grew closer, that the revolution would not cost the French "a drop of blood." The French Revolution would in fact become a bloody reign of terror in 1789. "Later in his life, probably when he was reviewing his correspondence in preparation to write his autobiography in 1821, Jefferson was somewhat embarrassed at his unrelieved optimism in the late 1780s… On at least one occasion toward the end of his life he doctored his correspondence, inserting a more cautionary statement designed to convince posterity that his affection for France had not blinded him to the possibility of unparalleled violence."[2]

During the spring of 1789 he worked closely with the Marquis de Lafayette, who was drafting a French Bill of Rights. Jefferson drafted the Charter of Rights, which he presented to Lafayette in June 1789; "it served as the basis for the Declaration of Rights that Lafayette presented to the National Assembly the following month."[3]

As the French do love all things French, perhaps this was the way it was meant to be:

The Huguenots depart France after the loss of their personal rights.

One century later the French Huguenot descendant Ephraim Brevard leads America to its first step of independence.

Once independence is established in America, through Jefferson and Lafayette, the fire of freedom is returned to France, where the personal rights of the French people are firmly restored (through a process that endured the twists and turns of the French Revolution and the rule of Napoleon).

Le Circle C'est Complete!

Postscript 2

A Return to Scotland

The Scotch-Irish brought their independence-minded spirit to the American frontier in the years leading up to the revolution. This spirit was born in Scotland, refined in Ireland, and it found expression in the Scotch-Irish settlements. The Scotch-Irish influence would occur mostly on the fringes of civilized America.

The Scottish Enlightenment, however, exerted its influence directly through the prime institutions of higher learning in America. Through this conduit the enlightenment of Francis Hutcheson, as taught at the University of Glasgow, Scotland, would become familiar to pre-Revolutionary America. In contrast to the more materialistic "life, liberty and property" of John Locke, Francis Hutcheson's "life, liberty and happiness" was predicated on the belief that mankind possessed a benevolent moral sense. According to scholar Arthur Herman, Francis Hutcheson created a new political and social vision of a free society that went far beyond John Locke and the English thinkers. Hutcheson believed in "the rights of resisting in the people, when their fundamental privileges [were] invaded." Hutcheson would popularize this concept with the words, "unalienable rights."[1]

The Scotland natives Dr. William Small (William and Mary College) and Dr. John Witherspoon (Princeton College) brought the Scottish Enlightenment directly to the intellectually elite of America. Hutcheson's "unalienable rights" would be used by Thomas

Jefferson to justify American independence in 1776 (also much later by Elizabeth Cady Stanton to justify women's suffrage and Dr. Martin Luther King, Jr., to justify civil rights). Witherspoon's influence on James Madison and his classmates would impact both the American Revolution and the U.S. Constitution. Thus the Scottish influence left its clear and indelible mark on American freedom and independence. In Scotland however, fate would take a different turn.

In 1707 Britain and Scotland were unified. According to Peter and Fiona Somerset Fry, "The English achieved by a mixture of bribes, threats, tricks and hard bargaining what they had failed to do by force of arms for centuries."[2] The union brought economic prosperity and stability to Scotland, but the struggle for political independence on the part of the Scottish people continued with little progress for two more centuries.

Then the Scottish National Party was formed in 1928 and finally began to dominate the political scene in the 1960s when Mrs. Winifred Ewing won the seat at Hamilton. This was the first victory in the latest chapter of successes in the movement towards political independence. Although home rule has not occurred yet, the Scots' "long history and their remarkable contribution towards the advancement of mankind fully equip them to meet this great opportunity."[3]

Postscript 3
Letters & Notes

The following portion of the letter from Ephraim Brevard to
W. Alexander concerns Liberty Academy, a Presbyterian school of
which Brevard was a trustee and teacher. This letter contains the
only known remaining example of Brevard's handwritten
signature as it would have appeared on the Mecklenburg
Resolves of May 31, 1775.[1]

Ephraim Brevard was elected to the Continental Congress on July 12, 1781.[2]

Monday in November next; they having been so elected by joint ballot of both Houses of Assembly.

(Signed)   ARCHIBALD CARY *Sp: Senate*
            BENJAMIN HARRISON *Sp: H. D.*

A Copy,
    JOHN BECKLEY *C. H. D.*

THE STATE of North Carolina to William Sharpe Samuel Johnston Ephraim Brevard and Benjamin Hawkins esquires

Whereas it appears on Record that you the said William Sharpe, Samuel Johnston, Ephraim Brevard and Bonjamin Hawkins at a Session of the General Assembly held at Wake Court House in the said State in the Months of June and July in this present Year were each of you duly elected Delegates for one Year to represent the said State in the Congress of the United States of America: that is to say you the said William Sharpe, Samuel Johnston and Ephraim Brevard on the twelfth day of July and you the said Benjamin Hawkins on the Fourteenth day of the same month.

THESE are therefore to make known, that you the said William Sharpe, Samuel Johnston, Ephraim Brevard and Benjamin Hawkins or any two or more of you are fully and duly authorised as Delegates to represent the said State for one year from the date of your Election when and wheresoever the said United States shall assemble or be assembled in Congress, and to advise, confer, debate, resolve and determine for and in behalf of the said State upon all matters and things which shall come before the said United States in Congress assembled agreably to the Articles of Confederation and Perpetual Union made and ratified between the said United States and not inconsistent with the Constitution and Laws of the Said State of North Carolina.

WITNESS Thomas Burke esquire, Governor, Captain General and Commander in Chief of the Said State under his Hand and the Great Seal of the Said State at Williamsborough in the County of Granville the thirteenth day of August Anno Dom 1781, and in the Sixth Year of our Independence.

THO^s BURKE
[With the Great Seal appendant]

By His Excellency's Command
    JN? HUSKE, *Secretary.*

No. 62. To Mr George Ewing — Commy. of Hides.

Head Qrs. Valley Forge January 27th 1778.

Sir

Col. Broadhead having procured three hundred pair of Shoes, you will deliver him as many Hides as you may judge necessary to pay for them.

By His Excellency's command

Rob. H. Harrison, Secy.

Head Quarters V. Forge Wednesday Jany. 14th 78

Parole Perseverance — Countersigns { Peace Plenty —

The Majors of Brigade will deliver a list of the Field Officers in the several Brigades to which they belong tomorow at orderly time —

The Court Martial which was to sit this day, to sit tomorrow ten o'clock at the Bake House near

Examples of Valley Forge correspondence of George Ewing and William Davidson.[3]

Lt. Col. Davidson presides over a general court martial at Valley Forge. Correspondence dated November 28, 1777.

now to be issued up to the on,

Sunday inclusively. —

At a general Court-Martial held 28.th of November last in the North-Carolina Brigade of which Lt Col. Davidson was President, Lieut Richard Whed by, charged with acting in an ungentlemanlike manner & encouraging Theft in the Army was tried and found guilty and Sentenced therefor to be discharg'd from the Service — The Commander in Chief approves the Sentence and orders it to be executed forthwith.

The Quarter-Master General is immediatel

- proper Place between or near th

William Davidson served with George Washington's Army at the battle of Germantown on October 4, 1777. This unsuccessful battle was Washington's final attempt to prevent the British occupation of Philadelphia. The British occupied Philadelphia until June 18, 1778 at which time they retreated to New York.

Washington placed Benedict Arnold in command of Philadelphia on June 19, 1778. In December George Washington established his winter headquarters at Middle Brook, New Jersey, and on December 19, 1778 Davidson received orders to report to Benedict Arnold at Philadelphia.[4] (Davidson would serve for several months in Philadelphia before being transferred back to New Jersey.)

George Washington's correspondence with Benedict Arnold concerning Davidson's arrival in Philadelphia indicated other more serious matters of concern for Washington regarding Benedict Arnold.[5]

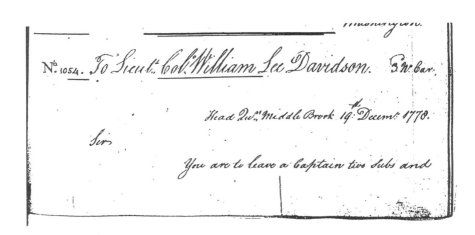

Official order of George Washington in transcriber's handwriting.

fifty men of the Detachment of Col: Hogan's Regiment at Trenton and proceed with the remainder to Philadelphia, upon your arrival at which place you are to make report to General Arnold or commanding Officer and take your directions from him. You are to leave word at Trenton for Col: Hogan to follow with the remainder of the Regiment (except the Captain and fifty who are to guard the Stores at Trenton) to Philadelphia. He is to take with him as many of his sick and convalescents as possible; those that cannot proceed beyond Trenton, must be left either there or at Princeton, with directions to join the Regiment as they recover. Col: Hogan is also, upon his arrival at Philadelphia, to take his orders from General Arnold or commanding Officer. Be pleased to leave a copy of this letter for him at Trenton.

> I am Sir
>> Your Most Obedt. Servt.
>>> G. Washington.

Head Quarters, Middle Brook, December 19, 1778.

Sir: You are to leave a Captain, two Subs and fifty Men of the detachment of Colo. Hogan's Regt. at Trenton and proceed with the remainder to Philadelphia, upon our arrival at which place you are to make report to General Arnold or commanding Officer and take your directions from him. You are to leave word at Trenton for Colo. Hogan to follow with the remainder of the Regt. (except the Captain and fifty who are to guard the Stores at Trenton) to Philada. He is to take with him as many of his sick and Convalescents as possible; those that cannot proceed beyond Trenton must be left either there or at Princetown, with directions to join the Regt. as they recover. Colo. Hogan is also upon his arrival at Philada. to take his orders from Genl. Arnold or commanding Officer. Be pleased to leave a Copy of this letter for him at Trenton.

To: Mr. General Arnold.   Phil^a

Head Qu^{rs} Middle Brook 13th Decem^r 1778.

Dear Sir,

Upon my arrival here I found your favour of the 5th. Your own letter communicated the first hint that I ever received of any representations or reports made by the Board of War to Congress respecting you or your command in Philadelphia. The Board some little time ago applied to me, for a Regiment or two to be stationed at Philadelphia and Trenton, to do the Town duties and guard the Stores, alledging, that the Militia complained of the hardship of being, turned out for these purposes. I have accordingly ordered down Col. Hogan's Regiment of North Carolina, which is as much as I can with propriety spare. I have never heard, nor is it my wish to be acquainted with the causes of the coolness between some Gentlemen composing the Board of War and yourself. I most sincerely hope that they may never rise to such a height as to oblige either party to make a public matter of it, as I am under more apprehensions on account of our own dissentions than of the effects of the Enemy.

        I am with great Regard

            Dear Sir Yours &c^a.

              GWashington.

Official order of George Washington in transcriber's handwriting.

Head Quarters, Middle Brook, December 13, 1778.

Dear Sir: Upon my arrival here I found your favor of the 5th. Your own letter communicated the first hint that I ever recd. of any representations on reports made by the Board of War to Congress respecting you or your command in Philada. The Board some little time ago applied to me for a Regiment or two to be stationed at Philada. and Trenton to do the Town Duties and guard the Stores, alledging that the militia complained of the hardship of being turned out for these purposes. I have accordingly ordered down Colo. Hogan's Regt. of North Carolina which is as much as I can with propriety spare. I have never heard, nor is it my wish to be acquainted with the causes of the coolness between some Gentlemen composing the Board of War and yourself. I most sincerely hope that they may never rise to such a height as to oblige either party to make a public matter of it, as I am under more apprehensions on account of our own dissentions than of the efforts of the Enemy.

The reality of George Washington's apprehensions would occur in September 1780 when Benedict Arnold would become the most notorious traitor in American history. Due to what Washington would call an act of "providence," the capture of John Andre (a British spy) would prevent Arnold from turning over West Point, its garrison of 4,000 men, and possibly Washington himself to Commander Henry Clinton and his British troops. Washington's close call and dark moment in September would be lightened by the information in W. L. Davidson's letter describing the Battle of King's Mountain, which he received in October 1780. Washington responded in his general orders of October 27th that the victory at King's Mountain "will in all probability have a very happy influence upon the successive operations in that quarter."

Some historians consider the Battle of King's Mountain to be the turning point of the Revolutionary War. William Davidson's letter to General Sumner was the first official communication describing that battle.

Camp Rocky River, October 10, 1780

Sir—I have the Pleasure of handing you very agreeable Intelligence from the West. Ferguson, the Great Partizan, has miscarried. This we are assured of by Mr. Tate, Brigade Major in General Sumpter's late Brigade. The particulars from that Gentleman's Mouth stand thus; that Colonels Campbell, Cleveland, Shelby, Sevier, Williams, Brandon, Lacey, etc., formed a Conjunct Body near Gilbert Town consisting of 3,000—From this Body were selected 1600 good Horse, who immediately went in search of Colonel Ferguson, who was making his way to Charlotte—Our people overtook him well posted on King's Mountain, and on the evening of the 7th Instant at 4 o'clock, began the attack which lasted forty seven minutes. Colonel Ferguson fell in the action, besides 150 of his men—810 were made prisoners, including the British—150 of the prisoners are wounded—1500 Stands of arms fell into our Hands. The enemy surrendered. We lost about 20 men among whom is Major Chronicle of Lincoln County, Colonel Williams is morally wounded, the number of our wounded cannot be ascertained. This blow will certainly affect the British very considerably. The designs of our conquering Friends near King's Mountain not certainly known, it is most probable that they will secure their prisoners in or over the Mountains and proceed toward Charlotte—The Brigade Major who gives us this was in action. The above is true. The Blow is great and I give you Joy upon the Occasion.

I am, Etc.,
Wm. Davidson[6]

The following letter from William Sharpe (a Continental Congressman from North Carolina) to William Lee Davidson, concerned the North Carolina prisoners of war (including Ephraim Brevard), who had been captured at the fall of Charleston, S.C., in May of 1780.

This remaining remnant of the complete letter was found among Lord Cornwallis's papers, as it had been removed from Davidson's possession by British soldiers after his death.

William Sharpe to William Lee Davidson[7]

William Sharpe to William Lee Davidson

Novr. 9th [1780][1]

P.S. I forgot to inform you[2] that Genl. Lincoln with upwards of an hundred Officers are lately exchanged. And that the commanders in Chief are about to negociate a general exchange, including the convention troops and our Militia. Genl. Washington is instructed to endeavour to obtain a condition, that, the convention and other british prisoners shall not take the field nor bear Arms before the first of May.[3]

However humanity dictated an immediate exchange, yet our present critical situation to the southward made it a great question in policy; was the exchange to take place immediately and the enemy at Liberty to Arm and send forth their liberated troops it might be a fatal stroke to the State of No. Carolina; because in that State we have not Arms, Stores &c at present to put into the hands of Our liberated troops & Militia in order to make a vigorous defence, therefore the Delegates of No. Carolina have been the means of keeping back the exchange a few weeks past and of quallifying the measure as above mentioned,[4] with a view to get Genl. Greene in command, get forward some Arms, Stores &c—and get time to draw out and organize a little Army, that may promise us some defence, all which I hope will sufficiently justify our conduct to our brave and virtuous Officers and Soldiers who are in a distressing captivity. We have been so opposed in this business of delaying the exchange, by some of our neighbouring Delegates, who has a passionate fondness for their friends, that we have been threatned with the displeasure of those in captivity. These things have but little effect on the minds of men determined to do what appears to be *right*. We are so well assured of the patriotism of Our Officers & Soldiers, that they would at the risk of their lives endure six months or perhaps twenty months longer confinement rather than obtain liberty at the risque of a whole State.   Wm. Sharpe

RC (PRO: Cornwallis Papers, P.R.O. 30/11/106). Addressed: "Genl. Davidson."
    [1] Only this partially dated postscript to Sharpe's intercepted letter has been found.

In January 1781 the traitor Benedict Arnold led British forces in a successful invasion of Virginia. Virginia's capital, Richmond, was plundered and burned by Arnold, after which his forces were marched to Portsmith, Virginia for winter quarters. On February 17, 1781, Governor Thomas Jefferson outlined the situation in a letter to Horatio Gates.

To Horatio Gates
Dear General   Richmond Feb. 17, 1781.
The situation of affairs here and in Caroline is such as must shortly turn up important events one way or the other. By letter from Genl. Greene dated Guilford C. house Feb. 10.Ld. Cornwallis rendered furious by the affair at the Cowpens and surprise of George town had burnt his own waggons to enable himself to move with facility, had pressed on to the vicinities of the Moravian towns and was still advancing. The prisoners taken at the Cowpens were saved by a hair's breadth accident, and Greene was retreating. His force 2000 regulars and no militia, Cornwallis's 3000. Genl. Davidson was killed in a skirmish. Arnold lies still at Portsmouth with 1500 men. A French 64. gun ship and 2 frigates of 36 each arrived in our bay three days ago. They would suffice to destroy the British shipping here (a 40., four frigates and a 20) could they get at them. But these are withdrawn up Elizabeth river which the 64. cannot enter. We have ordered about 700 riflemen from Washington Montgomery and Bedford and 500 common militia from Pittsylva. and Henry to reinforce Genl. Greene, and 500 new levies will march from Chestfd. C. H. in a few days. I have no doubt however that the Southwestern counties will have turned out in greater numbers before our orders reach them. I have been knocking at the door of Congress for aids of all kinds, but especially of arms ever since the middle of summer. The Speaker Harrison is gone to be heard on that subject. Justice indeed requires that we should be aided powerfully. Yet if they would repay us the arms we have lent them we should give the enemy trouble tho' abandoned to ourselves— ...
Thomas Jefferson[8]

Thomas Jefferson's unsuccessful tenure as a war governor for the state of Virginia would not detract from his great literary accomplishment. Jefferson's brilliant take on the enlightenment ideals of freedom and revolution are enshrined for posterity in the Declaration of Independence. Jefferson's lasting legacy is described by Joseph J. Ellis: "There never has been an American democracy without its powerful strand of individualism, and nothing suggests there ever will be. For better or worse, American political discourse is phrased in Jeffersonian terms as a conversation about sovereign individuals who only grudgingly and in special circumstance are prepared to compromise that sovereignty for larger social purposes."[9]

Thomas Jefferson's ideals for freedom continue to call out to a world in need. However, in 1776, they could not guarantee that America would in fact win its own freedom. The patriots that won this freedom faced reality and did what had to be done. Henry Knox was a Scotch-Irishman (his parents had migrated from Ireland), who tipped the scales mightily for American freedom. In 1775, Knox would conceive and carry out the incredible plan to transport the captured cannons at Fort Ticonderoga 300 miles in mid-winter to Boston, where they were used in a successful stand-off against the British. In 1776 he would direct the crossing of the Delaware under Washington's command that lead to the victories at Trenton and Princeton. Rev. Alexander MacWhorter would serve as a chaplain to Knox's artillery unit in the war year of 1778. There, he received a direct order from George Washington in October of 1778 to perform the duty of gaining intelligence from two British spies who were soon to be executed. Washington placed enough importance on this intelligence to request that it be transmitted directly back to him as soon as it was obtained. Along with the other victorious patriots, Knox and his men would do their duty through the remaining years of the war and in doing so they made American freedom a reality.

Thomas Jefferson's ideals for government were a noble effort but they were not workable in the real world. In a letter to Phillip Mazzei dated April 24, 1796, Jefferson would write, "Instead of that noble love of liberty, and that republican government [Articles of

Confederation], which carried us triumphantly through the dangers of the war [Revolutionary], an Anglo-Monarchio-Aristocratic party has arisen. Their avowed object is to impose on us the substance, as they have already given us the form of the British government." In his first inaugural address on March 4, 1804, Jefferson wrote for the "...support of the state governments in all their rights, as the most competent administrations for our domestic concerns and the surest bulwarks against anti-Republican tendencies." In a letter to states rights extremists John Taylor dated May 28, 1816, Jefferson clearly defines what he means by republicanism: "Were I to assign to this term a precise and definite idea, I would say purely and simply, it means a government by its citizens, acting directly and personally, according to rules established by the majority; and that every other government is more or less republican, in proportion as it has in its composition more or less of this ingredient of the direct action of the citizens."

In the 1790s, Thomas Jefferson called the Federalists "Monarchists" and "Tories" because in creating the U.S. Constitution they had moved far beyond the government of the Articles of Confederation and its one branch legislature of elected representatives. This confederation was the most republican form of representative government possible. Jefferson's idealistic hope for the election of 1800 was a return to these republican principles of the government of 1776. But in reality, all had observed the extreme inefficiencies of the pure republicanism of the Articles of Confederation during the Revolutionary War and afterword.

The U.S. Constitution created by the Federalists was less republican than the Articles of Confederation, but it would be very effective in the real world of efficient government. At least one historian suggests that Jefferson's ideology for government might have had a negative effect on the proceeding's successful efforts, had he directly influenced the Constitutional Settlement of 1787–1788.

Jefferson's post revolutionary ideas for constructing the federal government were based on states' rights and a decentralized agrarian economy. He believed that a strict agricultural economy would prevent the problems caused by the big business interests of the Industrial Revolution in Europe, consequently he was opposed to an economy based on manufacturing in the continental United States.[10] These ideas were out of step with his fellow Founding Fathers and found no lasting acceptance.

"—the principal formulator of the Constitution's doctrine was James Madison, friend and disciple of Jefferson;

—Madison under Witherspoon, like Jefferson under Small, had shaped his politics to Scottish Enlightenment ways;"[11]

Thomas Jefferson called his victory in the presidential election of 1800 "the Revolution of 1800" because his party had defeated the Federalists, but this would be more a victory of style than substance. The Republicans under Jefferson would eliminate the last vestiges of monarchial ceremony from American government, however the constitution that the Federalists had created remained unchanged and would prove to function equally well under a Republican administration. It was Jefferson's initial intention to reduce the power of the federal government, but his effective use of this very power made his first term in office one of the great presidencies of American history.

In reality, the real second revolution was produced by the hard work of James Madison (in collaboration with George Washington) during the months leading up to the Constitutional Convention and during the convention itself.[12]

Madison became the leader in the Continental Congress and at the Constitutional Convention, who successfully led the opposition to the ideas of the extreme monarchical Federalists (they supported a British-style of government) on the one hand and the Anti-Federalists (they were opposed to the U.S. Constitution) at the other extreme, producing a constitution of moderate Federalist doctrine, which the majority of Americans supported.[13] The U.S. Constitution would be tested by the Alien & Sedition Acts, but it had functioned successfully for more than a decade before Jefferson took office in 1800. By this time, the real post-revolution "revolution" was over.

James Madison's two-term presidency would follow Jefferson's two terms and after their deaths, Henry Clay of Kentucky would compare them. Author Ralph Ketcham's commentary outlines Clay's comparison: "Jefferson, Clay thought, 'had most genius—Madison most judgment and common sense.' Jefferson's enthusiasms often led him into 'rash and imprudent and impracticable measures [while] Madison [was] cool, dispassionate, practical, safe.' He [Clay] pronounced Madison, 'after Washington, our greatest statesman and first political writer,' but he agreed finally that Madison and Jefferson 'both were great and good, and though different—yet equal.' Madison did lack the dramatic and even reckless qualities some times useful in public life, but within his own chosen style of statesmanship, valuing prudence, wisdom and judgment, he was without peer."[14]

Though different, Jefferson and Madison would prove to be a complimentary pair. Thomas Jefferson's idealistic written expression of freedom's possibilities would set the stage for James Madison's realistic methodology for successful and fair government.

As author of the Declaration of Independence, Thomas Jefferson's enshrinement (the Jefferson Memorial) in Washington, D.C., is a valued statement of his importance to America's heritage. It would seem that America is still waiting for James Madison's enshrinement as the "Father of the U.S. Constitution" to become a reality in the City of Monuments on the Potomac.

Through the Federalist Papers, James Madison, Alexander Hamilton, and John Jay would provide the understanding necessary to persuade America to ratify the U.S. Constitution, which these leaders had worked long and hard for. Thomas Jefferson, who had no role in formulating the Constitution, as he was Minister to France from 1785 to 1789, suggested to Madison by letter that the Constitution should have a Bill of Rights.

Author Garry Wills elaborates: "Having a bill of rights was, of course, a whig tradition, harking back to Magna Carta through the 1689 Bill of Rights. In that sense it was "conservative" and represented concessions wrung from an executive by a legislature. Most states put bills of rights in their constitutions as a matter of course.

Those who opposed a bill of rights at the Constitutional Convention—including, at first, Madison himself, who drafted and steered through the final bill—were assuming that the individual was already protected by the states' bills; that the central government could not reach the individual except through the states, which had put impenetrable barriers around individual rights. Would it not be an act of usurpation to imply that the federal power could go around those barriers? The growth of the Bill of Rights was nudged along by antithetical developments. On the one hand, the states used the Bill of Rights as a further statement of limit on the central power; while, on the other, the effort to solicit popular support against state establishments made the framers themselves see their instrument as reaching individuals in new ways, who must therefore be assured of the customary exemptions."[15]

Upon first reading the new constitution in 1787, Jefferson would write: "How do you like our new constitution? I confess there are things in it which stagger all my dispositions to subscribe to what such an assembly has proposed. The house of federal representatives will not be adequate to the management of affairs either foreign or federal. Their President seems a bad edition of a Polish king. [Meaning he could serve for life as there were no term limits.]

"Indeed I think all the good of this new constitution might have been couched in three or four new articles to be added to the good, old, and venerable fabrick [Articles of Confederation], which should have been preserved even as a religious relique."[16]

Jefferson understood the inefficiences of the Articles of Confederation, which framed a one branch legislative government, but would be on the wrong side of history when it came to providing the ideas that produced effective government.

James Madison would use an efficiency argument for creating the three branches of the federal government as the powers of the Continental Congress (under the Articles of Confederation) were frequently mismanaged because these powers were not distributed effectively. In the U.S. Constitution, the treaty-making powers were given to the executive branch as the president would have the most energy and dispatch to deal effectively with foreign countries. Treaties would be approved by the senate because it would have "the institutional memory and continued membership needed to handle relations with other nations, where long-term agreements are desired… The house, by contrast, was designed with lower age requirements and shorter terms to reflect domestic concerns, especially over the economy… A separate judiciary was called for as well, again in the name of efficiency. For congress to set up ad hoc arbitration boards, courts that came and went, was a clumsy process."[17] Madison realized that an independent, tiered court system comprised of trained jurists would be most efficient.

Thomas Jefferson was opposed to Alexander Hamilton's National Bank plan and John Jay's treaty with Great Britain—both episodes occurred during the turbulent 1790s.

"I consider the foundation of the Constitution as laid on this ground: That 'all powers not delegated to the United States, by the Constitution, nor prohibited by it to the States, are reserved to the States or to the people.' [12th Amendment.] To take a single step beyond the boundaries thus specially drawn around the powers of Congress, is to take possession of a boundless field of power, no longer susceptible of any definition.

"The incorporation of a bank, and the powers assumed by this bill, have not, in my opinion, been delegated to the United States, by the Constitution."[18]

"The charter for the Bank of the United States was scheduled to lapse in March of 1811. This was, of course, the institution that Jefferson and Madison had denounced as unconstitutional, during Washington's presidency, when Hamilton won the battle to found it.[19]

"By 1811, Madison had changed his mind on the bank, though he did not want to make an open break with Jefferson on the issue. He privately assured people that his arguments against the bank, though sound at the time, had been rendered inapplicable by long usage (unconstitutional things become constitutional if they are accepted as such?). Gallatin was now an energetic promoter of the bank. Jefferson's embargo had slashed the Treasury's principal source of income, customs duties, and he needed loans that no other source would give on the terms available from the bank. The Republican party, born out of a hatred for the financial credit system, now depended on it for its survival."[20]

Author Joseph J. Ellis describes Thomas Jefferson's opposition to the Jay Treaty, which led to extreme measures. "He even went so far as to tell Monroe that he had no problem in shifting the main responsibility for approving all the treaties to the House and "in annihilating the whole treaty making power [of the executive branch], except as to making peace.

"These were radical prescriptions that, if taken seriously, would have thrown American foreign policy into the cauldron of domestic politics on every controversial occasion. They contrast with Madison's more narrow and careful constitutional argument, which became the official Republican position, that the House could block passage of the Jay Treaty because certain provisions required funding for their implementation and the House was the proper branch to decide all money bills. Madison's more careful argument made no frontal assault on executive power but still achieved the desired goal of allowing the Republican majority in the House to hold the Jay Treaty hostage. Jefferson's more extreme position reflected his more cavalier attitude toward constitutional questions in general. Unlike Madison, who had a deep appreciation for the Constitution as an artful arrangement of juxtaposed principles and powers with abiding influence over future generations, Jefferson tended to view it as a merely convenient agreement about political institutions that ought not to bind future generations or prevent the seminal source of all political power—popular opinion—from dictating government policy. His casual remarks in the spring of 1796 during the height of the debate over the Jay Treaty were uncharacteristic only in the sense that Jefferson customarily left constitutional questions in Madison's capable hands. But precisely because he did not feel the obligation to filter his opinions through Madison, his statements more accurately reflected his greater willingness to bend constitutional arguments to serve what he saw as a higher purpose, which in this case was defeat of the counterrevolutionary alliance with England. Upsetting delicate constitutional balances or setting dangerous precedents did not trouble him in such moments."[21]

Jefferson was opposed to an independent judiciary and the policies of Supreme Court Chief Justice John Marshall.

Author James F. Simon writes: "Jefferson's letter only reiterated his long-held view that the judiciary, like the other branches of the federal government, should be accountable to the people. Jefferson believed that Marshall's grand pronouncements on the Court's role as the final arbiter of the Constitution thoroughly distorted the framers' intentions. Under Jefferson's reading of the Constitution, the Court could no more tell the president or Congress what was constitutional than the president or Congress could dictate the Constitution's meaning to the Court. Each branch was responsible independently, for upholding the Constitution. If any erred egregiously, the people, through their federal and state representatives, could correct the error by constitutional amendment."[22]

"The former president continued to search for ways to curb the Marshall Court. The best remedy, Jefferson wrote Governor James Pleasants of Virginia, was to amend the Constitution so that the justices would serve six-year terms, renewable by the president and both houses of Congress. But nothing came of Jefferson's suggestion."[23]

The Sedition Act of 1798 was passed as a temporary measure set to expire on March 3, 1801. It was passed by the Federalists when war with France seemed imminent. This act made it a crime to speak or publish any false, scandalous, or malicious writing against the government. Though it was clearly unconstitutional, Thomas Jefferson would later as president use equally extreme measures. He imprisoned those who resisted his embargo act, by presidential discretion. Jefferson wrote the Kentucky Resolutions in secret two years before becoming president—his authorship was not made public until after his death.

Garry Wills writes that Jefferson's Kentucky Resolutions "have done far more damage, down through the years, than did the laws he wrote against [Alien & Sedition Acts]. They [Kentucky Resolutions] became a sacred text to the South as it took the road to the Civil War."[24]

Kenneth Stamp, in his book *The Causes of the Civil War*, writes: "The first of a series of resolutions adopted by the Kentucky legislature in 1798, and drafted by Thomas Jefferson, was one of the earliest systematic statements of the state-rights doctrine. From it one could easily infer the right of a state to secede from the Union.[25]

"*...Resolved,* that the several States composing the United States of America, are not united on the principle of unlimited submission to their general government; but that by compact under the style and title of a Constitution for the United States and of amendments thereto, they constituted a general government for special purposes, delegated to that government certain definite powers, reserving each State to itself, the residuary mass of right to their own self-government; and that whensoever the general government assumes undelegated powers, its acts are unauthoritative, void, and of no force: That to this compact each State acceded as a State, and is an integral party, its co-States forming, as to itself, the other party: That the government created by this compact was not made the exclusive or final judge of the extent of the powers delegated to itself; since that would have made its discretion, and not the Constitution, the measure of its powers; but that as in all other cases of compact among parties having no common Judge, *each party has an equal right to judge for itself, as well of infractions as of the mode and measure of redress.*"[26]

Some further comments on the Kentucky Resolutions by authors James F. Simon and Joseph J. Ellis. Simon begins: "Had Jefferson's original demand for state nullification of an unconstitutional act of Congress been enacted into law by the Kentucky legislature, it would have offered the Republicans a dramatic document to rally political support. But it also would have carried considerable risk, thereby giving credence to the Federalists' charge that the Republicans were attempting to break up the union. Madison's more moderate approach proved to be an effective political strategy. Madison called for repeal of the hated legislation [Alien & Sedition Acts] and, simultaneously, pilloried the Federalists for their sustained threats to democracy."[27]

Ellis continues: "Fortunately for Jefferson, the leadership of the Kentucky legislature decided to delete the sections of his draft endorsing nullification, presumably because such open defiance of federal law seemed excessive and unnecessarily risky. Madison's more judicious arguments, published as the Virginia Resolutions, were circulating in the national press and achieving the same goal— condemning the Sedition Act—but without recourse to nullification. Whereas Jefferson's line of thought led logically to the compact theory of the Constitution eventually embraced by the Confederacy in 1861, Madison's arguments led toward the modern doctrine of judicial review and constitutional guarantees for free speech and freedom of the press.[28]

"Madison's prudent and silent intervention rescued Jefferson from the secessionist implications of his revolutionary principles and artfully concealed the huge discrepancy between their respective views of the Constitution. The imperatives of their collaboration, plus the need to present a united front against the Federalists, took precedence over their incompatible notions of where sovereignty resided in the American republic."[29]

One year before his death, Jefferson once again considered making a public issue of state sovereignty but wisely reconsidered after receiving prudent council from his life-long friend James Madison.

Jefferson and Madison would create the Republican party (later to become the Democratic Party) in the late 1790s. The idea of parties was never a part of the Constitution and at this time Jefferson seemed to favor a one-party system.

"The Jefferson-Madison collaboration was not just committed to capturing the federal government for the Republicans. As Jefferson put it so graphically, their larger goal was "to sink federalism into an abyss from which there shall be no resurrection of it."[30]

Jefferson's vision would look beyond reality to a set of admirable but unrealistic ideals that captured his loyalty for a lifetime. Thomas Jefferson's ideas for government would have no lasting importance for America (though critical of the Constitution, he conceded that it was "the wisest ever yet presented to men"). While the unalienable rights to life, liberty, and happiness carry

Americans ever forward, Jefferson's ideology for government is no longer with us. "The New Deal was in fact the death knell for Jefferson's idea of a minimalist government."[31]

Thomas Jefferson's carefully preserved personal correspondence gives us a more intimate view of him than his political statements can reveal. We see that he was not an atheist, as he would have wanted us to know.

Thomas Jefferson's universe included God The Creator, but he was an aloof God that did not hear or respond to the prayers of mankind. Though Jefferson loved God and his fellow man, his religion did not include a prayerful foundation of a living and guiding faith. Jefferson believed that mankind had the capability of self perfection without the helping hand of God, but acknowledged that religion brought peace and order to society.

The words "with a firm reliance on the protection of divine providence" were added to the Declaration of Independence by the members of the Continental Congress and were not a part of Jefferson's original draft.

Shortly after Benjamin Franklin's return to Philadelphia from France (where he had been replaced as French minister by Thomas Jefferson), he would be welcomed home by Provost John Ewing and a delegation from the University of Pennsylvania. They gave a special tribute to Franklin, the University's founder.[32]

The following year Franklin was elected to be a delegate from Pennsylvania for the Constitutional Convention during the summer of 1787. His role would be more to keep the delegates in agreement than to lead them in a particular direction. However, on June 28th he moved that the convention begin its sessions with prayer. This motion was tabled and did not receive a vote.

But to Washington, as president of the convention, he spoke: "I have lived, Sir, a long time, and the longer I live the more convincing proofs I see of this truth: that God governs in the affairs of men. And if a sparrow cannot fall to the ground without His notice, is it probable that an empire can rise without His aid? ...I...believe that without His concurring aid we shall succeed in this political building no better than the builders of Babel."[33]

James Madison would be the most influential member of the Constitutional Convention. Madison's biographer, Ralph Ketcham, would write that Madison, though reticent about discussing religion, kept a prayer book that he used for family devotions, never attacked religion, and saw religion as a useful support for republican government.[34]

Madison understood the benefits that religion brought to a free society but he placed definitive boundaries between church and state when he wrote the First Amendment to the U.S. Constitution, which reads in part: "Congress shall make no law respecting an establishment of religion, or prohibiting the free exercise thereof..." This is the full extent of the U.S. Constitution's rules regarding religion.

In the years before Thomas Jefferson's Louisiana Purchase, the Western Migration of new settlers stopped short of the Mississippi River.

A few notes on the Davidson Family migration to Tennessee follow.

...The original advertisement in the *State Gazette* of North Carolina, of November 28th, 1788, announcing the departure of Judge McNairy's company for the Cumberland settlements, indicates the perils of the way: "Notice is hereby given, that the new road from Campbell's station to Nashville, was opened on the 25th of September, and the guard attended at that time to escort such persons as were ready to proceed to Nashville; that about sixty families went on, amongst whom were the widow and family of the late General Davidson, and John McNairy, judge of the Superior Court; and that on the 1st day of October next, the guard will attend at the same place for the same purpose."

... Before the end of October of 1788, the long train of emigrants, among whom was Mr. Solicitor Jackson, reached Nashville, to the great joy of the settlers there.

... Great news reached Nashville by this train; news that all was right with the new national Constitution, a majority of the States having accepted it; news that the Legislatures of the States were about choosing presidential electors, who would undoubtedly elect General Washington the first President of the republic. Washington was inaugurated in the April following the arrival of Jackson at his new home.[35]

The complete letter of Finis Ewing to General Andrew Jackson, dated November 14, 1813.

Ewingsville P. Office C. County, KY

Dear General

Permit an old acquaintance and an American to congratulate you, and my country on the late signal victory attained by your troops on the 9th Inst. I would ascribe to God as the prime cause, and honor you, with your valiant heroes as the instruments. Every intelligent true hearted American will duly estimate, and forever gratefully remember the skill and valor displayed on that occasion. Divine providence has given you almost unexampled success for the time your army has been in motion. I hope by his blessing that you will soon teach the British Allies in the South as impressive or more impressive lesson than they have been recently taught in the North. It is surely the prayer, the ardent prayer of all good men, that heaven may prosper you in your future cause.

Perhaps you may not yet know, that I had a very young son not yet 18 in the action with you (He is in Capt. David Smith's Company). I have heard that he has been preserved and that he acted bravely. I hope for the honor of his ancestors he did. He is you will recollect, a grandson of Genl. Davidson's, one of our Revolutionary Heroes, he is also his namesake. He was going to School at Mount Pleasant Academy in your state, when it was rumored that Huntsville would be attacked, and such was his ardour that he suddenly started off (no doubt feeling Sir, the force of your address on that occasion) from school to aid the brave Tenesseeans in repelling the enemy and chasting him for his temerity. His mother nor I knew anything of his going till after he was gone several days.

As he did go I am glad you were his commander. I indulged the hope, from your former friendship to myself and your uniform particular friendship to his Mother's Family that if anything should happen to him and you knew who he was, he would not be neglected, although a boy without relations and almost without acquaintances in the Army. I was pleased to hear one of his fellow soldiers (Capt. Smith's son) say that he acted bravely in the action, and was attentive to his duty and the orders of his officer generally. I know subordination is the life of a soldier in the army. But as the Boy has had a pretty good tour, as the object of the campaign cannot be materially effected by it, I would be glad he could now get an honorable discharge & return to his classical studies while there is an opportunity of his finishing his Education. But if you deem this improper, I hope you will make his situation as eligible as is consistent and give a moment of time to council him & caution him against vice.

I am Dear General your respectful
obedient servant
Finis Ewing[36]

Robert V. Remini writes: "Throughout Jackson's retirement, lasting nine years, he kept in active communication with his friends in Washington and tried on all important issues to intrude his presence and make his opinions known to the party and the nation." The following letter from William L. D. Ewing, acting as Speaker of the House of Representatives for the state of Illinois, requested political advice from Andrew Jackson who had retired from the Presidency in 1836.

Mar 14, 1840
Dear Sir:
Will you permit an old and devoted friend to presume on his acquaintance with, and respect for you to trespass a moment on your time? In the state of Illinois, we are destined to have a warm polytical contest at this approaching Presidential, and other elections. A large portion of our population consists of Tennesseans

and other western people. That population venerates the name of "Gen. Jackson" and have more confidence in his opinion of men… than any other living person (public or private) in the nation.

Now Sir: Will you, for the benefit of a great cause indulge me (not for my information) but for the information of many of my fellow citizens and thousands of your old and devoted friends, with your opinions and views on a few questions of exciting moment. What are your opinions of the relative claims of M. Van Buren and Gen. Harrison upon the people of the United States for the Presidency?

Are you friendly to the passage of the… Treasury Bill?

Your brief reply to the foregoing queries would be eminently useful to the "Democratic Cause" in this Country and highly gratifying to me as well as to many of your long true friends, who are cognizant of my addressing you this letter.

I have the honor to be with great respect

Yr. obt. Servt.

W. L. D. Ewing[37]

W. L. D. Ewing's intervention would help to prevent Abraham Lincoln's participation in a duel during his early political career.

This story of this episode is told by Douglas L. Wilson in an excerpt from *Honor's Voice: The Transformation of Abraham Lincoln.* A letter from Abraham Lincoln to his friend Joshua F. Speed gives Lincoln's final word on the duel.

"If Lincoln had misgivings about accepting Shields's challenge, they were apparently not evident to observers. He promptly named Dr. Merryman as his 'friend,' or second, the person designated in a formal duel to act for the principal in the necessary negotiations, ostensibly charged with arranging the terms and conditions of the prospective duel, in practice the seconds principally aimed at resolving the difficulty peacefully and avoiding an actual fight. Merryman, who, like his counterpart, Whiteside, published his version of events in the Springfield newspaper, implied that he enlisted in the affair because of his knowledge of the protocols of dueling, the infamous code duello. 'I knew Mr. Lincoln, was wholly unpracticed both as to the diplomacy and weapons commonly employed in similar affairs; and I felt it my duty, as a friend, to be with him, and so far as in my power, to prevent any advantage being taken of him as to either his honor or his life.'

"At their initial meeting the two seconds pledged themselves to work for a peaceful resolution of difficulties and proceeded to occupy the same buggy for part of the trip back to Springfield. But circumstances conspired against them, and they bungled their peacemaking effort. Arriving in Springfield late Monday evening, Lincoln's associates discovered that the duel was already widely known, and they heard rumors of an imminent arrest. Without consulting Whiteside, they made plans to dictate the terms of the duel—weapons, time, and place—and flee the city the next day. Whiteside's plan was apparently to get Governor Thomas Ford and the powerful Democratic leader General W. L. D. Ewing to talk the ungovernable Shields out of the duel, but before he could put it into action, Whiteside learned from Merryman on Tuesday that Lincoln had written out the terms and departed for Jacksonville. The incredulous Whiteside could neither agree to terms nor negotiate further under these conditions, nor could he consult his principal, who was still on his way back to Springfield with a lame horse. As a protest, he withdrew his pledge to Merryman, but he agreed to advise Shields of what had happened and to meet Lincoln's party in Missouri on Thursday, the appointed day.

"John J. Hardin, a leading Whig, was one of those who hurried to the scene to help effect a reconciliation and, in partnership with Revel W. English, a Democrat, offered to submit the case to impartial judges. To this end they drafted a formal note on the scene to Merryman and Whiteside that concluded: 'Let the whole difficulty be submitted to four or more gentlemen, to be selected by ourselves, who shall consider the affair, and report thereupon for your consideration.' Though this plan was ultimately not followed, it produced some progress, and Shields's friends, without his knowledge, eventually declared his offending note withdrawn. At this, but prior agreement, Lincoln's friends conveyed their principals' admission that he did write the September 2 letter 'solely for political effect' and his denial that he intended to injure 'the personal or private character of standing of Mr. Shields as a gentleman or a man.' With this, support for Shields apparently collapsed. According to Whiteside, 'This was all done without the knowledge or consent of Mr. Shields, and he refused to accede to it, until Dr. Hope, General Ewing, and myself declared the apology sufficient, and that we could not sustain him in going further.' This ended the duel, for though Shields would apparently have preferred to fight, his friends had effectively declared it unnecessary. His honor, in other words, was no longer in need of vindication.[38]

Springfield, October 4, 1842.
Dear Speed:—
You have heard of my duel with Shields, and I have now to inform you that the dueling business still rages in this city. Day before yesterday Shields challenged Butler, who accepted, proposed fighting next morning at sunrise in Bob Allen's meadow, one hundred yards distance, with rifles. To this Whiteside, Shields' second, said 'no' because of the law. Thus ended duel No. 2. Yesterday Whiteside chose to consider himself insulted by Dr. Merryman, so sent him a kind of quasi-challenge inviting him to meet him at the Planter's House in St. Louis, on the next Friday, to settle their difficulty. Merryman made me his friend, and sent Whiteside a note, inquiring to know if he meant his note as a challenge, and if so, that he would, according to the law in such case made and provided, prescribe the terms of the meeting. Whiteside returned for answer that if Merryman would meet him at the Planter's House as desired, he would challenge him. Merryman replied in a note, that he denied Whiteside's right to dictate time and place, but that he (Merryman) would wave the question of time, and meet him in Louisiana, Mo. Upon my presenting his note to Whiteside, and stating verbally its contents, he declined receiving it, saying he had business in St. Louis, and it was as near as Louisiana. Merryman then directed me to notify Whiteside that he should publish the correspondence between them, with such comments as he saw fit. This I did. Thus it stood at bed-time last night. This morning Whiteside, by his friend Shields, is praying for a new trial, on the ground that he was

mistaken in Merryman's proposition to meet him at Louisiana, Mo., thinking it was the State of Louisiana. This Merryman hoots at, and is preparing his publication; while the town is in a ferment, and a street-fight somewhat anticipated.

> Yours forever,
> Lincoln.[39]

Abraham Lincoln's youth shows in this episode of his early political life. He was 33 years old at this time and had not yet experienced the refining fires that would transform him into a man of God, and lead to his future greatness.

Rev. Finis Ewing's former associate, Rev. James Smith, would serve as minister to the Lincoln family in Springfield, Illinois from 1849 to 1856. "On 11 June 1861, Dr. Smith accepted Lincoln's invitation to visit the White House, on occasion of his eldest son's appointment as U.S. consul to Dundee, Scotland."[40] Later, Rev. Smith would be appointed to replace his son as consul, a post that Smith kept until his death on the eve of July 4, 1871, in his homeland of Scotland.

Mount Rushmore

Washington—The Father

our honorable father

Under Washington's command

The Patriots

won independence

and as Federalists

established the U.S. Constitution

General Henry Lee would call Washington

"First in war, first in peace,

first in the hearts of his countrymen."

Jefferson—The Idealist

his gift of five words

"all men are created equal"

would change the world

Under Jefferson, the Republicans

gave American government a new style

Jefferson's words:

"we are all Republicans—we are all Federalists"

would bring unity to a divided nation

Roosevelt—The Realist

the rough rider

his legacy

government's power

a gift given back

to the people

Lincoln—The Prophet

his reverent vision remains

"all are created equal"

his firm words remain a lasting legacy

"government of the people, by the people,

and for the people, shall not perish

from the earth"

Some details of F. Y. Ewing's return to the Midwest in 1838 with Jason Lee follow:

"... As stability increased, the fifty-one settlers of the Willamette Valley began to discuss the future. They had good farms and livestock. All around them was a plethora of soil awaiting development. But without political organization to guarantee land titles, they lacked security. Gathered at Lee's mission in March 1838, a group of them petitioned Congress for United States jurisdiction, writing confidently, 'We flatter ourselves that we are the germ of a great state.' Three dozen men signed the declaration, nine of them French Canadians. Jason Lee put the document into a tin box to carry horseback across the continent."[41]

"On the 26th of March, 1838, Mr. Lee left the Mission house, accompanied by Mr. Edwards, who has been before named, Mr. F.Y. Ewing, a gentleman well known in Missouri, and five Indians— three of the latter Nez Perces, and two Flat Heads. They came, for the most part, the way Mr. Lee went. On reaching the Walla Walla, they remained there until the 8th of May, waiting for the Fur company to set out, and with whom they traveled to Fort Hall. Here the greater part of the Fur company stopped, and the gentlemen who had it in charge, with a few men, continued on with Mr. Lee's party to the American Rendezvous on Wind river, a branch of the Yellow Stone. They numbered sixteen persons, and though this was the most dangerous portion of the route, they were not at all molested. From this point they proceed homeward with the American Fur company, having in their train thirty odd wagons and carts loaded with furs. On reaching Westport, near the Missouri line, Mr. Lee and his five Indians took canoes and descended the Missouri to Alton, proceeding about 50 miles a day. From Alton they went to St. Louis, and thence set out on their journey to New York, proceeding through Illinois to our town, whence they will continue by way of the lakes. Mr. L. was detained here til Wednesday by reason of the sickness of one of the Indians."[42]

F. Y. Ewing would arrive home safely and Oregon would finally achieve statehood in 1859. F. Y. Ewing's brother Robert C. Ewing was President of the First Constitutional Convention for

Montana's statehood (Montana was in the western most portion of the Louisiana Territory) in 1866, which was unsuccessful, as it was possibly a bit premature. Montana would not become a state until 1889, at which time it would utilize the model of government first devised by John Adams. John Adams' ideas on government have stood the test of time and Postscript 4 will more fully discuss their inception and importance.

HISTORICAL SOCIETY OF MONTANA

CONSTITUTIONAL CONVENTIONS OF MONTANA.

CONVENTION OF 1866.†

Held at Helena.
Convened April 9th, 1866.
Adjourned April 14th, 1866.

ROBERT C. EWING,* PRESIDENT.

MEMBERS.

SAMUEL W. BATCHELDER,*	Beaver Head County.
C. R. COOPER,*	Beaver Head County.
JOHN KEYSER,	Beaver Head County.
W. H. KING,*	Beaver Head County.
RICHARD McNEIL,*‡	Beaver Head County.
H. F. WRIGHT,*	Beaver Head County.
—— BLAKELY,	Deer Lodge County.
REUBEN BORTON,	Deer Lodge County.
FRED H. BURR,	Deer Lodge County.
MICHAEL HOLLAND,	Deer Lodge County.
DAVID L. IRVINE,*	Deer Lodge County.
WILLIAM L. IRVINE,*	Deer Lodge County.
ALEXANDER E. MAYHEW,	Deer Lodge County.
WASHINGTON J. McCORMICK,*	Deer Lodge County.
JAMES STUART,*	Deer Lodge County.
ROBERT C. EWING,*	Edgerton County.
JOHN H. SHOBER.	Edgerton County.
JOHN A. JOHNSTON,	Edgerton County.
A. S. MAXWELL,*	Edgerton County.
ROBERT B. PARROTT,	Edgerton County.
WILLIAM Y. PEMBERTON,	Edgerton County.
WILLIAM L. STEELE,	Edgerton County.
THOMAS E. TUTT,	Edgerton County.
ELIHU B. WATERBURY,*	Edgerton County.
ALEXANDER M. WOOLFOLK,	Gallatin County.
J. D. DAVIDSON,	Gallatin County.
H. P. DOWNS,	Gallatin County.
ANDREW J. HUNTER,*	Gallatin County.
A. METCALF,	Gallatin County.
W. B. MORRIS,	Jefferson County.
WILLIAM G. BARCLAY,*	Jefferson County.
THOMAS F. BOWLER,*	

43

An incident that occurred when John Adams was traveling by ship to take his post as a Minister to France in 1778 would illustrate his willingness to defend the government that he had helped to create.

John Adams was a passenger on the American fighting ship Boston and when cannon fire was exchanged with a heavily armed British merchantman, Adams did not seek safety down below but was in the thick of the fray. The American Captain Tucker noted that when a British cannonball struck Boston's mizzen yard, it was directly over the head of Adam's, who with musket in hand, was in the heart of the action. Captain Tucker's words follow: "I then went unto him and said 'My dear sir, how come you're here?' and with a smile he replied, 'I ought to do my share of the fighting.' This was sufficient for me to judge the bravery of my venerable and patriotic Adams."[44]

A Final Note

With the tragic events of September 11, 2001, now in the past, John Adams' words from the distant past lead us forward with hope: "Yesterday the greatest question was decided which ever was debated in America, and a greater perhaps, never was or will be decided among men. You will think me transported with Enthusiasm but I am not. I am well aware of the toil and blood and treasure, that it will cost us to maintain this Declaration, and support and defend these States. Yet through all the gloom I can see the rays of ravishing light and glory. I can see that the end is more than worth all the means. And that posterity will triumph in that day's transaction, even though we may rue it, which I trust in God we shall not."

These timeless words aptly apply to contemporary America— facing the challenge of the diverse, terrorized world of the third millenium. In the world of John Adams, there was only one threat— that of the British.

Britain and America, of course, have long since resolved their differences (incidentally, Scotland's Parliament recently reconvened after a lapse of more than two centuries) and rejoice in their birthright as close family members. But in 1776 this family was not a happy one.

Postscript 4
Government - Virtue - Revival

Government

"No one summed up better both the faith in the future and the obstacles on the way to it than the man who did as much to bring about independence as any man in America—John Adams. 'Yesterday the greatest question was decided, which ever was debated in America, and a greater perhaps, never was or will be decided among men...[1] You will think me transported with Enthusiasm but I am not. I am well aware of the toil and blood and treasure, that it will cost us to maintain this Declaration, and support and defend these States. Yet through all the gloom I can see the rays of ravishing light and glory. I can see that the end is more than worth all the means. And that posterity will triumph in that day's transaction, even although we should rue it, which I trust in God we shall not.' "[2]

"Soon after the passage of the resolution on independence on the second of July, 1776, the delegates took up the question of a constitution. A committee had been appointed on the eleventh of June to draft a constitution in anticipation of a vote in Congress declaring for independence. John Dickenson, reconciled to independence, was the principal author of the Articles of Confederation.[3]

"However inadequate a confederacy might be as a final form of national government, John Adams considered that such a grouping of independent governments now was the best way to win the war and insure the independence of the Colonies from the mother country."[4]

John Adams: "We must realize the Theories of the Wisest Writers and invite the People, to erect the whole Building with their own hands upon the broadest foundation. That this could be done only by Conventions of Representatives chosen by the people in the several Colonies, in the most exact proportions. That it was my Opinion, that Congress ought now to recommend to the People of every Colony to call such Conventions immediately and set up Governments of their own, under their own Authority: for the People were the Source of all Authority and Original of all Power."[5]

"Soon after his return to Congress, Adams was approached by William Hooper and John Penn, delegates from North Carolina, who were returning to that colony with the hope of stimulating it to draw up its own frame of government. Their friends had instructed them to bring along 'every hint (they) could collect concerning government,' and the two men had petitioned Adams, who had spoken so often to them of the proper principles of government, to put down his own thoughts. John found the suggestion irresistible."[6]

"In 1776 Adams published his *Thoughts On Government,* a series of essays urging the Virginia and North Carolina legislatures to establish mixed governments in their new constitutions. The pamphlet exerted a tremendous influence upon the framers of the state constitutions."[7]

"Adam's *Thoughts On Government* were prefaced with the observation that since 'the blessings of society depend entirely on constitutions of government' which generally last for many generations, 'there can be no employment more agreeable to a benevolent mind than a research after the best.' "[8]

"In 1787 Adams wrote the *Defence of the Constitutions of Government of the United States,* which remains the fullest exposition of mixed government theory by an American… Adams turned directly to the ancients for mixed government theory. In the *Defense,* he summarized the vague genesis of the theory in Plato's work and its development through Aristotle, Polybius, and Cicero. While respecting such modern authors as Niccolo, Machiavelli, James Harrington, Algernon Sidney, John Locke, and Montesquieu, Adams considered these theorists (particularly Montesquieu) overrated, emphasizing that 'the best part' of their writings came directly from the ancients."[9]

"The framers of the new state constitutions which emerged from the Revolution never doubted that their governments should be mixed. Rather, their real dilemma was how to mix them in a society which no longer possessed a monarch and which had never possessed a titled aristocracy. The framers decided that these essential roles should be played by an elective governor and a senate consisting of Harrington's 'natural aristocracy.' "[10]

"When the U.S. Constitution shifted the balance of power from the state governments to the federal government, it became imperative that the latter be mixed. Hence Adams was exceptionally pleased with the Constitution, with its balance between the one president, the few senators, and the representatives of the many."[11]

"James Madison also endorsed the Constitution as establishing a mixed government."[12]

Madison agreed with Adams that the principle of representation and the separation of powers had improved mixed government... In Federalist No. 10, Madison argued that "representative republics were more stable than the participatory democracies of ancient Greece and Rome."[13]

At the Constitutional Convention of 1787, James Madison's contributions would bestow upon him the title "Father of the U.S. Constitution." Madison's background included a classical Christian education which was standard fare for those of the Colonial era. "For Madison's generation the wisdom of Greece and Rome furnished, so to speak, the folklore, the morality plays, and the schoolboy texts on fundamental concepts of human nature and society... The other foundation stone of learning in Madison's day, and of his education, was the Christian tradition... So pervasive was Christian influence, especially in rearing children, that an education under other than Christian auspices was virtually unknown."[14]

James Madison's final two years of secondary education had been under the care of Reverend Thomas Martin. Martin was of Scotch-Irish descent, a graduate of Princeton College, and was influenced there by professors who had been participants in the First Great Awakening. Martin's guidance would help lead Madison to attend Princeton College in New Jersey rather than the more customary choice for a Virginian—the College of William and Mary, located in Williamsburg, Virginia.

As to his higher learning, "Madison's education at Princeton furnished him, from the wisdom of Greece and Rome, a lifelong realism about human nature, a comprehensive concept of political obligation, and a distinctive admiration of patience, prudence, and moderation. From the Christian tradition, he inherited a sense of the prime importance of conscience, a strict personal morality, an understanding of human dignity as well as depravity, and a conviction that vital religion could contribute importantly to the general welfare. From Locke, he learned that to be fully human, men had to be free, and that to be free, they had in some way to take part in their government."[15]

"… A disproportionate number of the leading lights in the Congress who later became drafters of the Constitution and Founding Fathers of the United States were graduates of Princeton."[16] "…Nine Princeton graduates—far more than from any other college—participated in the Constitutional Convention of 1787, where James Madison largely set the agenda."[17]

Ephraim Brevard was elected to the Continental Congress in 1781 and would have been a possible candidate for participation in the Constitutional Convention of 1787, had he survived the War of the Revolution. His presence would have raised the number of Princeton graduates participating to ten.

Thomas Jefferson was opposed to the idea of a strong federal constitution and government. In 1789, in a letter to James Madison, Jefferson speculated on an idealistic alternative to the new U.S. Constitution, which opposed the stability and long-term legality that the Constitution was designed to guarantee. In his response, Madison was diplomatic but called Jefferson's idea a dangerous fantasy.[18]

Virtue

In an excerpt from *Our Sacred Honor,* William Bennett makes the following comment: "In America, unlike any other country of the time, the Founders envisioned a land where people of all faiths could worship God without fear of persecution. The freedom to worship would, in turn, cultivate the piety and virtue necessary for the success of self-government. Washington noted that it would be folly to believe that national morality could be sustained without the support and guidance of religion. And although the founders provided the widest scope for religious liberty, they presupposed that the principles of the Judeo-Christian tradition would be enshrined in the hearts of all citizens. These religious principles, Benjamin Rush argued, should be encouraged for they 'promote the happiness of society and the safety and well being of civil government.' "[19]

Benjamin Rush wrote in 1798: "I proceed in the next place, to enquire, what mode of education we shall adopt so as to secure to the state all the advantages that are to be derived from the proper instruction of youth; and here I beg leave to remark, that the only foundation for a useful education in a republic is to be laid in Religion. Without this there can be no virtue, and without virtue there can be no liberty, and liberty is the object and life of all republican governments.

"Such is my veneration for every religion that reveals the attributes of the Deity, or a future state of rewards and punishments, that I had rather see the opinions of Confucius or Mohamed inculcated upon our youth, than see them grow up wholly devoid of a system of religious principles. But the religion I mean to recommend in this place is that of the New Testament.

"It is foreign to my purpose to hint at the arguments which establish the truth of the Christian revelation. My only business is to declare, that all its doctrines and precepts are calculated to promote the happiness of society, and the safety and well being of civil government. A Christian cannot fail of being a republican. The history of the creation of man, and of the relation of our species to each other by birth, which is recorded in the Old Testament, is the best refutation that can be given to the divine right of kings, and the strongest argument that can be used in favor of the original and natural equality of all mankind. A Christian, I say again, cannot fail of being a republican, for every precept of the Gospel inculcates those degrees of humility, self-denial and brotherly kindness, which are directly opposed to the pride of monarchy and the pageantry of a court. A Christian cannot fail of being useful to the republic, for his religion teacheth him, that no man 'liveth to himself.' And lastly, a Christian cannot fail of being wholly inoffensive, for his religion teacheth him, in a things to do to others what he would wish, in like circumstances, they should do to him."[20]

The Founding Fathers recognized the risks of government "of the people, by the people, and for the people," and of the importance of a virtuous population. In 1825 James Madison would voice the opinion that "Belief in a God all powerful, wise and good is so essential to the moral order of the world and to the happiness of man, that arguments which enforce it cannot be drawn from too many sources."[21]

Thomas Jefferson believed that individuals freed from oppression would naturally act in a manner that was to the benefit of the common good. John Adams would remind Jefferson in the correspondence of their twilight years that this idealist belief had always been an illusion.[22]

The following questions must be asked of a society that has lost its virtue (America today). Can virtue be regained? If so, how, and with what results? The United States of America has several times before reached a low ebb of virtue and morality—a state which was dramatically reversed over a relatively short period of time through true revival.

Revival

The Rev. Owen Murphy writes: "Today the word REVIVAL has largely lost its real meaning. Our present generation, never having witnessed the mighty movings of God in nation-wide spiritual awakening such as has taken place in past generations, has little conception of the magnitude of such a 'visitation.'

"REVIVAL is confused with EVANGELISM!

"Heaven-sent revival is not religious entertainment where crowds gather to hear outstanding preachers and musical programs, neither is it the result of sensational advertising—in a God-sent revival you don't spend money on advertising: people come because REVIVAL is there! Revival is an 'awareness of God' that grips the whole community, and the roadside, the tavern, as well as the church, becomes the place where men find Christ. Here is the vast difference between our modern evangelistic campaigns and true revival. In the former, hundreds may be brought to a knowledge of Christ, and churches experience seasons of blessings but as far as the community is concerned little impact is made; the taverns, dance halls, and movies are still crowded, and godlessness marches on. In revival, the Spirit of God like a cleansing flame sweeps through the community, Divine conviction grips people everywhere; the strongholds of the devil tremble and many close their doors, while multitudes turn to Christ!"[23]

Bob L. Eklund's words tell the history of American revival in this condensation of his work, *Spiritual Awakening:*

"Many of the first settlers came to America for religious and spiritual reasons. Their intent was very clear. When they reached the New World in 1607, one of their first concerns was to organize worship service. Deeply spiritual moral rules were followed in many of the early colonies. Indian evangelization was practiced, one of the most notable conversions being Pocahontas.

"Everyone went to church in the Puritan colonies. Although some of the later colonists were criminals and runaways, strong preaching in the pulpit resulted in many conversions and loyal church attendance until about 1650. During that time a preacher wrote home to England, from his New England preaching post, that he had never seen a beggar, never heard anyone swear an oath and had never seen a drunkard in his parish.

"By 1700, however, moral and spiritual conditions in the colonies had degenerated to a deplorable state. Clergy throughout the colonies were generally well paid. However, many lacked serious convictions about maintaining a serious prayer life. Many times they were the cause of open scandals in their communities. It was not unusual for unsaved preachers to preach to spiritually dead people in their churches. There was no discipline among the people or the preachers. When a few godly pastors tried to enforce discipline, churches in some areas of the new land revolted.

"Not one in 20 persons claimed to be a Christian; religion was in a state of decay. Church membership became nothing more than a political expediency since it was a requirement for citizenship. Wealth increased among the populace, and immorality was the order of the day. It was the age of enlightenment and reason, and deism was in vogue. Many Christian colleges operated in spiritual darkness. Samuel Blair, a pastor of the day, said that religion lay as it were dying and ready to expire its last breath of life in the visible church.

"A great darkness and anxiety existed at the beginning of the eighteenth century. God's people whose hearts were broken over the deplorable condition in America began to pray earnestly for God to heal their land.

"The forces that shaped this first great awakening in America were rooted in the pietism of Europe. Men such as Phillip Jacob Spencer, Hermann Francke, Count Von Zinzendorf, and other pietists in Germany, England, and other European nations insisted that Christian faith was a matter of the heart as well as the head.

"God's answer to the prayers of His people for awakening in America began in New England.

"Whitefield was a remarkable pulpiteer who came from England and toured all the colonies preaching the gospel. As a former schoolboy actor from England, he was perhaps the most remarkable of all the revivalists in this era. His visits to America served to unify awakening movements all up and down the Eastern seaboard. In Philadelphia, 8,000 people turned out to hear him preach from the courthouse steps. The city's population at that time was only 12,000.

"Results of the awakening were tremendous. Although accurate figures are hard to find, some conclude that during the 20 years from 1740 to 1760, the Congregational churches of New England grew by as many as 150 churches. In the years 1741-1742, 50,000 people were converted in New England alone! That represented one-fifth of the total population of New England.

"The first great awakening, as we have already seen, had great impact throughout the Colonies. As is always the case, however, the fires of awakening declined. Some local awakenings continued to occur; but for the most part, widespread awakening was only historical record. Several developments brought about the end of the first great awakening—religious controversy, jealous rivalries, and excesses.

"Society once again became immersed in immorality. Gambling and licentiousness were the order of the day. Drunkenness was commonplace. Three hundred thousand people in a population of five million were confirmed alcoholics. Profanity was used without reticence. Women were assaulted daily. Bank robberies were at an all time high. On the frontier, Peter Cartright, a prominent preacher, pointed out that Logan County, Ky., was nothing more than a vast harbor for criminals, cut-throats, and murderers.

"In 1782, only two students at Princeton University, established originally as a Presbyterian school, professed to be Christians. Harvard had only one professing believer. These and most other colleges had student bodies who joined the 'dirty speech movements.' Riots were common on campuses. Mock communions were held. One student group stole a Bible from a professor's desk and burned it.

"John Marshall, later chief justice of the Supreme Court, felt that the church was too far gone to salvage. Voltaire and Paine were predicting the death of Christianity within 30 years. For those who embraced any kind of faith at all in Christianity, most turned to Unitarianism or Universalism in New England and the Middle States. The churches had their backs to the wall, and there was nothing else to do but to go on bended knee to the Lord in prayer.

"There were three phases to the second awakening: the college campuses, the camp meetings and the missionary involvement of the local churches. If we had to choose a group in whom awakening initially began, it would be the college students.

"Hampton-Sidney College in Virginia, in 1787, is one example of campus awakening. Three students, concerned about the moral conditions at the school, covenanted together to pray once a week for awakening on the campus. Students who discovered them praying in the woods made fun of them. When the president of the college, John Blair Smith, learned of their prayer meeting, he invited them to his home for the prayer meeting. Soon other students joined the prayer meeting group. In the next year, 200 students were won to faith in Christ.

"Perhaps the most popular and widely known results of this second great awakening took place in camp meetings on Western Frontiers. E. M. Bounds, a chaplain in the Civil War and a pastor for 10 years afterward, once said, 'God's principal method is men.' And so it was on the frontier. Awakening was brought about through the camp meetings. One great camp meeting pastor was James McGready. He was born in Western Pennsylvania, but grew up in Guilford County, N.C., under the tutelage of a pastor there. During a preaching tour in Virginia, he stopped at Hampton-Sidney College and spent a summer in the president's home.

"Stirred by the movement of God at Hampton-Sidney, James McGready went back to North Carolina with a deep desire in his heart for God to send awakening. His preaching aroused opposition there and later in South Carolina also; but in addition to opposition there were great blessings, and many were saved. He moved to Logan County, Ky., where he pastored three churches. He drew up a prayer covenant, which called for prayer on Saturday evenings and Sundays. An all-day Saturday prayer and fasting meeting was held once a month.

"The original purpose of these gatherings was for the observation of the Lord's Supper, since there were so few pastors and churches on the Western Frontier. The people gathered in large crowds for these 'sacramental' meetings to partake of the Lord's Supper. These meetings soon became 'camp meetings' where awakening began to spread throughout the frontier. People came with the express purpose of getting right with God. The spiritual concern was intense. One participant, writing a description of what took place said, 'No person seemed to want to go home. Hunger and sleep seemed to affect nobody. Eternal things were the sincere and abiding concern of everyone.' The camp meetings spread everywhere, and by 1811, there were an estimated 500 camp meetings being held annually throughout America. One authority notes that in 1820 nearly 1000 were held.

"In 1800, frontier Kentucky's population was only about 221,000. The great Cane Ridge Revival, led by the Presbyterians in 1801, drew as many as 25,000 people at one time. One of eight people in Kentucky were at one place to hear the gospel preached. These awakened members went back to their towns and villages and established many churches."[24]

Charles Thompson writes: "The Cumberland Presbyterian Church was an indirect result of the powerful revival in Kentucky. It came about through a demand for an increase in the number of ministers to meet the new opportunities which the revival spirit had opened throughout the southern mountains.

"In February 1810, the independent Cumberland Presbytery was organized. This was the origin of the Cumberland Presbyterian Church. In three years and a half the Presbytery had grown to three Presbyteries which constituted the Cumberland Synod. Since then it has had continuous growth and is now (1903) a thoroughly organized denomination with 118 presbyteries, 2,944 congregations, 1,595 ministers and is not only doing its own work in the southern style but is carrying on a large home and foreign mission work."[25]

A large contingent of the Cumberland Presbyterians would later reunite with the traditional Presbyterians. A smaller remnant of the Cumberland Presbyterian Church survived this reunion and recently celebrated its bicentennial.

Eklund continues, "The Second Great Awakening was dynamic and created world-wide turning to Christ. By 1840, however, religious fervor was back to normal. A time of spiritual unconcern followed all across America. There were economic, political and religious reasons for the spiritual decline.

"Economic prosperity had turned men's thoughts from God to Gold. The Gold Rush of 1848, the building of the railroads, the increased production by farmers and the opening of vast tracts of land in the West and Northwest created a booming economy. By autumn of 1857, however, America was brought to her knees by a severe financial panic. Banks were failing, interest rates continued rising, businesses were declaring bankruptcy all over America, and many companies were laying off employees. In New York City alone, 30,000 people lost their jobs.

"In the midst of spiritual deadness, the Laymen's Prayer Movement began quietly at noon Wednesday, September 23, 1857 at the Old Dutch Church, located at the corner of Fulton and Williams Streets in the inner city of New York. The organizer of the prayer meetings was Jeremiah C. Lamphier. He was a Presbyterian businessman employed by the church as a lay missionary 'to reach the unchurched in the neighborhood.'

"Religion became the topic of the day. The secular press gave front-page coverage, describing the progress of the church work in various parts of the country. The usual front page items were overshadowed by revival news. Extra editions were published highlighting the revival. The famous Horace Greely sent a reporter racing around to the noon prayer meetings to see how many were praying. He could get to only 12 meetings in the one hour they met, but he counted 6,100 men praying.

"Wide-spread prayer meetings continued throughout the awakening. The 1858 Prayer Revival was to last a generation."[26]

In 1949 an awakening began in the Hebrides that led to a major transformation in these islands that lie off the western coast of Scotland. The power of this contemporary awakening may give a glimpse of the power of St. Patrick's original mission to Ireland, as well as St. Columba's subsequent mission to Scotland. One of the Hebrides Islands, Iona, was previously mentioned as the site of St. Columba's first monastery in Scotland. A Bible produced by St. Columba's monks in 700 A.D. at Iona has been preserved, and is still in existence as a lasting Christian influence.

The Rev. Owen Murphy gives a description of the revival in the Hebrides and his subsequent vision for revival in the United States. The following is condensed from Rev. Owen Murphy's book, *When God Stepped Down From Heaven:*

Chapter One

HOW IT BEGAN

Preparation must PRECEDE revival! The word of God, history, and the gracious visitation of God to the Hebrides all emphasize this fact. And that preparation must begin with God's people.

History turned another page when the Free Church Presbytery of Lewis met in the town of Stornoway to discuss the appalling spiritual conditions existing in their communities. While the haunts of sin were crowded, churches were almost empty. In many places youth had almost disappeared from the House of God and it seemed only a matter of time before many churches would have to close their doors. No one, however, ever dreamed for a moment that this special meeting was destined to be the preliminary to the amazing spiritual awakening that was to come.

Amongst the many who were deeply concerned about the desperate spiritual condition of the churches, was a little group of men who lived at Barvas, the district that was to become the centre of the outbreak of revival. As they met in a little wooden barn, greatly burdened for revival for their community, and began to pray, there suddenly dawned upon them, like a flash of light, the great fact of God as a COVENANT-KEEPING GOD, who had made COVENANT PROMISES!

"If this is true," they reasoned. "WE can enter into a covenant with Him, and, if we keep OUR part of it, then HE MUST KEEP HIS!" Has God given a "covenant promise" for REVIVAL? Immediately the words of God in II Chronicles. 7:14. came to them:

"IF MY PEOPLE, WHICH ARE CALLED BY MY NAME, SHALL HUMBLE THEMSELVES, AND PRAY, AND SEEK MY FACE, AND TURN FROM THEIR WICKED WAYS, THEN I WILL HEAR FROM HEAVEN…"

That night they entered into a solemn covenant with God, to take upon themselves the "burden" for revival for the community. to humble themselves, and to prevail in prayer UNTIL REVIVAL CAME!

Let me now take you to that little barn by the side of the road and see those men on their faces before God. They have gathered to pray but this is no ordinary prayer meeting. Here are men, led by their minister, who are there to do business with God, and at 10 o'clock at night they kneel down in the straw to plead with God that He would make bare His arm in revival.

For months they waited: for months they gathered in the little barn three nights a week and waited upon God until 4 and 5 o'clock in the morning, determined to wrestle with God until the answer had been given. Then, one night, a young man, a deacon from the Free Church, arose from his knees and began to read Psalm 24:

"WHO SHALL ASCEND INTO THE HILL OF THE LORD? OR WHO SHALL STAND IN HIS HOLY PLACE? HE THAT HATH CLEAN HANDS AND A PURE HEART—HE SHALL RECEIVE THE BLESSINGS OF THE LORD."

"Brethren," he said. "We have been praying for months for revival, waiting before God, but I would like to ask you now: ARE OUR HEARTS CLEAN? IS THE HEART PURE?" In response to this searching challenge they fell upon their knees in confession, and rededication, and again began to travail in prayer, even more earnestly. An hour later, three of them were lying prostrate upon the floor—they had PRAYED UNTIL THEY WERE EXHAUSTED! By five o'clock REVIVAL HAD COME! The barn was suddenly filled with the Glory of God, and the power of God that was let loose in that barn shook the whole community of Lewis.

That same morning, in a little cottage several miles away, lived two elderly sisters; one was 84 and the other 82 years of age. For many years they had sought the Face of God for revival and, knowing the others were waiting upon God, they had gathered around their little peat fire to spend the night in prayer. Suddenly, something happened! The Glory of God swept into their cottage. God then spoke to them. revealing to them the very man whom He was going to use—the Rev. Duncan

Campbell, a Presbyterian minister, and a mighty man of prayer.

"IN TWO WEEKS, said the Lord, I SHALL SEND UPON THIS COMMUNITY THE GREATEST SPIRITUAL AWAKENING IT HAS KNOWN!"

A wire was sent to the Man of God, but when he received it and discovered that he was already booked up for another meeting, he replied: "It is impossible for me to come at this time, but keep on praying and I will come next year." When the reply was given to the sisters, they answered: THAT IS WHAT MAN HAS SAID. GOD HAS SAID THAT HE WILL BE HERE IN TWO WEEKS! In the meantime. other letters began to reach him and strangely enough, his next meeting was cancelled. (How amazingly God can overrule!) The holiday Convention, which he was to address, was suddenly cancelled, owing to the Touring Board sweeping in and commandeering the hotels and boarding houses which the convention had been depending upon for accommodation for the many who were to attend the Convention. Within a fortnight he was in Barvas!

The first meeting was held in the old parish church. Many people had gathered in a great expectancy of a great "moving of God" but, strangely enough, nothing happened. It was just an ordinary service. Seeing the disappointment upon the preacher's face, one of the praying deacons came up to him: "DON'T BE DISCOURAGED" he said. IT IS COMING. I ALREADY HEAR THE RUMBLING OF HEAVEN'S CHARIOT WHEELS. WE WILL HAVE ANOTHER NIGHT OF PRAYER AND THEN WE WILL SEE WHAT GOD IS GOING TO DO!"

They went over to a near-by cottage, and about thirty knelt in prayer, and began to travail before the Lord. Three o'clock in the morning, God swept in and about a dozen were laid prostrate upon the floor, and lay there speechless. Something had happened! God had moved into action as He had promises; REVIVAL had come, and men and women were going to find deliverance. As they left that cottage that morning, they found men and women seeking God! Lights were burning in the homes along the road—no one seemed to think of sleep. Three men were found lying by the roadside, in a torment of conviction, crying for God to have mercy upon them! The

Spirit of God was moving into action, and soon the parish of Barvas was to be stirred from end to end.

Chapter Two
SCENES OF THE SUPERNATURAL

The events of the second night will never be forgotten by those who were privileged to attend. Buses came from the four corners of the island, crowding the church. Seven men were being driven to the meeting in a butcher's truck, when suddenly the Spirit of God fell upon them in great conviction, and all were converted before they reached the church! As the preacher delivered his message, tremendous conviction of sin swept down upon the people! Tears rolled down the faces of the people, and from every part of the building came cries of men and women crying for mercy. So deep was the distress of some that their voices could be heard outside in the road. A young man beneath the pulpit cried out: "O God, hell is too good for me!"

The meeting closed when the people began to move out. As the last person was about to leave, a young man began to pray. Under a tremendous burden of intercession, he prayed for three quarters of an hour and, as he prayed, the people kept gathering until there were twice as many outside the church as there were inside! When the young man stopped praying, the Elder gave out Psalm 132, and as the great congregation sang the old hymn, the people streamed back into the church again, and the meeting went on until 4 a.m.

The moment people took their seats, the Spirit of God in awful conviction began to sweep through the church, and hardened sinners began to weep and confess their sins.

Just as the meeting was closing, a messenger hurried up to the preacher, very excited:

"COME WITH ME! THERE'S A CROWD OF PEOPLE OUTSIDE THE POLICE STATION; THEY ARE WEEPING AND IN AWFUL DISTRESS. WE DON'T KNOW WHAT'S WRONG WITH THEM, BUT THEY ARE CALLING FOR SOMEONE TO COME AND PRAY WITH THEM."

Describing the scenes outside the police station, which reminded one of the amazing days of Charles Finney, and the Welsh Revival, the minister declared:

"I SAW A SIGHT I NEVER THOUGHT WAS POSSIBLE. SOMETHING I SHALL NEVER FORGET. UNDER A STARLIT SKY, MEN AND WOMEN WERE KNEELING EVERYWHERE, BY THE ROADSIDE, OUTSIDE THE COTTAGES, EVEN BEHIND THE PEAT STACKS, CRYING FOR GOD TO HAVE MERCY UPON THEM!"

Nearly 600 people, who had been making their way to the church, when suddenly the Spirit of God had fallen upon them in great conviction-like Paul on the way to Damascus-causing them to fall to their knees in repentance!

REVIVAL HAD SURELY COME! For five weeks it swept on in that one Parish. Duncan Campbell conducted four services nightly; in one church at 7 o'clock, in another at 10, in a third at midnight, and back to the first one at 3 o'clock, and home between 5 and 6 o'clock—tired, but very happy to be in the midst of such a wonderful moving of God.

After five weeks in this district the revival began to spread and what had taken place in Barvas, was repeated in other districts.

As men and women throughout the island began to grip God in desperate intercession and prayer for revival, the Spirit of God swept on in increasing power. ARNOL, a small community, came within the path of this spiritual tornado. Gripped by a spirit of religious indifference, it was reckoned that hardly a young person darkened the House of God, the Sabbath being given over to the drinking house, poaching, and other sinful pleasures. News of the gracious moving of God having spread through the island, it was here where an opposition meeting was held, lest a similar visitation fall upon Arnol. Although the church was crowded with those who came from the various parts of the island, very few people from Arnol attended the services. In desperation, the little prayer band made their way to the farmhouse to plead the promises of God. Just after midnight, a young man rose to his feet and prayed a prayer that will never be forgotten by those who were present.

"LORD, YOU MADE A PROMISE, ARE YOU GOING TO FULFILL IT? WE BELIEVE THAT YOU ARE A COVENANT KEEPING GOD. WILL YOU BE TRUE TO YOUR COVENANT? YOU HAVE SAID THAT YOU WILL POUR WATER UPON HIM THAT IS THIRSTY AND FLOODS UPON THE DRY GROUND. LORD, I KNOW HOW THESE MINISTERS STAND IN YOUR PRESENCE, BUT IF I KNOW MY OWN HEART I KNOW WHERE I STAND, AND I TELL THEE NOW THAT I AM THIRSTY. OH, I AM THIRSTY FOR A MANIFESTATION OF THE PRESENCE AND POWER OF GOD! AND "LORD, BEFORE I SIT DOWN, I WANT TO TELL YOU THAT YOUR HONOUR IS AT STAKE!"

(Have you ever prayed like that? Here is a man praying the prayer of faith that Heaven must answer! One could imagine the angels of Heaven looking over the battlements of Glory and saying: "This is a man who believes God! This is a man who dares to stand firm upon the promise of God and take from God what has been promised!")

Then came the answer! There are those in Arnol today who will verify the fact that while the brother prayed the house shook like a leaf (just as in Acts 4) as God turned loose His mighty power! Dishes rattled upon the sideboard; an elder exclaimed: "An earth tremor?" Then wave after wave of Divine Power swept throughout the room. Simultaneously, the Spirit of God swept through the village. PEOPLE COULD NOT SLEEP; HOUSES WERE LIT ALL NIGHT; PEOPLE WALKED THE STREETS IN GREAT CONVICTION; OTHERS KNELT BY THEIR BEDSIDES CRYING FOR GOD TO PARDON THEM! As the praying men left the prayer meeting, the preacher walked into a house for a glass of milk and found the lady of the house, with seven others, down upon their knees, crying for pardon. Within 48 hours the drinking house, usually crowded with the drinking men of the village, was closed. Today, it is in ruins. Fourteen young men who had been drinking there, were gloriously converted. Those same men could be found three times a week, with others, down upon their knees before God, from 10 o'clock until after midnight praying for their old associates and the spread of revival. It was in this village that within 48 hours nearly every young person between the ages of 12 and 20 had surrendered to Christ, and it was reckoned that every young man between the ages of 18 and 35 could be found in the prayer meetings!

In BERNERAY things were very difficult as the stream of religious life was very low; churches were empty and prayer meeting were practically nil. In view of this, a wire was sent to the praying men of Barvas to come and assist in prayer, and bring with them Donald Smith, the 17-year-old boy to whom God had imparted the amazing ministry of prayer. Halfway through his message, the preacher stopped. and called out: "DONALD WILL YOU LEAD US IN PRAYER?" Standing to his feet, he began to pour out his heart before God in agonizing intercession for the people of the island, and reminding God that He was the great "Covenant-keeping God." Suddenly, it seemed as though the heavens were rent and God swept into the church. People everywhere were stricken by the Power of God, as the Spirit swept through in great convicting power. Outside, startling things were taking place. Simultaneously the Spirit of God had swept over the homes and area around the village, and everywhere people came under great conviction of sin. Fishermen out in their boats, men behind their looms, men at the pit bank, a merchant out with his truck, school teachers examining their papers, were gripped by God and by 10 o'clock the roads were black with people, streaming from every direction to the church. As the preacher came out of the church, the Spirit of God swept in among the people on the road, as a wind. They gripped each other in fear. In agony of soul they trembled, many wept and some fell to the ground in great conviction of sin. Three men were found lying by the side of the road, in such distress of soul that they could not even speak—yet they had never been near the church!

So tremendous was the supernatural moving of God in conviction of sin, not a home, not a family, not an individual escaped fearful conviction, and even the routine of business was stopped that the island might seek the Face of God like Nineveh of Bible days. The town was changed, lives and homes transformed. and even the fishing fleet, as it sailed out into the bays, took with it a Presenter, to lead them in prayer and singing of hymns.

Chapter Five

THE SECRET OF THE VISITATION OF GOD!

The HEBRIDES revival was a MANIFESTATION OF GOD! Something greater than organization, something more wonderful than a new approach in dynamic evangelism-this was GOD AT WORK! GOD IN ACTION, independent of special PERSONALITIES! And, behind the mighty" "turning loose" of the irresistible power of God, there was a "SECRET"—ONE MINISTER AND SEVEN MEMBERS OF HIS CHURCH, in a little wooden barn by the side of the road, who were prepared to 'stand in the gap" and PAY THE FULL PRICE THAT GOD HAD DEMANDED that revival might come!

What Was the "Secret" Of These Men?

(1) THEIR FAITH IN A"COVENANT-KEEPING"GOD!

Here were men who believed the tremendous fact that REVIVAL lay within their power. through the "Covenant" promises of God. Had God not declared:

"IF MY PEOPLE, WHO ARE CALLED BY MY NAME, WILL HUMBLE THEMSELVES, AND PRAY, AND SEEK MY FACE, AND TURN FROM THEIR WICKED WAYS; THEN I WILL HEAR FROM HEAVEN, AND WILL FORGIVE THEIR SIN, AND WILL HEAL THEIR LAND." (11 Chron. 7:14)

(2) THEIR HUMBLING BEFORE GOD!

"If my people... will HUMBLE themselves!" God is holy, and humanity must humble itself before Deity. Before man can stand upon Holy Ground he must be clean. Watch the drama of the barn by the roadside unfold itself as one of the men, slowly rising from the straw, takes up the Word and begins to read from Psalm 24.

"WHO SHALL ASCEND INTO THE HILL OF THE LORD? WHO SHALL STAND IN HIS HOLY PLACE? HE THAT HATH CLEAN HANDS, AND A PURE HEART; WHO HATH NOT LIFTED UP HIS SOULD UNTO VANITY, NOR SWORN DECEITFULLY; HE SHALL RECEIVE THE BLESSING OF THE LORD."

(3) THEIR TRAVAILING AND PREVAILING IN PRAYER!

Every revival that has broken upon the face of the earth has been preceded by the people of God upon their knees travailing before God.

For long, weary months, undeterred by the cold and discomforts of the barn; undeterred by the seeming "silence" of God; undeterred by the fact that no one else seemed concerned about revival and the world seemed to be as godless as ever; they travailed before God. Kneeling in the straw, or upon their faces before the Lord in agony of soul, they cried unto the Throne.

And how they prayed; not the half-hearted, sentimental, churchly, half-doubting prayers to which we are accustomed today and which accomplish so little. As one listened to men literally wrestling with God, drawing into the spiritual conflict every power and energy they possessed, one was reminded of the prayer of the Master In Gethsemane:

"Who, in the days of His flesh… offered up prayers and supplications with strong crying and tears…"

The men who had covenanted to stand in the gap for revival, PRAYED! In desperation, they stormed the throne of God. Burning passion, concern for the lost, and absolute confidence in God, gripped every word that fell from their praying lips. They prayed until they lay helpless and exhausted. What depths of reaching out to God! They prayed until they travailed, and they travailed until they PREVAILED! They prayed UNTIL GOD ANSWERED! TRAVAIL must always precede PREVAIL! "When Zion travailed she brought forth."

Such, then is REVIVAL. A mighty, sovereign moving of God in answer to the cries of men and women who have gone down upon their knees to travail before God. A visitation of God, through His Spirit, that pours tormenting CONVICTION OF SIN upon the ungodly, wherever they may be, until multitudes have turned to Christ. A demonstration of God that closes the dens of iniquity, transforms the lives and homes of multitudes, fills the churches, and causes the influence of spiritual values to be felt throughout a whole nation. A genuine "moving of God" that lays a spiritual foundation for the blessing of God in future generations.

THIS IS REVIVAL!

With the ashes of past revivals before us—for those scenes today are only history—we may ask the question: CAN THOSE SCENES BE REPEATED? CAN GOD SEND A SIMILAR REVIVAL IN OUR DAY? The writer is convinced that God can do more than that, God is WAITING TO DO IT. In every age, the revival resources of God have been waiting to be 'turned loose" when God could find MEN who could stand before Him in holiness, prayer, and faith and make it possible, and to those who travel the highways of the world, there are obvious and encouraging signs that God is again "preparing the way" for a new spiritual awakening.

HEBRIDES which although just the size of a "man's hand," is not only one of the most stirring events of our day, but under the blessing of God is challenging men and women everywhere to "stand in the gap" for revival in our day.

The spiritual awakening of the Hebrides, between 1949 and '52 has stirred the hearts of God's people, not because of its size, but because of its QUALITY, and challenge for TODAY! In spite of the scattered nature of the country and difficulty of transport, the rugged and unemotional nature of the people and limited population, the fact that hundreds have turned to Christ in life-changing conversion, accompanied by such God-given scenes, inspires us with new FATIH for a far greater awakening in our own land. Just as the tidings of the great awakening of America, in 1857, swept across the ocean and brought REVIVAL to Ireland in '59. So it may be, in the purposes of God, that attention has been focused upon that which God wrought in the Hebrides, that its CHALLENGE OF INTERCESSION may cause a flame of REVIVAL to be kindled IN AMERICA, that will cause the whole land to be swept with a mighty Holy Ghost [Holy Spirit] revival.[27]

Postscript 5
The World According to Thomas Jefferson

Thomas Jefferson's place in history is assured. During Jefferson's lifetime, history took a marked turn of events and Jefferson did his part to steer America through the first of it.

He was a champion of individual rights and a student of the enlightenment that led to governments of common sense. The Declaration of Independence remains a timeless document that continues to set the standard for freedom, equality, and the ideal of fair government. Fair government is government of and for the people. It would also become government separate from the church, not an idea exclusive to Jefferson—William Penn would establish freedom of religion in the colony of Pennsylvania in 1682—but one that his legislation made a reality in Virginia (though James Madison "maneuvered Jefferson's statute into law after Jefferson had failed."[1]). Through these efforts Jefferson helped set America on a new and revolutionary course that was, as it turns out, the correct one. In contrast, Thomas Jefferson's ideals for post-revolutionary America were not shared by the majority of the Founding Fathers; and if enacted, would have resulted in an entirely different American creation.

The ideas Jefferson brought forth to create Virginia's new government followed John Adam's *Thoughts On Government,* but replaced Adam's more effective strong executive branch with a weak executive called an administrator.[2] On the federal level, Thomas Jefferson was opposed to a strong government constitution and supported instead a modification of the existing Articles of Confederation, in which the states would exclusively control domestic issues and the federal government would exclusively control international issues.[3] Jefferson was opposed to a standing army and navy, preferring to rely on a militia force for the nation's military requirements.[4] The War of 1812 proved Jefferson's vision for American government and defense to be dangerously wrong on both counts. In reality, a strong federal government and military (the militia was ineffective throughout most of this war) under President James Madison would be vital to the safeguarding of America's sovereignty and freedom during this war and would set the standard for America's future security. While in the earlier time that James Madison's vital contributions helped to create the powerful United States Constitution (including "the guarantee of religious freedom in the Federal Bill of Rights"[5]), Thomas Jefferson was serving as a minister to France.

Jefferson helped to create the French Declaration of the Rights of Man, which served a similar purpose in France, as had the Declaration of Independence in America. Jefferson was present when the French Revolution began and stated: "It is impossible to conceive of a greater fermentation than has worked in Paris, nor do I believe that so great a fermentation ever produced so little injury in any other place. I have been through it daily, have observed the mobs with my own eyes, and declare to you that I saw so plainly the legitimacy of them that I have slept in my house as quietly through the whole as I ever did in the most peaceful moments. The National Assembly have now a clean canvas to work on here as we had in America... I will agree to be stoned as a false prophet if all does not end well in this country."[6]

In this statement, Jefferson was dead wrong, as the French Revolution (though it did result in reforms) was a bloody Reign of Terror that lasted for a decade and ended with Napoleon as dictator (a French Republic would come later—much later than Jefferson anticipated).

Jefferson would also err in his condemnation of the Christian Trinity. Jefferson believed that the Apostle Paul was the "first corrupter of the doctrines of Jesus."[7] In addition, there were other corrupters but Jefferson produced the remedy. "I have made a wee-little book... which I call the *Philosophy of Jesus*; it is a paradigma of his [Jesus'] doctrines, made by cutting the texts out of the [*New Testament*] and arranging them on the pages of a blank book in a certain order of time and subject."[8] Jefferson apparently had no difficulty in recognizing the corruptions that required removal. "The matter which is evidently his [Jesus]... is as easily distinguishable as diamonds in a dunghill."[9] Jefferson continued, "If a history of his [Jesus'] life can be added, written with the same view of the subject, the world will... at length see the immortal merit of this first of human sages..."[10] In a letter to F. A. Van Der Kemp dated April 25, 1816, Jefferson suggested a future collaboration to publish this work anonymously in England to hide his connection with it. It is uncertain when *The Jefferson Bible* was first published. But an edition was made available for presentation to new U.S. senators beginning in 1904 and it is available in print today. He apparently expected his revised Bible to influence public opinion and reveal the real Jesus, who had been "dressed up in the rags of an imposter" by the disciples.

In 1822, Jefferson would state, "I rejoice that in this blessed country of free inquiry and belief, which has surrendered its creed and conscience to neither kings nor priests, the genuine doctrine of one only God is reviving and I trust that there is not a young man now living in the United States that will not die a Unitarian."[11]

Jefferson's new bible and his false prophecy would, in reality, not disturb the rock solid foundation of the Christian faith; as the multitude of believers in The Father, The Son, and The Holy Spirit, through free choice, continue to attest to their firm convictions. As true believers, they would not choose to cast the first stone, but would simply offer prayer for Jefferson's soul.

It is an important fact that America's cherished freedom of speech allows Jefferson's words from the past or any citizen's words in the present to speak freely for or against any issue including religion.

Thomas Jefferson tried to follow Jesus' teachings (he called them "of fine imagination, correct morality and of the most lovely benevolence[12]), but Jefferson called himself an "Epicurean" in that he relied on himself and his senses only—rejecting the possibility of any supernatural help from a living God.[13] This would also be known as a deist philosophy.

Although Jefferson was a deist, his stand on religious freedom would help establish a new creation—a country whose citizens each enjoy the unalienable right and total freedom to accept no God, an aloof God, or a living God. This would prove to be an environment in which faith would flourish.

The Jefferson Bible would end abruptly with these hopeless words: "Now in the place where he was crucified, there was a garden, and in the garden, a new sepulchre, wherein was never man yet laid. There laid they Jesus. And rolled a great stone to the door of the sepulchre and departed."

Postscript 6

The Founding Fathers & the Power of Prayer

Francis Hutcheson would disagree with the English deist viewpoint that God was distant and unconcerned with the fate of us here on earth.[1] So would most of the Founding Fathers.

In *America's Providential History,* Mark Beliles and Stephen K. McDowell would write: Webster's 1828 Dictionary defines "providence" as "the care and superintendence which God exercises over His creatures. By 'Divine Providence' is understood 'God Himself.' " This definition, written in the times in which our Founders lived, is significant, for it helps us to see what they meant when they used this term in their writings. They also used many other names for God other than simply "God" or "Jesus." George Washington's writings reveal 54 different titles, Abraham Lincoln used 49 and Robert E. Lee used 45. This reflects the depth of understanding our Founding Fathers had of God and His involvement in human affairs.

Here are some statements that reveal how America's Founders recognized God's hand in history (as listed in *America's Providential History*):

William Bradford, Governor of the Pilgrims

"But these things did not dismay them… for their desires were set on the ways of God, and to enjoy His ordinances; but they rested on His Providence and knew whom they had believed."

Declaration of Independence

"And for the support of this Declaration, with a firm reliance on the Protection of Divine Providence, we mutually pledge to each other our Lives, our Fortunes and our Sacred Honor."

Benjamin Franklin addressing the Constitutional Convention

"How has it happened, Sir, that we have not hitherto once thought of humbly appealing to the Father of lights to illuminate our understanding? In the beginning of the contest with Great Britain, when we were sensible to danger, we had daily prayers in this room for Divine protection. Our prayers, Sir, were heard and they were graciously answered… I have lived, Sir, a long time and the longer I live, the more convincing proofs I see of this truth—that God governs in the affairs of men. And if a sparrow cannot fall to the ground without His notice, is it probable that an empire can rise without His aid? We have been assured, Sir, in the sacred writings that 'except the Lord build the house, they labor in vain that build it.' …I firmly believe this…"

The United States House of Representatives, 1854

"The people of these United States, from their earliest history to the present time, have been led by the hand of a Kind Providence, and are indebted for the countless blessings of the past and present, and dependent for continued prosperity in the future upon Almighty God… The great vital and conservative element in our system is the belief of our people in the pure doctrines and divine truths of the gospel of Jesus Christ."

George Washington's Thanksgiving Proclamation, 1789

"It is the duty of all nations to acknowledge the Providence of Almighty God, to obey His will, to be grateful for His benefits, and humbly to implore His protection and favor."

In *America's Providential History,* Mark Beliles and Stephen K. McDowell continued: "During the first days of July 1776, the Continental Congress was considering one of the most historical events of all time—the declaration by thirteen colonies to become the new nation of the United States of America.

On the issue of independence, all the colonies were agreed, but a few of the most cautious delegates still were not sure about the timing. Rev. John Witherspoon, a delegate from New Jersey, answered their concerns as he said, 'There is a tide in the affairs of men. We perceive it now before us. To hesitate is to consent to our own slavery. That noble instrument should be subscribed to this very morning by every pen in this house. Though these gray hairs must soon descend to the sepulchre, I would infinitely rather that they descend thither by the hand of the executioner than desert at the crisis the sacred cause of my country!"

The delegates went on to approve the Declaration of Independence. After the announcement of the vote, silence moved over the Congress as the men contemplated the magnitude of what they had just done. Some wept openly, while others bowed in prayer. After signing the Declaration with unusually large writing, the President of the Continental Congress, John Hancock, broke the silence as he declared, "His majesty can now read my name without glasses. And he can also double the price on my head." Then he went on to say at this tense moment, 'We must be unanimous; there must be no pulling different ways; we must all hang together.'

Benjamin Franklin responded in his characteristic wit, "Yes, we must indeed all hang together, or most assuredly we shall all hang separately!"

A brief chuckle followed and then Samuel Adams, whom men of that day ascribed "the greatest part in the greatest revolution of the world," rose and stated, "We have this day restored the Sovereign to Whom alone men ought to be obedient. He reigns in heaven… and from the rising to the setting sun, may His kingdom come."

The men who helped give birth to America understood what was taking place. They saw in the establishment of America the first true Christian nation in history.

As Franklin suggested, they did "hang together," but even so, many of these signers as well as tens of thousands of colonists lost their lives, property, families and reputations in order to purchase liberty for themselves and their posterity.

What was it that motivated these people to risk everything in order that they might have freedom? What was it that brought about the events leading to the colonists declaring their independence?

John Adams, our second President and a leader in the cause of independence, revealed what he and many others thought as he wrote on the day that the colonies declared their independence: "It is the will of Heaven that the two countries should be sundered forever; it may be the will of Heaven that America shall suffer calamities still more wasting and distresses yet more dreadful. If this is to be the case, the furnace of affliction produces refinement in states as well as individuals; but I submit all my hopes and fears to an overruling Providence, in which, unfashionable as the faith may be, I firmly believe."

John Hancock echoed the reliance upon God and the belief that the destiny of nations is in the hand of God as he said: "Let us humbly commit our righteous cause to the great Lord of the Universe... Let us joyfully leave our concerns in the hands of Him who raises up and puts down the empires and kingdoms of the earth as He pleases."

This firm reliance upon God was so universally adhered to among those in America that the Continental Congress insisted it be included in the Declaration of Independence. While reviewing Thomas Jefferson's original draft of the Declaration, the committee assigned to the task added the words, "they are endowed by their Creator with certain unalienable rights." Then, when the Declaration was debated before Congress, they added the phrase, "appealing to the Supreme Judge of the World, for the rectitude of our intentions," as well as the words "with a firm reliance on the protection of divine Providence."

Authors Mark Beliles and Stephen K. McDowell continued: "[During the Revolution] Washington was very instrumental in securing chaplains for the army. Rev. Henry Muhlenberg relates how General Washington "rode around among his army... and admonished each and every one to fear God, to put away the wickedness that has set in and become so general, and to practice the Christian virtues."

It was said of Washington, in a sketch written by an American gentleman in London in 1779 that "he regularly attends divine service in his tent every morning and evening, and seems very fervent in his prayers." General Knox was one among many who gave testimony of Washington frequently visiting secluded groves to lay the cause of his bleeding country at the throne of grace.

A number of people have recorded the story of how a Tory Quaker, Isaac Potts, came upon Washington while he was on his knees in prayer in the woods. Benson J. Lossing relates that Potts later made the following remarks to his wife: "If there is anyone on this earth whom the Lord will listen to, it is George Washington; and I feel a presentiment that under such a commander there can be no doubt of our eventually establishing our independence, and that God in his providence has willed it so."

On May 6, 1982, President Reagan remarked on this event in his National Day of Prayer Proclamation: "The most sublime picture in American history is of George Washington on his knees in the snow at Valley Forge. That image personifies a people who know that it is not enough to depend on our own courage and goodness; we must also seek help from God, our Father and Preserver."[2]

In conclusion, as authors Mark Beliles and Stephen K. McDowell so succinctly illustrated in the previous pages in excerpts from their book *America's Providential History,* America has always been and remains a nation under God. Even though its citizens have total freedom to accept or reject the idea of a living God—a God who is accessible through the power of prayer to individuals and nations.

Perhaps the growing number of religion-based schools in America will increasingly promote the purity of the separation of church and state, while insuring the promise of a nation that continues to live under God's will.

The King James version of the Bible expresses the hope that belief in a living God brings: "… and they found the stone rolled away from the sepulchre. And they entered in, and found not the body of the Lord Jesus… And two men stood beside them in shining garments and… said unto them, why seek ye the living among the dead. He is not here, but is risen…"

.

Postscript 7
Of Our God

In *Scottish World,* George Shepperson writes: the Scotch-Irish "were, in the main, Presbyterians, and they stood by the English language of the 1611 authorized version of the Bible. This King James version of the Bible occupies an important place in the social and religious history of the United States; and it is arguable that the Ulster Scots, with their devotion to it, did much to implant it in the affections of the emerging nation."[1]

"The Ulster Scots had no religious or sentimental attachment to the institution of monarchy. On the eve of the American Revolution, most of them were already inclined toward a break with Britain. To the British government, indeed, their Presbyterian churches were 'sedition shops' for from the Ulster Scots on the frontier of Virginia and North Carolina came some of the first advances toward a declaration of American independence."[2]

The Scotch-Irish, in their long-sought search for freedom, helped to spark the American Revolution. The refining fire of their struggles brought them into a close relationship with God. These revolutionaries understood and followed the Bible. They served God and country.

If we allow this same spirit that lived in them to revive us, we too, can truly pledge our mutual cooperation, our lives, our fortunes, and our most sacred honor to our God, to our country, and to one another.

Saint Patrick 5th Century A.D

And He has given to Him all power

over every name

of beings celestial

and terrestrial

and of the lower regions

and every tongue should confess to Him

That Jesus Christ is Lord and God

Whom we believe

and we look hopefully for His advent

soon to be

the judge of the living and the dead

who will give back to each according

to his own deeds

and he has poured out abundantly

among us the Holy Spirit

a gift and pledge of immortality

who makes those believing and

obeying

that they may be sons of God and

fellow heirs of Christ

Whom we confess and adore

one God in a Trinity of sacred name.[3]

The Religion of Experience

When the Heavens open wide

and

The Divine Flame descends

Heaven is at hand

Blessed is

The love of Christ

that passeth knowledge

and

The peace of God

that passeth understanding

What Jesus Means to Me
Elizabeth Brown
10 years old. Born February 22, 1989

Jesus to me is my rock and my shield. He protects me from harm. Jesus is my one and only Savior. Jesus died for me and you. He is always with me whether I'm at home, school or ballet. He is always with me. When I cry he is here for me. He is not just with Anne or Mom, He is always with me.

Jesus is the KING of the Universe. No one can take God's place. Jesus is beyond perfect. He never fails or breaks promises like I do. He is an unfailing everlasting God and I know that well. Jesus loves me so much I can't and never will be able to explain how much.

F. Y. Ewing

At some point past middle age, F. Y. Ewing would write of "a glorious reunion with those beloved departed ones, in that beautiful immortality, where there is no more sin, suffering or death—which result is to be alone reached through the grace of our dear Redeemer."

On February 12, 1880, F. Y. Ewing would add: "As I grow older I live more in the past, yet not without a very hopeful vision of that beautiful country "beyond the River."

A universal statement of an equal creation as truth is confirmed in the following verse:

There is neither

Jew nor Greek

There is neither

Slave nor Free

There is neither

Male nor Female

For you are all

One

in

Christ Jesus

—Galatians 3:28

Revolutionary Spirit

The cycle of life continues:

left to himself man is lost

in a hopeless labyrinth

of his own creation

but when awakened by the

refreshing and renewing breeze

that comes from Heaven

man's face turns to God

and through Jesus

he is found.

—William L. Brown, Jr., 1995

Postscript 8
Genealogy

In *The Scotch Irish in America,* Henry Jones Ford writes, "Andrew Jackson, James K. Polk, James Buchanan, Andrew Johnson, Chester A. Arthur and William McKinley are of Ulster ancestry. General Grant has Scotch ancestry on his father's side, Scotch-Irish on his mother's side. Benjamin Harrison, Grover Cleveland and Theodore Roosevelt have Scotch-Irish ancestry on the mother's side. The paternal ancestry of James Munroe and Rutherford B. Hayes goes to Scotland direct. Since Mr. Reid's book was published, the Presidency has been attained by Woodrow Wilson, whose presumably authorized biography in *Who's Who* states that he is Scotch-Irish on both sides."

The Ewing Family Members as listed in the *Ewing Genealogy,* by P. K. Ewing in 1919:

Rev. Finis Ewing, p. 58
Margaret Davidson Ewing, p. 58
W. L. D. Ewing, p. 59
Ephraim Brevard Ewing, p. 70
Finis Young (F. Y.) Ewing, p. 69
Robert C. Ewing, p. 70
Senator Thomas Ewing, Sr., p. 5
Thomas Ewing, Jr. (Civil War), p. 9-10
Rev. John Ewing, p. 11
Nathaniel Ewing, p. 15
William L. Ewing, p. 14-15
George Ewing (Valley Forge), p. 13
George Ewing (Texas Revolution), p. 17
Young Ewing, p. 51
Adlai Ewing Stevenson, p. 17

Adlai Ewing Stevenson, the Democratic candidate for U.S. President in 1952 and 1956, was the grandson of U.S. Vice President Adlai Ewing Stevenson, who served from 1893 to 1897. They were descendants of Ephraim Brevard's brother, Hugh Brevard, and Finis Ewing's cousin, Nathaniel Ewing.

Ephraim Brevard Ewing's daughter Anna would wed Francis Marion Cockrell of Warrensburg, Missouri, who served five terms as a U.S. senator in the post Civil War era. Their son Ewing Cockrell served in political office and as a judge in Missouri from 1905 to 1927, until becoming president of the U.S. Federation of Justice in 1928. In 1951 he was nominated for the Nobel Peace Prize. "…In 1944 [he] compiled a declaration of 'Ten Fundamental Peace Policies' that was published internationally and was approved by 65 government and industry leaders."[1] Ewing and 28 other nominees worldwide, including Nehru of India, lost out to prize winner Leon Jenhaux of France. Earlier in 1916, when Ewing Cockrell was a name known countywide but not yet worldwide, one family in Johnson County, Missouri, though not related, chose to name their son Ewing after Ewing Cockrell. The boy's middle name would be Marion, but this name was from his maternal grandfather John Marion Winders and not from Cockrell's father Francis Marion Cockrell.[2] When grown this young man would leave his parents farm and move to Kansas City, Missouri, where he would have a bright future. Ewing Marion Kauffman would eventually become a legend in pharmaceutical sales and major league baseball ownership. In death, he left a lasting legacy to his adopted city—the City of Fountains.

The Davidson and Brevard families of *Revolutionary Spirit* would be distantly related to James Madison and George Washington through the matrimony of the great niece (Mary Anna Morrison) of William Lee Davidson II and Alexander Brevard. Brevard and Davidson had married two of the daughters of John Davidson of Mecklenburg County, North Carolina, with a third daughter being the grandmother of Mary Anna.

Mary Anna would become the second wife of Thomas "Stonewall" Jackson of Civil War fame. The wedding ceremony would take place at Davidson College in Davidson, North Carolina, where Mary Anna's father served as the college president.

Jackson's cousin John G. Jackson had married Dolly Madison's sister Polly. This wedding took place at the Madison's home in Virginia and James Madison gave away the bride. Earlier George Steptoe Washington (George Washington's nephew) had married another of Dolly's sisters (Lucy) and subsequently Lucy and George Steptoe had hosted James and Dolly's wedding at Steptoe's Virginia estate, which was known as Harewood.

Postscript 9

The Declarations

The Mecklenburg Resolves

The Mecklenburg Resolves of May 31, 1775, appeared in the *South Carolina Gazette and Country Journal* on Tuesday, June 13, 1775, published in "Charles-Town," South Carolina, as follows:

Charlotte-Town, Mecklenburg County, May 31, 1775.

This day the Committee of this county met, and passed the following Resolves:

WHEREAS by an Address presented to his Majesty by both Houses of Parliament, in February last, the American colonies are declared to be in a state of actual rebellion, we conceive, that all laws and commissions confirmed by, or derived from the authority of the King or Parliament, are annulled and vacated, and the former civil constitution of these colonies, for the present, wholly suspended. To provide, in some degree, for the exigencies of this county, in the present alarming period, we deem it proper and necessary to pass the following Resolves, viz.

That all commissions, civil and military, heretofore granted by the Crown, to be exercised in these colonies, are null and void, and the constitution of each particular colony wholly suspended.

That the Provincial Congress of each province, under the direction of the great Continental Congress, is invested with all legislative and executive powers within their respective provinces; and that no other legislative or executive power, does, or can exist, at this time, in any of these colonies.

As all former laws are now suspended in this province, and the Congress have not yet provided others, we judge it necessary, for better preservation of good order, to form certain rules and regulations for the internal government of this county, until laws shall be provided for us by the Congress.

That the inhabitants of this county do meet on a certain day appointed by this Committee, and having formed themselves into nine companies, (to wit) eight in the county, and one in the town of Charlotte, do chuse a Colonel and other military officers, who shall hold and exercise their several powers by virtue of this choice, and independent of the Crown of Great-Britain, and former constitution of this province.

That for the better preservation of the peace and administration of justice, each of those companies do chuse from their own body, two discreet freeholders, who shall be empowered, each by himself and singly, to decide and determine all matters of controversy, arising within said company, under the sum of twenty shillings; and jointly and together, all controversies under the sum of forty shillings; yet so as that their decisions may admit of appeal to the Convention of the Select-Men of the county; and also that any one of these men, shall have power to examine and commit to confinement persons accused of pettit larceny.

That those two Select-Men, thus chosen, do jointly and together chuse from the body of their particular company, two persons properly qualified to act as Constables, who may assist them in the execution of their office.

That upon the complaint of any persons to either of these Select-Men, he do issue his warrant, directed to the Constable, commanding him to bring the aggressor before him or them, to answer said complaint.

That these eighteen Select-Men, thus appointed, do meet every third Thursday in January, April, July, and October, at the Court-House, in Charlotte, to hear and determine all matters of controversy, for sums exceeding forty shillings, also appeals; and in cases of felony, to commit the person or persons convicted thereof to close confinement, until the Provincial Congress shall provide and establish laws and modes of proceeding in all such cases.

That these eighteen Select-Men, thus convened, do chuse a Clerk, to record the transactions of said Convention, and that said clerk, upon the application of any person or persons aggrieved, do issue his warrant to one of the Constables of the company to which the offender belongs, directing said Constable to summons and warn said offender to appear before the Convention, at their next sitting, to answer the aforesaid complaint.

That any person making complaint upon oath, to the Clerk, or any member of the Convention, that he has reason to suspect, that any person or persons indebted to him, in a sum above forty shillings, intend clandestinely to withdraw from the county, without paying such debt, the Clerk or such member shall issue his warrant to the Constable, commanding him to take said person or persons into safe custody, until the next sitting of the Convention.

That when a debtor for a sum below forty shillings shall abscond and leave the county, the warrant granted as aforesaid, shall extend to any goods or chattels of said debtor, as may be found, and such goods or chattels be seized and held in custody by the Constable, for the space of thirty days; in which time, if the debtor fail to return and discharge the debt, the Constable shall return the warrant to one of the Select-Men of the company, where the goods are found, who, shall issue orders to the Constable to sell such a part of said goods, as shall amount to the sum due: That when the debt exceeds forty shillings, the return shall be made to the Convention, who shall issue orders for sale.

That all receivers and collectors of quit-rents, public and county taxes, do pay the same into the bands of the chairman of this Committee, to be by them disbursed as the public exigencies may require; and that such receivers and collectors proceed no further in their office, until they be approved of by, and have given to, this Committee, good and sufficient security, for a faithful return of such monies when collected.

That the Committee be accountable to the county for the application of all monies received from such public officers.

That all these officers hold their commissions during the pleasure of their several constituents.

That this Committee will sustain all damages that ever hereafter may accrue to all or any of these officers thus appointed, and thus acting, on account of their obedience and conformity to these Resolves.

That whatever person shall hereafter receive a commission from the Crown, or attempt to exercise any such commission heretofore received, shall be deemed an enemy to his country, and upon information being made to the Captain of the company in which he resides, the said company shall cause him to be apprehended, and conveyed before the two Select-Men of the said company, who, upon proof of the fact, shall commit him, the said offender, to safe custody, until the next sitting of the Committee, who shall deal with him as prudence may direct.

That any person refusing to yield obedience to the above Resolves, shall be considered equally criminal, and liable to the same punishment, as the offenders above last mentioned.

That these Resolves be in full force and virtue, until instructions from the Provincial Congress, regulating the jurisprudence of the province, shall provide otherwise, or the legislative body of Great-Britain, resign its unjust and arbitrary pretentions with respect to America.

That the eight militia companies in the county, provide themselves with proper arms and accoutrements, and hold themselves in readiness to execute the commands and directions of the General Congress of this province and this Committee.

That the Committee appoint Colonel Thomas Polk, and Doctor Joseph Kenedy, to purchase 300 lb. of powder, 600 lb. of lead, 1000 flints, for the use of the militia of this county, and deposit the same in such place as the committee may hereafter direct.

Signed by order of the Committee,

EPH. BREVARD, Clerk of the Committee.

The Declarations of Jefferson
and of the Congress

This section is excerpted from Julian P. Boyd's *The Papers of Thomas Jefferson* (Volume 1:315-19. 19 volumes, Princeton, 1950-74). Thomas Jefferson wrote:

I will state the form of the declaration as originally reported. The parts struck out by Congress shall be distinguished by a black line drawn under them; & those inserted by them shall be placed in the margin or in a concurrent column:

A Declaration by the representatives of the United states of America, in [General] Congress assembled

When in the course of human events it becomes necessary for one people to dissolve the political bands which have connected them with another, and to assume among the powers of the earth the separate & equal station to which the laws of nature and of nature's god entitle them, a decent respect to the opinions of mankind requires that they should declare the causes which impel them to the separation.

We hold these truths to be self evident: that all men are created equal; that they are endowed by their creator with ∧ [inherent and] inalienable rights; that among   ∧ certain
these are life, liberty & the pursuit of happiness: that to secure these rights, governments are instituted among ₁nen, deriving their just powers from the consent of the governed; that whenever any form of government becomes destructive of these ends, it is the right of the people to alter or to abolish it, & to institute new government, laying it's foundation on such principles, & organising it's powers in such form, as to them shall seem most likely to effect their safety & happiness. Prudence indeed will dictate that governments long established should not be changed for light & transient causes; and accordingly all experience hath shewn that mankind are more disposed to suffer while evils are sufferable than to

right themselves by abolishing the forms to which they are accustomed. But when a long train of abuses & usurpations [begun at a distinguished period and] pursuing invariably the same object, evinces a design to reduce them under absolute despotism it is their right, it is their duty to throw off such government, & to provide new guards for their future security. Such has been the patient sufferance of these colonies; & such is now the necessity which constrains them to _∧ [expunge] their former systems of government. The history of the present king of Great Britain is a history of _∧ [unremitting] injuries & usurpations, [among which appears no solitary fact to contradict the uniform tenor of the rest but all have] _∧ in direct object the establishment of an absolute tyranny over these states. To prove this let facts be submitted to a candid world [for the truth of which we pledge a faith yet unsullied by falsehood.]

_∧ alter

_∧ repeated

_∧ all having

He has refused his assent to laws the most wholsome & necessary for the public good.

He has forbidden his governors to pass laws of immediate & pressing importance, unless suspended in their operation till his assent should be obtained; & when so suspended, he has utterly neglected to attend to them.

He has refused to pass other laws for the accommodation of large districts of people, unless those people would relinquish the right of representation in the legislature, a right inestimable to them, & formidable to tyrants only.

He has called together legislative bodies at places unusual, uncomfortable, and distant from the depository of their public records, for the sole purpose of fatiguing them into compliance with his measures.

He has dissolved representative houses repeatedly [& continually] for opposing with manly firmness his invasions on the rights of the people.

He has refused for a long time after such dissolutions to cause others to be elected, whereby the legislative powers, incapable of annihilation, have returned to the people at large for their exercise, the state remaining in the mean time exposed to all the dangers of invasion from without & convulsions within.

He has endeavored to prevent the population of these states; for that purpose obstructing the laws for naturalization of foreigners, refusing to pass others to encourage their migrations hither, & raising the conditions of new appropriations of lands.

He has ∧ [suffered] the administration of justice [totally to cease in some of these states] ∧ refusing his assent to laws for establishing judiciary powers.   ∧ obstructed ∧ by

He has made [our] judges dependant on his will alone, for the tenure of their offices, & the amount & paiment of their salaries.

He has erected a multitude of new offices [by a self assumed power] and sent hither swarms of new officers to harrass our people and eat out their substance.

He has kept among us in times of peace standing armies [and ships of war] without the consent of our legislatures.

He has affected to render the military independant of, & superior to the civil power.

He has combined with others to subject us to a jurisdiction foreign to our constitutions & unacknoleged by our laws, giving his assent to their acts of pretended legislation for quartering large bodies of armed troops among us; for protecting them by a mock-trial from punishment for any murders which they should commit on the inhabitants of these states; for cutting off our trade with all parts of the world; for imposing taxes on us without our consent; for depriving us ∧ of the benefits   ∧ in many cases
of trial by jury; for transporting us beyond seas to be tried for pretended offences; for abolishing the free system of English laws in a neighboring province, establishing therein an arbitrary government, and enlarging it's boundaries, so as to render it at once an example and fit instrument for introducing the same absolute rule into these ∧ [states]; for taking away our charters, abol-   ∧ colonies
ishing our most valuable laws, and altering fundamentally the forms of our governments; for suspending our own legislatures, & declaring themselves invested with power to legislate for us in all cases whatsoever.

He has abdicated government here ∧ [withdrawing his governors, and declaring us out of his allegiance & protection.]   ∧ by declaring us out of his protection & waging war against us.

He has plundered our seas, ravaged our coasts, burnt our towns, & destroyed the lives of our people.

He is at this time transporting large armies of foreign

mercenaries to compleat the works of death, desolation & tyranny already begun with circumstances of cruelty and perfidy ∧ unworthy the head of a civilized nation.

_{∧ scarcely paralleled in the most barbarous ages, & totally}

He has constrained our fellow citizens taken captive on the high seas to bear arms against their country, to become the executioners of their friends & brethren, or to fall themselves by their hands.

He has ∧ endeavored to bring on the inhabitants of our frontiers the merciless Indian savages, whose known rule of warfare is an undistinguished destruction of all ages, sexes, & conditions [of existence.]

_{∧ excited domestic insurrections amongst us, & has}

[He has incited treasonable insurrections of our fellow-citizens, with the allurements of forfeiture & confiscation of our property.

He has waged cruel war against human nature itself, violating it's most sacred rights of life and liberty in the persons of a distant people who never offended him, captivating & carrying them into slavery in another hemisphere or to incur miserable death in their transportation thither. This piratical warfare, the opprobrium of *infidel* powers, is the warfare of the *Christian* king of Great Britain. Determined to keep open a market where *Men* should be bought & sold, he has prostituted his negative for suppressing every legislative attempt to prohibit or to restrain this execrable commerce. And that this assemblage of horrors might want no fact of distinguished die, he is now exciting those very people to rise in arms among us, and to purchase that liberty of which he has deprived them, by murdering the people on whom he also obtruded them: thus paying off former crimes committed against the *Liberties* of one people, with crimes which he urges them to commit against the *lives* of another.]

In every stage of these oppressions we have petitioned for redress in the most humble terms: our repeated petitions have been answered only by repeated injuries. A prince whose character is thus marked by every act which may define a tyrant is unfit to be the ruler of a ∧ people [who mean to be free. Future ages will scarcely believe that the hardiness of one man adventured, within the short compass of twelve years only, to lay a foundation so broad & so undisguised for tyranny over a people fostered & fixed in principles of freedom.]

_{∧ free}

Nor have we been wanting in attentions to our British brethren. We have warned them from time to time of attempts by their legislature to extend ∧ [a] jurisdiction over ∧ [these our states.] We have reminded them of the circumstances of our emigration & settlement here, [no one of which could warrant so strange a pretension: that these were effected at the expence of our own blood & treasure, unassisted by the wealth or the strength of Great Britain: that in constituting indeed our several forms of government, we had adopted one common king, thereby laying a foundation for perpetual league & amity with them: but that submission to their parliament was no part of our constitution, nor ever in idea, if history may be credited: and,] we ∧ appealed to their native justice and magnanimity ∧ [as well as to] the ties of our common kindred to disavow these usurpations which ∧ [were likely to] interrupt our connection and correspondence. They too have been deaf to the voice of justice & of consanguinity, [and when occasions have been given them, by the regular course of their laws, of removing from their councils the disturbers of our harmony, they have, by their free election, re-established them in power. At this very time too they are permitting their chief magistrate to send over not only souldiers of our common blood, but Scotch & foreign mercenaries to invade & destroy us. These facts have given the last stab to agonizing affection, and manly spirit bids us to renounce for ever these unfeeling brethren. We must endeavor to forget our former love for them, and to hold them as we hold the rest of mankind enemies in war, in peace friends. We might have been a free and a great people together; but a communication of grandeur & of freedom it seems is below their dignity. Be it so, since they will have it. The road to happiness & to glory is open to us too. We will tread it apart from them, and] ∧ acquiesce in the necessity which denounces our [eternal] separation ∧ !

∧ an unwarrantable
∧ us

∧ have
∧ and we have conjured them by
∧ would inevitably

∧ we must therefore

∧ and hold them as we hold the rest of mankind, enemies in war, in peace friends.

We therefore the representatives of the United states of America in General Congress assembled do in the name, & by the authority of the good people of these [states reject & renounce all allegiance & subjection to the kings of Great Britain & all others who may hereafter claim by, through or under them: we utterly dissolve all political connection which may heretofore have subsisted between us & the people or parliament of Great Britain: & finally we do assert & declare these colonies to be free & independant states,] & that as free & independant states, they have full power to levy war, conclude peace, contract alliances, establish commerce, & to do all other acts & things which independant states may of right do. And for the support of this declaration we mutually pledge to each other our lives, our fortunes & our sacred honour.

We therefore the representatives of the United states of America in General Congress assembled, appealing to the supreme judge of the world for the rectitude of our intentions, do in the name, & by the authority of the good people of these colonies, solemnly publish & declare that these United colonies are & of right ought to be free & independant states; that they are absolved from all allegiance to the British crown, and that all political connection between them & the state of Great Britain is, & ought to be, totally dissolved; & that as free & independant states they have full power to levy war, conclude peace, contract alliances, establish commerce & to do all other acts & things which independant states may of right do.
And for the support of this declaration, with a firm reliance on the protection of divine providence we mutually pledge to each other our lives, our fortunes & our sacred honour.

The following is called the Mecklenburg Declaration of Independence of May 20, 1775; however, it was actually written by John McKnitt Alexander, in an attempt to reconstruct the original (which was actually dated May 31st) after it had been destroyed in a fire in April 1800.

The Mecklenburg Declaration of Independence

Resolved, 1. That whoever directly or indirectly abetted, or in any way, form or manner, countenanced the unchartered and dangerous invasion of our rights, as claimed by Great Britain, is an enemy to this country, to America, and to the inherent, and inalienable rights of man.

Resolved, 2. That we, the citizens of Mecklenburg county, do hereby dissolve the political bands which have connected us to the mother country, and hereby absolve ourselves from all allegiance to the British Crown and abjure all political connection, contract, or association with that nation, who have wantonly trampled on our rights and liberties, and inhumanly shed the blood of American patriots at Lexington.

Resolved, 3. That we do hereby declare ourselves a free and independent people: are, and of right ought to be a sovereign, and self-governing association, under the control of no power, other than that of our God, and the general government of the congress; to the maintenance of which independence, we solemnly pledge to each other our mutual co-operation, our lives, our fortunes, and our most sacred honor.

Resolved, 4. That, as we acknowledge the existence and control of no law, or legal officer, civil or military, within this country, we do hereby ordain and adopt, as a rule of life, all, each, and every one of our former laws; wherein, nevertheless, the crown of Great Britain never can be considered as holding rights, privileges, immunities, or authority therein.

Resolved, 5. That it is also further decreed that all, each and every military officer in this county is hereby retained in his former command and authority, he acting conformably to these regulations. And that every member present of this delegation shall henceforth be a civil officer, viz: a justice of the peace, in the character of a committeeman, to issue process, hear and determine all matters of controversy, according to said adopted laws; and to preserve peace, union and harmony in said county; and to use every exertion to spread the love of country, and fire of freedom throughout America, until a more general and organized government be established in this province.

Reprinted from the Southern Historical Collection,
The Library of The University of North Carolina at Chapel Hill.

John McKnitt Alexander's written statement (dated
September 3, 1800), found in the mid-1800s with the Davie copy of
the Mecklenburg Declaration of May 20, 1775. In it he explains that
he wrote the declaration from memory after the April 6, 1800, fire in
which the original was destroyed.

Postscript 10

The North Carolina State Flag

The date given on the North Carolina state flag for the first Declaration of Independence is May 20, 1775. There has been speculation by some that the possibly mistaken date of May 20, 1775, given for the Mecklenburg Resolves was due to a continued usage of the Julian calendar by some colonists in North Carolina, even though the British Empire had officially converted to the Gregorian calendar in 1752. At that time, the difference between the two calendars was 11 days. Thus, if the Julian calendar was used to give the May 20, 1775 date, a switch to the Gregorian calendar would give the correct date of May 31, 1775. Though the date May 20, 1775 is of interest, the date May 31, 1775 is one of historical importance for the state of North Carolina and America.

Epilogue

The framers of the U.S. Constitution were in general recipients of a classical Christian education as it was the only education system available during the Colonial era. This education would give the future framers a detailed knowledge of Greece and Rome. In particular, they learned the history of these ancient governments.

They knew of Julius Caesar's rise to power and the details of his misuse of power. They knew standing armies were necessary for the security of nations, but they must be watched closely. They studied the government confederations of Greece such as the Achaen League (280–140 B.C.) and the Lucian League (200–43 B.C.), which failed due to inadequate federal power.

They also knew well that the simple participatory direct democracy of Athens was subject to grave disorder and mob rule. (Even Jefferson himself was distrustful of the electorate in the early 1780s—possibly because of his knowledge of this history).

They understood the histories of the mixed governments of Greece and Rome, which were mixed in the sense that an emperor might share power with a senate and/or a general assembly. The successes and failures of these governments could be understood in the light of how well or how poorly these mixes were balanced.

The ideas of seventeenth century Englishman James Harrington on mixed government were influential in America. Mixed governments originated to protect the vested interests of different factions of a society. For instance, the House of Lords represented the titled aristocracy of England in Parliament. In America there was no titled aristocracy, but there would be a talented and influential minority. Harrington's mixed government consisted of a senate of natural aristocracy (those with the most talent), a large assembly elected from the common people, and an executive to provide a balance of power.

John Adams believed that a bicameral (two house) legislature was important in that it would keep the representatives of the more powerful natural aristocracy separate from the representatives of the many. In a unicameral (one house) legislature he believed the representatives of the powerful few could more easily impose their will on the representatives of the many.

Adams pointed out that the downfall of Athen's unstable and short-lived democracy was the imbalance of the three orders of government. Adams believed that through a proper balancing of the president, the senate and the assembly; and through the modern innovations of representation, the separation of powers, and the veto power of each order, America could avoid the "tumultuous commotions like the raging waves of the sea" that plagued the popular assembly of Athens.

The U.S. Constitution created by the Federalists would be a hybrid of mixed government and representative democracy. Congress being the branch of government that was most democratic (as its representatives were elected directly by the people) was given the most power. Also, means were devised to give it some control over the other two less democratic branches.

The representatives of the U.S. House would be directly elected by the people (a pure representative democracy). The U.S. Senators would be elected by the state legislatures, who in turn were elected by the people (one step removed from representative democracy). The U.S. President would be elected by presidential electors who were appointed by the state legislatures who had been elected by the people (somewhat more removed from a representative democracy).

The U.S. Federal judges would be appointed by the President and approved by the U.S. Senate (the most removed from a representative democracy).

After Thomas Jefferson's election to the U.S. Presidency in 1800, the Republicans would successfully govern utilizing this same hybrid of mixed government and representative democracy. Jefferson's election was not a revolution that saved American government nor did it make him the patriot that saved the Revolution.

Though there were extremists on both sides, the war of words between the Federalists and the Republicans would not really change the political landscape appreciably. (The founders' intimate knowledge of the many intrigues of the classical era may have contributed to the mutual mistrust, hysteria, insecurity and exaggerated hype between the Federalists and Republicans during the 1790s).

Moderate Federalists eventually became moderate Republicans. The minority monarchial extremist Federalists gradually faded away. The issues of the state's rights extremist Republicans would grow, split the nation, and were finally extinguished by the Civil War. The Whigs would replace the Federalists and then be replaced by the new Republicans—the original Republicans would become the Democratic Party. Though not part of the framers' plan, the eventual formation of two major political parties provided an orderly system for the politics of democracy.

Over time the Founding Fathers' concern that America's representative democracy might repeat the failure of Athens' direct democracy gave way to increased confidence in the success of representative democracy.

In 1826 the first reform (under President John Quincy Adams) required the Electoral College to follow the popular vote of each state in presidential elections. The second reform in 1913 (under President Woodrow Wilson) was the Seventeenth Amendment, which provided for the direct election of U.S. Senators.

Currently the Supreme Court is probably too far removed from the direct vote of the people. Author Mark Levins suggested possibilities of giving congress a veto (2/3 majority of both houses required) over Supreme Court rulings with 12-year renewable terms for the judges would be worthy of a constitutional amendment. This third reform would likely bring the judicial branch of the federal government back into a more proper balance. A Supreme Court more accountable to the people would certainly give Thomas Jefferson a belated, but much needed, sigh of relief.

The experiment that formed America remains a work in progress (though people of faith have always seen Providence at work in this process). No one founding father could fulfill all of the roles necessary or have all the right answers to produce this American creation. The Founding Fathers wrote with posterity in mind, but in his memoirs and elsewhere, Thomas Jefferson didn't need to try to convince us that he had done everything. History shows that Jefferson's true accomplishments are more than enough to deserve America's most sincere appreciation.

Bibliography

A History of the City of Newark, N.J. Lewis Historical Publishing Co., New York, 1913.

A Recorded Tradition. Lexington, Missouri Historical Society, Missouri.

Adams, John. *The Works of John Adams.*

Andrae, Rolla P. *A True Brief History of Daniel Boone.* Miller Publishing, Washington, MO, 1985.

Arnow, Harriett Simpson. *The Flowering of the Cumberland.* University of Nebraska Press, Lincoln, 1963.

Babits, Lawrence E. *A Devil of a Whipping: The Battle of Cowpens.* The University of North Carolina, Chapel Hill, NC, 1998.

Bailyn, Bernard. *Pamphlets of the American Revolution, 1750-1776.* Belknap Press of Harvard University Press, Cambridge, MA, 1965.

Bainton, Roland H. *The Reformation of the Sixteenth Century.* Beacon Press, Boston, 1952.

Bancroft, George. *The History of the United States.* 7:370.

Barry, Louise. *The Beginning of the West.* Kansas State Historical Society, 1972.

Bateman, Newton, and Paul Selby, *Historical Encyclopedia of Illinois.* Munsell Publishing, Chicago, 1910.

Beaty, Mary D. *A History of Davidson College.* Briarpatch Press, Davidson, NC, 1988.

Beliles, Mark A., & Stephen K. McDowell, *America's Providential History.* Providence Foundation, Charlottesville, VA, 1989.

Bennett, William J., ed. *Our Sacred Honor.* Simon & Schuster, New York, 1997.

Benton, Thomas Hart. *Thirty Years View.* D. Appleton, New York, 1854-1856.

Bernstein, R. B. *Thomas Jefferson.* Oxford University Press, 2003.

Boyd, Julian. *The Declaration of Independence.*

Buchanan, John. *The Road to Guilford Courthouse.* John Wiley & Sons, New York, 1997.

Burnett, Edmond Cody. *The Continental Congress.* W. W. Norton, New York, 1964.

Cahill, Thomas. *How the Irish Saved Civilization.* Anchor Books Doubleday, New York, 1995.

Campbell, Thomas, and Milton L. Baughn, and Ben M. Barrus, *A People Called Cumberland Presbyterians.* Frontier Press, Memphis, TN, 1972.

Carver-Briggs, Noel, & Royston Gambier, *Huguenot Ancestry.* Chichester, Phillimore, 1985.

Chambers, William Nisbet. *Old Bullion Benton.* Little, Brown, Boston, 1956.

Clayton, W. W. *The History of Davidson County, Tennessee 1880.* Reproduced Charles Elder, Nashville, TN, 1971.

Cobb, Hubbard. *American Battlefields.* Macmillan, New York, 1995.

Commager, H. S., and R. B. Morris, eds., *The Spirit of Seventy-Six.* DaCapo Press, New York, 1995.

Cordry, Eugene Allen. *History of New Lebanon, Cooper County, Missouri.* VKM Publishing, Fort Worth, TX, 1976.

Cossitt, Rev. F. R. *The Life and Times of Finis Ewing.* Cumberland Presbyterian Church Archives, 1853.

Davidson, Chalmers G. "Early History about the Stevensons and Brevards (N.C.)." *The State Magazine,* August 1952.

Davidson, Chalmers Gaston. *Piedmont Partisan.* Davidson College, Davidson, NC, 1951.

Davidson, John. *William Lee Davidson Papers.* Davidson College Press, Davidson, NC.

Davidson, Marshall B. *The Horizon Concise History of France.* American Heritage Publishing, New York, 1971.

Devoto, Bernard. *Across the Wide Missouri.* Houghton Mifflin, Boston, 1947.

Dillon, Richard. *Captain John Sutter: Sacramento Valley's Sainted Sinner.* Western Tanager, Santa Cruz, 1981.

Donaldson, Gordon. *Scotland: The Shaping of a Nation.* David and Charles Publishers, London, 1974.

Dulles, Foster Rhea. *The United States since 1865.* University of Michigan Press, Ann Arbor, 1971.

Dunne, Gerald T. *The Missouri Supreme Court.* University of Missouri Press, Columbia, MO, 1993.

Eklund, Rev. Robert L. *Spiritual Awakening.* Home Mission Board of the Southern Baptist Convention, Atlanta, GA, 1989.

Ellis, Joseph J. *American Sphinx.* Alfred A. Knopf, New York, 1997.

Ellis, Joseph J. *The Founding Brothers.* Alfred A. Knopf, New York, 2001.

Ewing, Prestley Kittredge. *The Ewing Genealogy.* Hercules Printing and Book Company, Houston, TX, 1919.

Ewing, Robert C. *Aunt Peggy.* Cumberland Presbyterian Publishing House, 1876.

Eyre-Todd, George. *The Highland Clans of Scotland: Their History and Traditions.* Garnier, Charleston, SC, 1969.

Farrand, Max, ed. *Benjamin Franklin Memoirs.* 1936.

Fetter, Frank Whitson. *The Revision of the Declaration of Independence in 1941.*

Finch, Robert. *Introduction to A Sand County Almanac.* Brewster, Massachusetts, 1987.

Ford, Henry Jones. *The Scotch Irish in America.* Anchor Books, Hamden, CT, 1966.

Ford, Paul Leicester. *The Writings of Thomas Jefferson.* New York, 1892-1899.

Fosdick, Lucian. *The Huguenots in France.* Genealogical Publishing, Baltimore, MD, 1973.

Fuller, Edmund & David E. Greens, *God in the White House.* Crown Publishers, New York, 1968.

Gender and Justice Task Force Report.

George Washington Papers, 3b. Varik Transcripts, Letterbook 5. *The Writings of George Washington.* Vol. 13.

Graham, James. *The Life of General Daniel Morgan.* Zebrowski Historical Services Publishing Company, New York, 1993.

Griffin, Edward D., Sermon at MacWhorter's Funeral, July 22, 1807.

Hafen, LeRoy R., ed. *Mountain Men and the Fur Trade of the Far West.* Vol. 2. Arthur H. Clark, 1972, 1982.

Henderson, Archibald. *North Carolina: The Old North State and the New.* Lewis Publishing, Chicago, 1941.

Herman, Arthur. *How the Scots Invented the Modern World.* Crown Publishers, New York, 2001.

Herndon, William H., and Jesse W. Weik, *Herndon's Life of Lincoln.* DaCapo, New York, 1983.

Houghton, S. M. *Sketches from Church History.* The Banner of Truth Trust, Edinburgh, 1980.

Howard, Helen Addison. *The Saga of Chief Joseph.* University of Nebraska Press, Lincoln & London, 1941.

Howlett, D. R., ed. *The Confession of Saint Patrick.* Triumph Books, Liguori, MO, 1994.

Hoyte Papers, Southern Historical Collection, Library of the University of North Carolina at Chapel Hill, NC.

Hoyte, William Henry. *The Mecklenburg Declaration is Spurious.* G. P. Putnam & Sons, 1907.

Hughs, Kathleen. *The Irish World.* Harry N. Abrams, New York, 1977.

Hunter, C. L. *Sketches of Western North Carolina.* Regional Publishing, Baltimore, MD, 1970.

Hutcheson, Francis. *An Inquiry into the Origin of Our Ideas of Beauty and Virtue.* 1725.

Jefferson, Thomas. Inaugural Address.

Jefferson, Thomas. *Opinion on the Constitutionality of a National Bank.* February 15, 1791.

Jefferson, Thomas. *The Jefferson Bible.* Beacon Press, Boston, 1989.

Jefferson, Thomas. *The Writings of Thomas Jefferson (Library Edition).* Library of Congress.

Jensen, Merrill. *The Founding of a Nation.* Oxford University Press, London, 1968.

Jones, Colin. *Cambridge Illustrated History of France.* Cambridge University Press, 1994.

Journal of the Historical Society of Montana.

Kennedy, John F. *Profiles in Courage.* Harper and Row, New York, 1955.

Ketcham, Ralph. *James Madison: A Biography.* University of Virginia Press, Charlottesville, 1990.

King, Jr., Martin Luther. *I Have a Dream.* Edited by James Melvin Washington. Harper Collins, San Francisco, 1986.

Kohn, Bernice. *The Spirit and the Letter: The Struggle for Rights in America.* Viking Press, New York, 1974.

Kopper, Phillip. *Washington: Seasons of the Capitol.* Elliott & Clark, Washington, D.C., 1992.

Lavender, David. *The Great West.* Houghton Mifflin.

Leckie, Robert. *George Washington's War.* HarperCollins, New York, 1992.

Lee, General Henry. *The Revolutionary War Memoirs of General Henry Lee.* DaCapo Press, New York, 1998.

Lee, Richard Henry. *Record of the Continental Congress, July 2, 1776.* Journals of the Continental Congress.

Leibiger, Stuart. *Founding Friendship.* University of Virginia Press, Charlottesville, 1999.

Levon, Jacques. *History of France.* Leon Amial Publishing, New York.

Leyburn, James G. *The Scotch Irish: A Social History.* University of North Carolina Press, Chapel Hill, 1962.

Linder, Usher F. *Reminiscences of the Early Bench and Bar of Illinois.* Chicago Legal News Company, Chicago, 1879.

Lipscomb, Andrew A., and Albert Ellery Bergh, *The Writings of Thomas Jefferson.* Thomas Jefferson Memorial Association, Washington, D.C., 1903.

Maclean, Fitzroy. *A Concise History of Scotland.* Thames and Hudson, London, 1970.

Maier, Pauline. *American Scripture.* Alfred A. Knopf, New York, 1997.

Malone, Dumas, ed. *Dictionary of American Biography.* Charles Scribner's Sons, New York, 1931.

Malone, Dumas. *Thomas Jefferson and His Time: The Sage of Monticello.* Little Brown, Boston, 1981.

Martin, Josiah. *Almon's Remembrancer.* August 8, 1775.

Martin, Josiah. *Colonial Records of North Carolina.*

McCullough, David. *John Adams.* Simon & Schuster, New York, 2001.

McLuhan, T. C. *Touch the Earth.* Promontory Press, New York, 1971.

McNitt, V. V. *Chain of Error and the Mecklenburg Declaration of Independence.* Hampton Hills Press, Palmer, MA, & New York, 1960.

Merrill, Jr., Boynton. *Jefferson's Nephews: A Frontier Tragedy.* Princeton University Press, Princeton, NJ, 1976.

Meyers, William Starr. *The Story of New Jersey.* Lewis Historical Publishing Co., New York.

Missouri Historical Review.

Missouri Supreme Court Journal. Summer 1993.

Mitchison, Rosalind. *A History of Scotland.* Methuen, London, 1970.

Monaghan, Jay. *Civil War on the Western Border, 1854-1865.* University of Nebraska Press, Lincoln.

Morgan, Anne. *Prescription for Success – The Life and Values of Ewing Marion Kauffman.* Andrews & McMeel, Kansas City, MO, 1995.

Morgan, Edmund S. *The Birth of the Republic.* University of Chicago Press, Chicago & London, 1956.

Murphy, Rev. Owen. *When God Stepped Down from Heaven.*

Nies, Judith. *Native American History.* Ballantine Books, New York, 1996.

Nofi, Albert A. *The Alamo and the Texas War for Independence.* DaCapo Press, New York, 1994.

Noll, Hatch and Marsden, *The Search for Christian America.*

Oberdorfer, Don. *Princeton University: The First 250 Years.* Trustees of Princeton University, Princeton, NJ.

Official Manual of the State of Missouri, *Journal of the Missouri Supreme Court* 1:1, 2 1986.

Official Manual of the State of Missouri: Missouri Supreme Court Records.

Oregon Historical Quarterly. March 1958.

Patterson, Edith Meyer. *Petticoat Patriots of the American Revolution.* Vanguard Press, New York, 1976.

Patterson, Rev. R. *Biography of Rev. John Ewing.* 2 vols., 1809.

Peden, William, ed. *Notes on the State of Virginia.* University of North Carolina Press, Chapel Hill, 1955.

Pennsylvania Evening Post. April 26, 1777.

Powell, William S. *North Carolina: A History.* University of North Carolina Press, Chapel Hill, 1977.

Powell, William S., ed. *Biographical Dictionary of North Carolina.* University of North Carolina Press, Chapel Hill, 1979.

Quisenberry, A. C. *Kentucky in the War of 1812.* Genealogical Publications, Baltimore, MD, 1969.

Remini, Robert V. *The Life of Andrew Jackson.* Penguin Books, New York, 1988.

Richard, Carl J. *The Founders and the Classics.* Harvard University Press, Cambridge, MA, 1995.

Risjord, Norman K. *Thomas Jefferson.* Madison House, Madison, WI, 1994.

Roeder, Richard B. *Montana: A History of Two Centuries.* University of Washington Press, 1976.

Roosevelt, Theodore. *Thomas Hart Benton.* Haskell House Publishers, 1968.

Scottish World. Harry Abrams, New York, 1981.

Shackford, James Atkins. *David Crockett: The Man and the Legend.* University of Nebraska Press, Lincoln & London, 1994.

Simon, James F. *What Kind of Nation.* Simon & Schuster, New York, 2002.

Smith, Elbert B. *Magnificent Missourian.* J. B. Lippincott, New York, 1958.

Smith, Page. *A New Age Begins Now.* McGraw-Hill, New York.

Smith, Page. *John Adams.* Vols. 1 & 2. Doubleday, New York, 1962.

Smith, Rev. James. *History of the Cumberland Presbyterian Church.*

Somerset Fry, Peter & Fiona Somerset Fry, *The History of Scotland.* Rutledge Press, New York & London, 1982.

Stamp, Kenneth M., ed. *The Causes of the Civil War.* Prentice-Hall, Englewood Cliffs, NJ, 1959.

Stephens, John Vant. *The Genesis of the Cumberland Presbyterian Church.* Lane Seminary Building, Cincinnati, OH, 1941.

Tarleton, Banastre. *A History of the Campaigns of 1780 and 1781 in the Southern Provinces of North America.*

Temple, Wayne C. *Abraham Lincoln: From Skeptic to Prophet.* Mayhaven Publishing, Mohomet, IL, 1995.

Temple, Wayne C. *The Quill of the Cumberland Presbyterian Church Archives.* Winter 1985.

Theobald, Francoise, ed. *A History of Women.* Harvard University Press, 1994.

Thompson, Dr. Charles Lemuel. *The Presbyterians.* Baker & Taylor, New York, 1903.

Van Doren, Carl. *Benjamin Franklin.* Penguin Books, 1938.

Wertenbaker, Thomas Jefferson. *Princeton 1746-1896.* Princeton University Press, Princeton, NJ, 1946.

Wheeler, John H. *Historical Sketches of North Carolina.* Regional Publishing, Baltimore, MD, 1974.

Williams, John Hoyte. *Sam Houston: A Biography of the Father of Texas.* Simon & Schuster, New York, 1993.

Wills, Garry. *A Necessary Evil, A History of American Distrust of Government.* Simon & Schuster, New York, 1999.

Wills, Garry. *Inventing America: Jefferson's Declaration of Independence.* Doubleday, New York, 1978.

Wills, Garry. *James Madison.* Henry Holt & Co., New York, 2002.

Wills, Garry. *Under God.* Simon & Schuster, New York, 1990.

Wilson, Douglas L. *Honor's Voice: The Transformation of Abraham Lincoln.* Alfred A. Knopf, New York, 1998.

Withers, W. A. *Biographical History of North Carolina.* Edited by Samuel Ashe. 1905.

Suggested Readings

Chief Joseph

Howard, Helen Addison. *The Saga of Chief Joseph.* University of Nebraska Press, Lincoln & London, 1941.

Christian

Beliles, Mark A., & Stephen K. McDowell. *America's Providential History.* Providence Foundation, Charlottesville, VA, 1989.

Bennett, William, ed. *Our Sacred Honor.* Simon & Schuster, New York, 1997.

Cahill, Thomas. *How the Irish Saved Civilization.* Anchor Books Doubleday, New York, 1995.

Civil Rights

King, Jr., Martin Luther. *I Have a Dream.* Edited by James Melvin Washington. Harper-San Francisco, San Francisco, 1986.

Davy Crockett

Shackford, James Atkins. *David Crockett: The Man and the Legend.* University of Nebraska Press, Lincoln & London, 1994.

Sam Houston

Williams, John Hoyte. *Sam Houston: A Biography of the Father of Texas.* Simon & Schuster, New York, 1993.

Andrew Jackson

Remini, Robert V. *The Life of Andrew Jackson.* Penguin Books, New York, 1988.

Thomas Jefferson & The Declaration of Independence

Ellis, Joseph J. *American Sphinx.* Alfred A. Knopf, New York, 1997.

Maier, Pauline. *American Scripture.* Alfred A. Knopf, New York, 1997.

Risjord, Norman K. *Thomas Jefferson.* Madison House, Madison, WI, 1994.

Wills, Garry. *Inventing America: Jefferson's Declaration of Independence.* Doubleday, Garden City, NJ, 1978.

For selected comments, see the following:

The Jefferson Bible. Introduction, F. Forrester Church; afterword, Jaroslav Pelikan. Beacon Press, 1989.

Ellis, Joseph. *American Sphinx.* Alfred A. Knopf, New York, 1997. 101-103, 111, 300.

McCullough, David. *John Adams.* Simon & Schuster, New York, 2001. 313, 314, 521.

Abraham Lincoln

Temple, Wayne C. *Abraham Lincoln: From Skeptic to Prophet.* Mayhaven Publishing, Mohamet, IL, 1995.

Wilson, Douglas. *Honor's Voice: The Transformation.* Alfred A. Knopf, New York, 1998.

Revolutionary War

Buchanan, John. *The Road to Guilford Courthouse.* John Wiley & Sons, New York, 1997.

Cobb, Hubbard. *American Battlefields.* MacMillan, USA, 1995.

Commager, H. S., & R. B. Morris, eds. *The Spirit of Seventy-Six.* DaCapo Press, New York, 1995.

Leckie, Robert. *George Washington's War.* HarperCollins, New York, 1992.

Morgan, Edmund S. *The Birth of the Republic.* University of Chicago Press, Chicago & London, 1956.

Influence of Classical History in America

Richard, Carl J. *The Founders and the Classics.* Harvard University Press, Cambridge, MA, 1995.

Endnotes

Introduction
[1] Mark A. Beliles and Stephen K. McDowell, *America's Providential History* (Charlottesville: Providence Foundation, 1989), 141.

Chapter 1
[1] D. R. Howlett, *The Confession of Saint Patrick* (Missouri: Triumph Books, 1994), 46-47.

[2] Thomas Cahill, *How the Irish Saved Civilization* (New York: Anchor Books, Doubleday, 1995), 102.

[3] Howlett, 70.

[4] Cahill, 105, 109, 114.

[5] Kathleen Hughs, *The Irish World* (New York: Harry Abrams, 1977), 57.

[6] Cahill, 110-11.

[7] *Scottish World* (New York: Harry Abrams, 1981), 50.

[8] Peter and Fiona Somerset Fry, *The History of Scotland* (New York & London: Rutledge Press, 1982), 78.

[9] *Scottish World,* 71.

[10] Somerset Fry, 78.

[11] Rosalind Mitchison, *A History of Scotland* (London: Methuen, 1970), 43.

[12] Gordon Donaldson, *Scotland: The Shaping of a Nation* (London: David and Charles Publishers, 1974), 36.

[13] Roland H. Bainton, *The Reformation of the Sixteenth Century* (Boston: Beacon Press, 1952), 57.

[14] Somerset Fry, 129.

[15] James G. Leyburn, *The Scotch Irish: A Social History* (Chapel Hill: University of North Carolina Press, 1962), 111.

[16] Prestley Kittredge Ewing, *The Ewing Genealogy* (Houston: Hercules Printing & Book Company, 1919), 3-4.

[17] George Eyre-Todd, *The Highland Clans of Scotland: Their History and Traditions* (Charleston: Garnier, 1969), 68-69, 406-407.

[18] William S. Powell, *The Biographical Dictionary of North Carolina* (Chapel Hill: University of North Carolina Press, 1979), 27-28.

[19] Lucian Fosdick, *The Huguenots in France* (Baltimore, MD: Genealogical Publishing, 1973), 25-38.

[20] S. M. Houghton, *Sketches from Church History* (Edinburgh: The Banner of Truth Trust, 1980), 131.

[21] Fosdick, 41, 43.

[22] Noel Carver-Briggs and Royston Gambier, *Huguenot Ancestry* (Phillimore: Chichester, 1985), 1, 31.

[23] Houghton, 137.

[24] Leyburn, 128, 157-58.

Chapter 2

[1] Leyburn, 210.

[2] Ibid., 215.

[3] William S. Powell, *North Carolina: A History* (Chapel Hill & London: University of North Carolina Press, 1977), 51.

[4] Ibid., 61.

[5] Letter from Thomas Jefferson to William Small, May 7, 1775, *The Thomas Jefferson Papers Series 1*. Library of Congress.

[6] V. V. McNitt, *Chain of Error and the Mecklenburg Declaration of Independence* (New York: Hampton Hills Press, 1960), 38.

[7] John Davidson, *William Lee Davidson Papers* (Davidson, NC: Davidson College Press).

[8] William Henry Hoyte, *The Mecklenburg Declaration is Spurious* (G. P. Putnam's Son, 1907), 64.

[9] Archibald Henderson, *North Carolina: The Old North State and the New* (Chicago: Lewis Publishing, 1941), 294-98.

[10] Powell, 62.

[11] John Wheeler, *Historical Sketches of North Carolina* (Baltimore, MD: Regional Publishing, 1974), 372.

[12] Powell, 62.

[13] Ibid., 65.

[14] Paul Leicester Ford, *The Writings of Thomas Jefferson,* 10 vols. (New York, 1892-1899), 10:267-68.

[15] Hoyte, 1-5.

[16] John Adams, *Works of Adams,* 10:380-81.

[17] Ford, *Thomas Jefferson,* 10:136-39.

[18] Letter from John Adams to Thomas Jefferson, July 21, 1819.

[19] Hoyte, 14-15.

[20] Josiah Martin, *Almon's Remembrancer,* August 8, 1775.

[21] Peter Force quoted from Hoyte, 18.

[22] Ibid., 28-29.

[23] Josiah Martin, *Colonial Records of North Carolina,* 10:41-50.

[24] Hoyte, 143.

[25] Edmond Cody Burnett, *The Continental Congress* (New York: W. W. Norton, 1964), 54, 61.

[26] Hoyte, 22, 25.

[27] Ibid., 49.

[28] Garry Wills, *Inventing America: Jefferson's Declaration of Independence* (New York: Doubleday, 1978), 176.

[29] Norman K. Risjord, *Thomas Jefferson* (Madison, WI: Madison House, 1994), 4.

[30] Ibid., 6.

[31] W. A. Withers, *Biographical History of North Carolina,* Samuel Ashe, ed., 8 vols. (1905), 389-90.

[32] Powell, *History,* 66-67.

[33] Don Oberdorfer, *Princeton University: The First 250 Years* (Princeton, NJ: Trustees of Princeton University), 10-11.

[34] Thomas Jefferson Wertenbaker, *Princeton 1746-1896* (Princeton, NJ: Princeton University Press, 1946), 111-12.

[35] Arthur Herman, *How the Scots Invented the Modern World* (New York: Crown Publishers, 2001), 202-203.

[36] Wertenbaker, 23.

[37] Herman, 204, 207.

[38] Oberdorfer, 42.

[39] Wertenbaker, 94.

[40] Wills, *Inventing America,* 201.

[41] Bernard Bailyn, *Pamphlets of the American Revolution, 1750-1776* (Cambridge, MA: Belknap Press of Harvard University Press, 1965), 32.

[42] Wills, *Inventing America,* 217.

[43] Francis Hutcheson, *An Inquiry into the Origin of our Ideas of Beauty and Virtue* (1725).

[44] Wills, *Inventing America,* 207-9, 211.

[45] Ibid., 84.

[46] Ibid., 84.

[47] Hoyte, 28-29.

[48] Wills, *Inventing America,* 216-17, 290-91.

[49] Ford, *Thomas Jefferson,* 10:343.

[50] John Adams, *The Works of John Adams,* 2:514n Lucas.

[51] Ibid., 10:380-81.

[52] Robert Finch, *Introduction to A Sand County Almanac* (Massachusetts: Brewster, 1987), xxii.

[53] Richard Henry Lee, *Record of the Continental Congress, July 2, 1776.*

Chapter 3

[1] Burnett, 198-99, 204.

[2] Edmund S. Morgan, *The Birth of the Republic* (Chicago: University of Chicago Press, 1956), 78, 80-82, 84-85.

[3] John Buchanan, *The Road to Guilford Courthouse* (New York: John Wiley & Sons, 1997), 150, 152, 153, 155, 172.

[4] Henderson, 346.

[5] Buchanan, 133, 190-91, 194, 206-8, 213, 232, 242.

[6] Chalmers Gaston Davidson, *Piedmont Partisan* (Davidson, NC: Davidson College, 1951), 85-86.

[7] Robert Leckie, *George Washington's War* (New York: HarperCollins, 1992), 588-89.

[8] Henderson, 353.

[9] Davidson, *Partisan,* 89-91.

[10] Morgan, 85.

[11] Leckie, 595.

[12] Henderson, 356-58.

[13] Davidson, *Partisan,* 104-7.

[14] Buchanan, 285, 315-18.

[15] James Graham, *The Life of General Daniel Morgan* (New York: Zebrowski Historical Services Publishing Company, 1993), 296.

[16] Lawrence E. Babits, *A Devil of a Whipping: The Battle of Cowpens* (Chapel Hill: The University of North Carolina, 1998), 106-9.

[17] Graham, 321.

[18] Henderson, 358.

[19] Leckie, 606.

[20] Buchanan, 343-44.

[21] Leckie, 606-8.

[22] Davidson, 122.

[23] Leckie, 608.

[24] Morgan, 85.

[25] Leckie, 630-31.

[26] Risjord, 40-41.

[27] David McCullough, *John Adams* (New York: Simon & Schuster, 2001), 314.

[28] Risjord, 46-47.

[29] Morgan, 85-86.

[30] C. L. Hunter, *Sketches of Western North Carolina* (Baltimore, MD: Regional Publishing, 1970), 232-39.

[31] Chalmers G. Davidson, "Early History about the Stevensons and Brevards (N.C.)," *State Magazine,* August 16, 1952.

[32] Edward D. Griffin, Sermon at MacWhorter's Funeral, July 22, 1807.

[33] *A History of the City of Newark, N.J.* (New York: Lewis Historical Publishing Co., 1913), 1:271-72; Noll, Hatch and Marsden, *The Search for Christian America*

[34] *Pennsylvania Evening Post,* April 26, 1777. *Dictionary of American Biography,* Dumas Malone, ed. (New York: Charles Scribner's Sons, 1930-1931), 6:175.

[35] *A History of the City of Newark, N.J.,* 273-74.

[36] William Starr Meyers, *The Story of New Jersey* (New York: Lewis Historical Publishing Co.), 1:299-300.

[37] Davidson, *Partisan.*

[38] Rev. R. Patterson, *Biography of Rev. John Ewing* 2 vols., 1809.

[39] Ewing, *Genealogy,* 13.

[40] McCullough, *John Adams,* 313-14.

[41] W. W. Clayton, *The History of Davidson County, Tennessee (1880)* (Nashville: Reproduced by Charles Elder, 1971), 139-41.

[42] Withers, 391.

[43] General Henry Lee, *The Revolutionary War Memoirs of General Henry Lee* (New York: DaCapo Press, 1998), 586.

[44] Charles Royster, Introduction to Lee, *The Revolutionary War Memoirs of General Henry Lee* (New York: DaCapo Press, 1998), i-vii.

[45] H. S. Commager and R. B. Morris, eds., *The Spirit of Seventy-Six* (New York: DaCapo Press, 1995), 1195.

Chapter 4

[1] Rolla P. Andrae, *A True Brief History of Daniel Boone* (Washington, MO: Miller Publishing, 1985), 59.

[2] Harriet Simpson Arnow, *The Flowering of the Cumberland* (Lincoln: University of Nebraska Press, 1963), 376-77.

[3] Clayton, 44.

[4] Robert C. Ewing, *Aunt Peggy* (Cumberland Presbyterian Publishing House, 1876), 15-18.

[5] Reverend F. R. Cossitt, D.D., *The Life and Times of Finis Ewing* (Cumberland Presbyterian Church, 1853), 23-29.

[6] John Vant Stephens, *The Genesis of the Cumberland Presbyterian Church* (Cincinnati, OH: Lane Seminary Building, 1941), 22-25.

[7] *A Recorded Tradition* (Missouri: Lexington, Missouri Historical Society).

[8] Thomas Hart Benton, *Thirty Years View* (New York: Appleton, 1856), 737.

[9] Finis Ewing, Letter to Andrew Jackson, October 14, 1828, Andrew Jackson Papers.

[10] Robert V. Remini, *The Life of Andrew Jackson* (New York: Penguin Books, 1988), 162-63.

[11] Andrew Jackson, Letter to Finis Ewing, November 17, 1828, Andrew Jackson Papers.

[12] Remini, 170-71, 340.

[13] Wayne C. Temple, *Abraham Lincoln: From Skeptic to Prophet* (Mohomet, IL: Mayhaven Publishing, 1995), 38.

[14] Remini, 340-41, 356, 358.

[15] Clayton, 137, 159.

[16] Hubbard Cobb, *American Battlefields* (New York: Macmillan, 1995), 96-110.

[17] Ibid., 112.

[18] Kentucky Historical Society

[19] A. C. Quisenberry, *Kentucky in the War of 1812* (Baltimore, MD: Genealogical Publishing, 1969), 88.

[20] Finis Ewing, Letter to General Andrew Jackson, November 24, 1813, Andrew Jackson Papers.

[21] Remini, 6.

[22] Cobb, 118.

[23] Remini, 3-4.

[24] Clayton, 162.

[25] Albert A. Nofi, *The Alamo and the Texas War for Independence* (New York: DaCapo Press, 1994), 54-56.

[26] John Hoyte Williams, *Sam Houston: A Biography of the Father of Texas* (New York: Simon & Schuster, 1993), 161.

[27] Nofi, 55.

[28] James Atkins Shackford, *David Crockett: The Man and the Legend* (Lincoln: University of Nebraska Press, 1994), 168.

[29] Pauline Maier, *American Scripture* (New York: Alfred A. Knopf, 1997), 184-85.

[30] William Peden, ed., *Notes on the State of Virginia* (Chapel Hill: University of North Carolina Press, 1955), 162-63.

[31] Boynton Merrill Jr., *Jefferson's Nephews: A Frontier Tragedy* (Princeton: Princeton University Press, 1976), 256-57, 270-71, 293-97, 301, 325-26.

[32] Dumas Malone, *Thomas Jefferson and His Time: The Sage of Monticello* (Boston: Little Brown, 1981), 511-12.

[33] Letter from Thomas Jefferson to William Short, April 13, 1820. *The Writings of Thomas Jefferson,* Lipscomb and Bergh, eds., (Thomas Jefferson Memorial Association, 1903), 15:244.

[34] Letter from Thomas Jefferson to William Short, October 31, 1819. *The Writings of Thomas Jefferson,* Lipscomb and Bergh, eds., (Thomas Jefferson Memorial Association, 1903), 15:221.

[35] Ewing, *Aunt Peggy,* 91-92.

[36] Eugene Allen Cordry, *History of New Lebanon, Cooper County, Missouri* (Fort Worth, TX: VKM Publishing, 1976), 51.

[37] Rev. Finis Ewing, Letter dated May 22, 1822, Cumberland Presbyterian Church Archives, Memphis, TN.

[38] Campbell, Baughn, and Barrus, *A People Called Cumberland Presbyterians* (Memphis, TN: Frontier Press, 1972), 148.

[39] Joseph J. Ellis, *The Founding Brothers* (New York: Alfred A. Knopf, 2001), 118-19.

[40] *A History of Rev. Finis Ewing,* condensed from Cossitt, and from Rev. James Smith, *A History of the Cumberland Presbyterian Church,* 41-42. Cumberland Presbyterian Archives, Memphis, TN.

[41] Cordry, 36.

[42] Cossitt, 273, 289.

[43] Newton Bateman and Paul Selby, *Historical Encyclopedia of Illinois* (Chicago: Munsell Publishing, 1910), 160.

[44] Douglas L. Wilson, *Honor's Voice: The Transformation of Abraham Lincoln* (New York: Alfred A. Knopf, 1998), 145, 167.

[45] Usher F. Linder, *Reminiscences of the Early Bench and Bar of Illinois* (Chicago: Chicago Legal News Company, 1879), 62-63.

[46] Bateman and Selby, 160.

[47] *A Recorded Tradition* (Lexington, MO: Lexington Missouri Historical Society).

Chapter 5

[1] Maier, 202-3.

[2] Temple, 36, 40-41, 56, 58-59, 284-85.

[3] Maier, 205, 207.

[4] Joseph J. Ellis, *American Sphinx* (New York: Alfred A. Knopf, 1997), 264-65.

[5] John F. Kennedy, *Profiles in Courage* (New York: Harper & Row, 1955), 101.

[6] *Missouri Historical Review* 39:327-31.

[7] William Nisbet Chambers, *Old Bullion Benton* (Boston: Little, Brown, 1956), 144.

[8] Elbert B. Smith, *Magnificent Missourian* (New York: J. B. Lippincott, 1958), 322.

[9] Theodore Roosevelt, *Thomas Hart Benton* (Haskell House Publishers, 1968), brief excerpts.

[10] Smith, *Missourian,* 322, 325.

[11] Chambers, 427.

[12] Kennedy, 99.

[13] Official Manual of the State of Missouri, *Journal of the Missouri Supreme Court* 1:1, 2 (1986).

[14] Jay Monaghan, *Civil War on the Western Border 1854-1865* (Lincoln: University of Nebraska Press), 170, 182, 251.

[15] Richard B. Roeder, *Montana: A History of Two Centuries* (University of Washington Press, 1976), 153.

[16] Monaghan, 281, 289, 298, 306-7, 346, 348-49.

[17] Official Manual of the State of Missouri: Missouri Supreme Court Records.

[18] *Missouri Historical Review* (October 1906-July 1907), 1:110-15.

[19] *Missouri Historical Review* 1:117-18.

[20] *Missouri Historical Review* 68:338-39.

[21] Foster Rhea Dulles, *The United States since 1865* (Ann Arbor: University of Michigan Press, 1971), 131, 179-80.

[22] Mary D. Beaty, *A History of Davidson College* (Davidson, NC: Briarpatch Press, 1988), 233.

[23] Dulles, 211-12.

[24] Martin Luther King, Jr., *I Have a Dream,* James Melvin Washington, ed. (San Francisco: HarperCollins, 1986), 102-6, 111.

[25] Ibid.

[26] Remini, 219.

[27] Shackford, 116.

[28] Helen Addison Howard, *The Saga of Chief Joseph* (Lincoln: University of Nebraska Press, 1941), 21, 23, 28-29, 31-32, 37-38.

[29] Bernard Devoto, *Across the Wide Missouri* (Boston: Houghton Mifflin, 1947), 353-54.

[30] Richard Dillon, *Captain John Sutter: Sacramento Valley's Sainted Sinner* (Santa Cruz: Western Tanager, 1981), 56.

[31] LeRoy R. Haten, ed., *Mountain Men and Fur Traders of the Far West* (Arthur H. Clark Company, 1972), 2:378-79, 361.

[32] Howard, book cover.

[33] T. C. McLuhan, *Touch the Earth* (New York: Promontory Press, 1971), 123-24.

[34] Judith Nies, *Native American History* (New York: Ballantine Books, 1966), 367, 374-75, 380, 397-98.

[35] Gerald T. Dunne, *The Missouri Supreme Court* (Columbia, MO: University of Missouri Press, 1993), 80-82.

[36] Edith Patterson Meyer, *Petticoat Patriots of the American Revolution* (New York: Vanguard Press, 1976), 132.

[37] Hunter, 142-46.

[38] Bernice Kohn, *The Spirit and the Letter: The Struggle for Rights in America* (New York: Viking Press, 1974), 126.

[39] Missouri Public Library Archives, Kansas City.

[40] *Gender and Justice Task Force Report,* 16.

[41] *Missouri Supreme Court Journal* Vol. 5, No. 1, Summer 1993.

Chapter 6

[1] Phillip Kopper, *Washington: Seasons of the Capitol* (Washington, D.C.: Elliott & Clark, 1992), 17, 21, 53.

[2] Maier, 210-12.

[3] Wills, *Inventing America,* 167, 169, 180-81, 191.

[4] Somerset Fry, 135; and McNitt, 117.

[5] George Bancroft, *The History of the United States,* 7:370.

[6] Banastre Tarleton, *A History of the Campaigns of 1780 and 1781 in the Southern Provinces of North America,* 160.

Postscript 1

[1] Henry Jones Ford, *The Scotch Irish in America* (Hamden, CT: Anchor Books, 1966), 475-77.

[2] Ellis, *American Sphinx,* 107-8.

[3] Ibid., 109.

Postscript 2

[1] Herman, 63, 70.

[2] Somerset Fry, 188.

[3] Ibid., 224.

Postscript 3

[1] Hoyte Papers #3410, tol 247, Southern Historical Collection, Library of the University of North Carolina at Chapel Hill.

[2] *Journals of the Continental Congress,* 21:1103-4.

[3] George Washington Papers, 3b. Varik Transcripts, Letterbook 5, image 21, 23-25.

[4] *The Writings of George Washington,* Vol. 13.

[5] Ibid.

[6] Letter from William Lee Davidson to General Sumner, October 10, 1780. William Lee Davidson Papers, Davidson College, Davidson, NC.

[7] Letter from William Sharpe to William Lee Davidson, November 9, 1780. William Lee Davidson Papers, Davidson College, Davidson, NC.

[8] Letter from Thomas Jefferson to Horatio Gates, February 17, 1781. *The Thomas Jefferson Papers Series 1.* Library of Congress.

[9] Ellis, *American Sphinx,* 300-1.

[10] R. B. Bernstein, *Thomas Jefferson* (Oxford University Press, 2003). 192.

[11] Wills, *Inventing America,* 352.

[12] Stuart Leibiger, *Founding Friendship* (Charlottesville: University of Virginia Press, 1999), 58.

[13] Ibid., 97.

[14] Ralph Ketcham, *James Madison: A Biography* (Charlottesville: University of Virginia Press, 1990), 671.

[15] Wills, *Inventing America,* 356.

[16] Letter from Thomas Jefferson to John Adams, November 13, 1787. *The Thomas Jefferson Papers Series 1.* Library of Congress.

[17] Garry Wills, *A Necessary Evil, A History of American Distrust of Government* (New York: Simon & Schuster, 1999), 73-4.

[18] Thomas Jefferson, *Opinion on the Constitutionality of a National Bank,* February 15, 1791.

[19] Garry Wills, *James Madison* (New York: Henry Holt & Co., 2002), 75.

[20] Ibid., 76.

[21] Ellis, *American Sphinx,* 162.

[22] James F. Simon, *What Kind of Nation* (New York: Simon & Schuster, 2002), 286.

[23] Ibid., 287.

[24] Wills, *A Necessary Evil,* 144.

[25] Kenneth M. Stamp, *The Causes of the Civil War* (Englewood Cliffs, NJ: Prentice-Hall, 1959), 34-35.

[26] *The Writings of Thomas Jefferson* (Washington: Memorial Edition: 1904), 17:379-91.

[27] Simon, 61.

[28] Ellis, *Founding Brothers,* 200-1.

[29] Ibid., 201.

[30] Ibid., 203.

[31] Ellis, *American Sphinx,* 294.

[32] Carl Van Doren, *Benjamin Franklin* (Penguin Books, 1938), 731.

[33] Max Farrand, ed., *Benjamin Franklin Memoirs* (1936), 1:450-52.

[34] Ketcham, 56-7.

[35] James Parton, *The Life of Andrew Jackson* (Cambridge, MA: Houghton Mifflin & Co., 1860), 121, 124.

[36] Letter from Finis Ewing to Andrew Jackson, November 14, 1813, Andrew Jackson Papers.

[37] Letter from W. L. D. Ewing to Andrew Jackson, March 14, 1840, Andrew Jackson Papers.

[38] Wilson, 278-83.

[39] Letter from Abraham Lincoln to Joshua Speed, October 14, 1842.

[40] Wayne C. Temple, *The Quill of the Cumberland Presbyterian Church Archives,* 2:1 (Winter 1985), 156-162.

[41] David Lavender, *The Great West* (Houghton Mifflin), 231.

[42] *Oregon Historical Quarterly,* 59:1 (March 1958).

[43] *Journal of the Historical Society of Montana,* 2:394.

[44] McCullough, *John Adams,* 185-86.

Postscript 4

[1] Merrill Jensen, *The Founding of a Nation* (London: Oxford University Press, 1968), 703.

[2] Ibid., 704.

[3] Page Smith, *A New Age Now Begins* (New York: McGraw-Hill), 1:844.

[4] Page Smith, *John Adams* (New York: Doubleday, 1962), 2:176.

[5] Ibid., 177.

[6] Smith, *Adams,* 1:245.

[7] Carl J. Richard, *The Founders and the Classics* (Cambridge, MA: Harvard University Press), 132.

[8] Smith, 1:245.

[9] Richard, 133.

[10] Ibid., 131.

[11] Ibid., 139.

[12] Ibid., 139.

[13] Ibid., 141.

[14] Ketcham, 46.

[15] Ibid., 21-24, 50.

[16] Wertenbacker, 31.

[17] Ibid., ix

[18] Ellis, *American Sphinx,* 110-12.

[19] William J. Bennett, *Our Sacred Honor* (New York: Simon & Schuster, 1997), 367.

[20] Ibid., 412-13.

[21] Ketcham, 667.

[22] Ellis, *American Sphinx,* 300.

[23] Rev. Owen Murphy, *When God Stepped Down from Heaven.*

[24] Rev. Robert L. Eklund, *Spiritual Awakening* (Atlanta, GA: Home Mission Board of the Southern Baptist Convention, 1989).

[25] Charles Lemuel Thompson, D.D., *The Presbyterians* (New York: Baker & Taylor, 1903), 138-40.

[26] Eklund.

[27] Murphy.

Postscript 5

[1] Garry Wills, *Under God* (New York: Simon & Schuster, 1990), 373.

[2] Ellis, *American Sphinx,* 47.

[3] Ibid., 100-2.

[4] Thomas Jefferson, Inaugural Address, March 4, 1801. *The Thomas Jefferson Papers Series 1.* Library of Congress.

[5] Wills, *Under God,* 373.

[6] Letter from Thomas Jefferson to Comte Jean Diodate, August 3, 1789.

[7] Thomas Jefferson, *The Jefferson Bible* (Boston: Beacon Press, 1989), 156.

[8] Paul Leicester Ford, ed., Letter from Thomas Jefferson to Charles Thompson, January 9, 1816. *The Works of Thomas Jefferson* (New York: G.P. Putnam's Sons, 1905), 11:499.

[9] Letter from Thomas Jefferson to John Adams, October 13, 1813. *The Writings of Thomas Jefferson,* Lipscomb and Bergh, eds., (Washington, D.C.: Thomas Jefferson Memorial Association, 1903), 13:390.

[10] Letter from Thomas Jefferson to F. A. Van Der Kemp, April 25, 1816. *The Writings of Thomas Jefferson,* Lipscomb and Bergh, eds., (Washington, D.C.: Thomas Jefferson Memorial Association, 1903), 15:2-3.

[11] Letter from Thomas Jefferson to Dr. Benjamin Waterhouse, June 26, 1822. *The Writings of Thomas Jefferson,* Lipscomb and Bergh, eds., (Washington, D.C.: Thomas Jefferson Memorial Association, 1903), 15:383-85.

[12] Letter from Thomas Jefferson to William Short, April 13, 1820. *The Writings of Thomas Jefferson,* Lipscomb and Bergh, eds., (Washington, D.C.: Thomas Jefferson Memorial Association, 1903), 15:244.

[13] Edmund Fuller and David E. Greens, *God in the White House* (New York: Crown Publishers, 1968), 33.

Postscript 6
[1] Herman, 59-60.
[2] Beliles and McDowell, 6-7, 148-49, 156-57.

Postscript 7
[1] George Shepperson, *Scottish World,* 239.
[2] Ibid., 239.
[3] Howlett, 49-50.